A PERSONAL GUIDE TO THE B
AND AMUSEMENT/WA

(MY FAVORITE PARK AND RIDES FROM AROUND THE WORLD)

BY PETE TRABUCCO

PICTURES BY JOEL ROGERS

Published by Starry Night Publishing.Com

Rochester, New York

Copyright 2017 Pete Trabucco

Pete Trabucco

Well, it took a while, but it was finally time to do another book. There are so many people to thank this time around. First of all. I want to thank Joel Rogers from Coaster Gallery.com who supplied all the pictures for this book. He also supplied the pictures from book one as well. I would also like to thank my nephew. Andrew Trabucco, Shannon Struthers and Gretchyn Boshart for helping me edit, fact find and compile lists for many of these amusement parks, roller coasters, and thrill rides that you see on these pages. Again, no one can undertake a project such as this without the support and love of one's own family. I would like to again thank my beautiful wife, mentor, and best friend Dorie who has always stood by and of course, to my daughter Jennifer, the reason why I wrote these books in the first place. This book is also dedicated to my mom who is no longer with me today but still very close in my heart and in my thoughts. She always wanted me to be a writer. How am I doing Mom? Finally, I need to also thank my family and all those who I met along the way on this journey and have supported me along the way. Many of them I can truly call my forever friends. Thanks, guys!

It's been a wild ride folks, and that ride continues…

Pete

Contents

Foreword by Joel Rogers 7

So Why Write Another Book on Roller Coasters and Amusement Parks? 9

A Funny Thing Happened While Visiting the Park 11

My Continuing Search for the Ultimate Scream Machine 15

Why Roller Coasters (My Story) 17

A Brief History of Roller Coasters Then and Now 21

Is This Ride Really Safe? 23

Fighting the Fear of Coasters 25

Types of Roller Coasters 33

The Mighty Wood Roller Coaster 34

Steel Marvels (There are many types out there) 35

The Best Mass-Produced Coasters in the Nation 39

The Best Wood and Steel Roller Coasters Around 43

My Favorite Wooden Roller Coasters Around the Nation 81

My Favorite Late Addition Roller Coaster List 113

My Top Amusement Parks (In North America) 115

My Top Sixteen European Amusement Parks Across the Pond 139

My Top (US) Amusement Parks to Visit During Christmastime 145

The Best Amusement Parks to Hit for Halloween 149

The Top Ten Water Parks Around the Nation 153

Non Roller Coaster Adventures Worth Mentioning 159

Tips for Families When Traveling on Vacation 165

Amusement Park Safety- Have fun but be Safe 169

The Future of Coasters 173

Roller Coaster and Dark Ride Clubs 175

Listing of North American Amusement Parks 179

Roller Coaster Terminology 187

About the Author 195

Foreword by Joel Rogers

I love roller coasters. I have personally ridden on over 750 different roller coasters in a dozen countries. But, when people ask me to name my favorite coaster, I must confess I don't have an answer.

There are so many things that make a roller coaster great. Is it the thrill of going fast? Sure! Do g-forces and airtime make for a good ride? Possibly. Is it the engineering and design work involved that makes a ride exciting? Probably. Is it the number of loops? Not necessarily, but one thing is for sure, there is so much more to it.

In the late 1990s, I got to ride Leap-The-Dips, the world's oldest operating roller coaster. Lakemont Park was holding an exclusive event for roller coaster fans, but the fall weather that day was rainy and cold. Because so many enthusiasts had traveled to ride the 1903 side-friction coaster, they reluctantly opened it. But they warned us that the ride would be extremely slow that day because of the poor weather conditions. My brother, my wife, and I were on one of the first cars to run early that morning, and sure enough, our car ended up slowly grinding to a halt. We literally had to reach out, grab the nearby wood beams, and pull our train back to the station. So if I were to simply measure the speed or the g-forces, this ride would have been a total dud. But the overall experience, the fun with my family, the historic nature of the coaster, and the craziness of pulling ourselves back to the loading platform made it one of the best and most memorable coaster rides I have been on.

I realize that it is just not the ride that brings me joy, but it is often the social aspect. Some of my fondest childhood memories are of going to amusement parks with my family and friends. And now that I am older, I am enjoying introducing my children to the thrill of roller coasters.

I love the wide variety of coaster designs. There used to be two basic types of coasters: wood and steel. But the amazing new designs, especially the ones from the Rocky Mountain Construction Company, are making the wood versus steel categorization blurry at best. Today, you can experience flying coasters, shuttle coasters, suspended rides, inverted rides, floorless trains, rides with no loops, rides with many loops, racing coasters, spinning coasters, indoor coasters, themed coasters, wing coasters, and stand-up coasters.

The diversity of roller coasters is one of the reasons I love photographing them. I have posted thousands of my pictures on CoasterGallery.com so others can appreciate the designs and engineering that went into making these thrill rides. I was thrilled when Pete asked me to supply the pictures for this book. It was a chance to collaborate with another coaster enthusiast on a project that would allow readers to appreciate a wide variety of parks and rides.

In this book, Pete has listed some of his favorite roller coasters. It obviously is not an all-inclusive list because he hasn't been on every ride, and new coasters are being built every year, but it is a great list. He has covered some of the best roller coasters around!

I recently rode the famous Coney Island Cyclone with Pete while he was working on his Thrill Ride Maniacs show. (By the time you read this, the show might be on the air.) From our discussions and his lists of favorite coasters, I know that he and I have similar taste in roller coasters. And nearly all the rides he talks about in this book I would gladly ride again and again.

What will you find in this book? Pete will introduce you to a number of different roller coasters that he counts as being among his favorite rides. I hope they whet your appetite to do some riding yourself. So now, go through this book, learn about some of the world's best roller coasters, and pick up some travel and amusement park tips. Then go out and ride some of these amazing thrill machines yourself!

Joel Rogers
www.coastergllery.com

So Why Write Another Book on Roller Coasters and Amusement Parks?

Many people asked me, "So why write a second book on amusement parks and roller coasters?" Well, my answer was easy. With the success of the first edition and the fact that I have had such media success with my first outing, the answer was quite simply. "Why not?" With hundreds of media interviews, a radio show, and a reality show still in the works, a second addition seemed to be the natural progression in the process. It is also a way for me to pay it forward and, like last time, a good portion of the revenue from this book will again go to charity. Also, when you add the fact that literally hundreds of new rides and attractions are added to America's parks every year, it seemed like a no-brainer. Some of these newer rides are even bigger and faster and even more thrilling than the rides already out there, and it would be a crying shame not to add as many as I could. However, there is one problem. This industry changes every day and part of the problem of even writing a book like this one is that (like in the technical world of computers and cell phones) change happens almost on a dime. The fact is that what is new and hot today may not be hot tomorrow. Unlike radio/television or the Internet, there is a definite lag time from the time one writes a book to when it actually gets published and released. Sometimes that delay can take up to a year! **It's important to know that rides that appear in this book might have closed down or had their names changed during the production process of this publication.**

But, this time around I wanted to make sure I not only cover the best amusement parks and roller coasters (that I have ridden) around the nation, but I also wanted to talk about our nation's best water parks and finest thrill rides (non-roller coaster attractions like "Tower of Terror") that can be found in the United States. As I was putting together my new (and improved) list of roller coasters, thrill rides, and amusement parks, it suddenly occurred to me that I shouldn't stop there. Why not include the best of the best in the United Kingdom (Great Britain) as well. Many of the best amusement parks and rides can also be found just over the pond. Rides and attractions that actually rival what we have here in the United States and in North America. After all, the same manufactures are building them. My second edition would not be complete without at least mentioning all the fun you can have over there. You might ask, "What about all those fantastic parks that can be found in Asia and elsewhere? Why not include them in this edition as well?" Unfortunately, the fact is that there are so many fantastic amusement parks and roller coasters around the world that to include them in this second edition would be absolutely impossible to do. The only solution that I could come up would be to include some of these rides and attractions in a third edition sometime down the road.

The intention of this book is to explore the best coasters and parks around the country that I have experienced firsthand—to explain why these rides are so breathtaking and to help you make a decision on where to sit and when the best time would be to ride the rails. The book has also been published in paperback so you can carry it with you (in you backpack) when you visit these parks and get some key information on all these thrill rides while you are still in the parks. But it is also written to help those of you who simply fear coasters and just want to overcome their fears of these monsters of the midway using a method that I used on myself in the past.

In this latest edition (which is my personal guide to the best amusement and water parks), you can expect to find the most- innovative and most interesting rides I have ridden and that this industry has to offer. That was my plan for this project and I believe we have succeeded towards that end. You will also find everyday tips for amusement park safety and a section on how to plan and pack for your amusement park experience. There are also tips to getting through security for you and your family as well. Finally for those who are still afraid of roller coasters and thrill rides, I have more tips on how to enjoy the ride and beat that beast "in everyone's head" that I call the "fear factor." So sit down and strap yourself in for another edition **in** my personal guide to ride series!

A Funny Thing Happened
While Visiting the Park

There is a certain magic to being at an amusement park that you just don't experience anywhere else. So who are the people that visit these lands of imagination and fantasy?

A Funny Thing while visiting the park…

Not too long ago, I found myself at an amusement park on what turned out to be a very beautiful summer day. It was your typical Saturday in the park, and I was at a smaller but absolutely beautiful park on the East Coast. This particular park had a great old wooden roller coaster, and I came to the park that day just to ride this classic puppy. This wooden marvel is still a fan favorite and actually has a great water park attached to it. I really enjoyed going to these types of parks because, unlike the larger parks, it is here that you will discover the true flavor of the local community and of these parks. After a fantastic day of seeing the sites and what I thought was an amazing tiger show, I noticed they also had a boat and a decent-sized lake It is not really a big boat, but it did fit around ten to fifteen people. It was a nice day around eighty degrees, so I thought I would take a boat ride to see the park from a different angle. The ride also had a canopy. The first fifteen minutes of the boat ride was uneventful, but as we were heading back to the dock, the little boat's engine cut out. We were in fact stranded and that's when this experience became etched in my brain and something I would never forget.

There were about a half dozen other passengers on this little boat, and all of us were wondering what we would be doing for the next ten to twenty minutes. At this time, I was just about finishing up my first book and doing some research for a second one when I had an idea. In most parks, you only get to go on the rides with your friends, but I learned early on that there is so much more about being at an amusement park than just the rides and shows that you will find there. It's about the people that go to these parks that really make the story worthwhile.

While visiting La Ronde, an amusement park in Montreal, Canada, I realized that laughter is universal in any language. I couldn't speak the language of most of the guests at that park on that day but knew pretty much what they were saying and how they were feeling. I actually communicated successfully with everyone that day, and I was able to do it with just my smile and body language. It's the people that make these amusement parks what they are, but I wondered to myself, who were they? Why were they here? How did it come about that I was to meet them here today on this broken-down boat in the middle of a lake.

While stuck on this boat and waiting for help to arrive, I thought it would be a great opportunity to find out who the other passengers were and why were they here today? When I started this inquiry, I thought I would just get the standard answers that I thought I would typically get. Answers like, to have fun or to do something different, but the answer I received actually shaped my thoughts about why people go to these fabulous places in the first place. Sitting right next to me was a young couple that I would say were in their early twenties. From the way they looked and talked with each other, I deduced they were just dating. They seemed nervous and on their best behavior, and it looked like it might be their first or second date. His name was John and hers, Linda. Linda absolutely loved amusement parks. Her parents used to take her to one every month when she was very young and have loved them since. John, meanwhile not so much! It was their second date together, and I actually felt I was intruding on their time. But being the noisy guy that I am, I continued my line of questioning. John was the nervous type, and you could clearly see he was very conservative and did not like taking chances or talking with strangers. They were total opposites of each other, yet they still went on this second date here! John even went on the popular roller coaster at this park. The same ride that was in fact the main reason for me coming to this park in the first place. It was a classic wood coaster and not very tame, but he did it because that's what she liked to do. Talk about getting some brownie points! This guy was willing to take what he truly thought was his life into his hands to just be with her. Now that's true love!

While telling his story, he had an "AHA" moment and realized that he also liked to go to these parks because it made her so happy. Turns out he would be totally hooked on the experience in the next few years himself. Now that's a great start to true love if I do say so myself. It was really fun to watch them both, which, by the way, reminded me of myself many years ago when I made what I thought was a similar sacrifice for my future wife and daughter. All I could do is wish this couple the best of luck. Many a romances seem to start right here at places like these!

The second couple on board were retiree's from the town of Allentown, Pennsylvania. They had to be in their late sixties or quite possibly,-early seventies. Just by looking at them, one can see that they had been married a very long time and were quite comfortable with each other. They were also empty nesters for a long time, from the looks of it. Her name was Maria, and for forty years, she was a hardworking housewife and mother who took care of all life's problems and issues as well as most of the bills. From what I could gather in my short time with her is that she was also very good at it. Her husband, Sam, shared some similarities with me. He had been a successful salesman who traveled a lot, and together, they had three fantastic kids. They weren't at the park for their children or their grandchildren. They were actually at the park for themselves. When I asked why, they said that they were there just to remember! Over forty years of marriage and great memories of times past that they shared in this very park, and believe me, it was evident to see what this meant to their relationship. Sam told me that, over the years, it was automatic that they would ride this same boat every time they were in the park and added, in the many years they had ridden this attraction, that it "never got stuck" not even once! Guess it was this old boat's time to become retired and time for me to tell a new story.

The next individual on the boat was Ryan. He was also a salesman, and today, he was just flying solo and killing some time. He was actually in town (just flew in) and in the middle of some serious meetings. He was looking for a break in the day and thought it would be a great idea to just come to the park to forget about his problems. Coming to the park actually relieved some of the stress he had, and he found that being there and watching other people on the rides, the animals, and relaxing in the shade of this old boat actually did wonders to rejuvenate his soul. Like many people, he always had a soft spot for roller coasters, especially the wooden ones. In fact, he was at the park to ride one of best wood coasters (just like me) from around the country. He missed home, thought of his kids and the fun he would be having with them at this park if they were there. He didn't talk about his wife and I determined that she was no longer in the picture and not a topic he wanted to talk about. I was glad to talk with Ryan. For the rest of the day (even after the boat situation was resolved), it was great hanging out with him.

The next two people on the boat were a grandfather (named Jake) and his nine –year-old granddaughter, Samantha. When we ended up in the middle of the lake, it was clear that they were both a little nervous about the present situation. When I came over to talk with them, it seemed talking about something else had definitely helped to alleviate their fear of the situation. Everyone started to have some fun, telling me their stories. I helped them with their situation and now it was their turn to tell me what brought them to this particular place in time. It seems that Jake simply wanted to spend some time with little Sam. He didn't see her as much as he liked to and admitted that it was many years since he was in this very park. Samantha was fearless for her age and she took her poor grandfather on all the crazy rides at the park. Even though it was plain to see that her not-so-enthusiastic grandfather was just toughing it out, in the end, he was making her happy, forming a bond with her and actually having fun as well.

The final group of people stuck on board our small little vessel were three teenagers, Matthew, Bob, and Teresa. (They were around fifteen to sixteen years of age) and to say the least, they were not happy campers. All three loved, and I mean *loved* roller coasters and thrill rides. They (like me) even kept track of all the rides they had been riding. Bob's family also belonged to a coaster enthusiast club, and it was safe to say he had taken advantage of all the extended ride time these groups were granted. They were here today to add a famous wood roller coaster to their lists. It was Teresa's idea to come on this boat and right now was not the most popular person in the group. It was true they had ridden the best rides at this park a dozen or so times, but still, a teenager stuck on a boat with nothing happening is not good! They wanted to know about other parks and all the rides that I have been lucky enough to experience. I was happy to tell them about my experiences and was about as cool as a middle-aged man can get with **a** teenager. About an hour later, we were pulled into the dock, and we were all able to go back to the park and back to our lives. However, I will never forget these people coming from different places in life, all looking for something different and finding what was ailing them (together) in the melting pot of a typical American amusement park like this one. That's one day I won't forget.

Pete Trabucco

My Continuing Search for the Ultimate Scream Machine

On the following pages, I have included many of the best ultimate scream machines around the country that I have been lucky enough to ride over the past decade. This list does not include all of them because there are still many roller coasters I have not been able to experience firsthand, so if yours is not on the list, it doesn't mean it isn't a great ride. These are my favorites thrill rides and roller coasters and, if yours is not included here, chances are it was not in operation during the creation of this book, or I never had the opportunity to actually ride it. However, the coasters listed here have consistently been represented on many of the top one hundred roller coaster lists distributed throughout the nation. I can honestly tell you that I have truly enjoyed each and every one of these rides, and I always look forward to riding these coasters again! Whether you prefer wood roller coasters or today's steel mega-marvels each coaster seat really gives you the chance to experience the world from an entirely new and very different perspective. Like flying an airplane (which as you all know is another one of my hobbies), your viewpoint of the world vastly changes and can help in altering how you perceive yourself as well as others around you. Besides, where else can you scream your head off without getting arrested) and ride something that will both exhilarate and scare the heck out of you all at the same time? In the end for me, the best part about riding coasters is the chance to experience them with the people that I love as well.

With thousands of new gravity-defying contraptions across the nation and more cropping up every day, roller coasters and thrill rides are truly the driving forces behind any amusement park and, in most cases, are the sole basis of that amusement park's very existence. Over the past Fifteen years, America (and the rest of the world) has experienced a renaissance in the creation of new roller coasters, and because of this, we have seen many great advances in roller coaster technology. You can literally see (and experience) this in today's newest roller coasters in terms of their overall size, height, and the production time it takes the get the ride operational.

You can also find many different types of roller coasters around the country that will surely amaze you. There are flying coasters (such as Superman, Batwing, and Stealth); linear induction coasters (like Rock n Roller Coaster at MGM Disney World, or Volcano at Kings Dominion), floorless wonders (like Bizarro and Kraken); and mega-coasters (like Millennium Force at Cedar Point and Superman Ride of Steel at Six Flags, New England or Leviathan at Canada's Wonderland.) There are also four-dimensional coasters (like X2 at Six Flags, Magic Mountain) as well as dive coasters, wing coasters, and super-hydraulic mega-coasters that have come into the mix. The world's fastest ride, the Formula Rossa in Abu Dhabi, clocks in at 150 miles per hour at Ferrari World. and with the introduction of the 420-foot marvel Top Speed Dragster at Cedar Point in Sandusky, Ohio and tallest roller coaster in the world, the behemoth 455-foot high Kingda Ka at Six Flags Great Adventure, who knows where ride manufacturers will take us next? All of these rides seem to exhibit extended ride elements that literally defy or at least bend the laws of physics, as we know them. In this industry, the sky is the limit and the possibilities now seem to be endless. Indeed, it is a great time to be a roller coaster enthusiast.

But why do people ride these coasters in the first place? Why subject yourself to the terror? Perhaps, the anticipation and screams you witness while waiting in line for the ride itself? And why subject yourself to that moment of truth when those ride gates open, and you find yourself strapping in like a test pilot to the latest contraption and heading up a towering lift hill, if there is even a lift hill to head up?

I guess there is something to be said for facing your fears head-on, and that is why most people do it. What was it that President Franklin D. Roosevelt once said regarding overcoming the fear element in life? He said, "There is nothing to fear but fear itself." His statement was not intended for a coaster enthusiast, yet it goes a long way in explaining why people challenge themselves on these roller coasters and other thrill rides. It seems that facing your fears head-on and overcoming them really does make you feel good about yourself and the world that you live in. I guess that's the challenge of trying new and different things, and in the hobby of roller coastering (as in most other things) in general. It's a doorway to one more new and different experiences in life. It brings out the classic fight or flight impulse embedded in all of us, a behavior very evident when it comes to these mega-coaster thrill rides and ultimately our own secret fears.

After interviewing thousands of people on this topic, I think it's safe to say that people ride coasters for many different reasons. Some just love the thrill of trying something new, different, and exciting. Others see it as a way to unload their stress after a hard day's work. Still others want to be challenged and see how far they can push their own physical and emotional envelopes, or what I like to call the "pucker factor." (That factor will make you break out in a cold hard sweat and have your mouth and lips sucking for as much air as possible.) I am sure if you ask ten people why they ride roller coasters, you will get ten different answers. Everyone has a story to tell. All of them are interesting and seem to follow a logical path as to why we "*coaster*" No matter the answer, riders usually fall into one of two categories.

The first group are the thrill seekers. They come from all walks of life, different parts of the world, different jobs. Their common thread is simply the need to experience life on the edge. They're often referred to as adrenaline junkies. They thrive on the rush of adrenaline that comes with things like thrill rides. In fact, they seek it out, crave it even.

When you have ruled out the adrenaline junkies, which usually leaves the rest of us, a more subdued set of folks. People that truly want to experience this thrill but, alas, can't seem to take that first step past their fear.

So which group are you? In the end, whether you ride roller coasters or not, just visiting a park can help you escape life's daily pressures and make you feel like a kid all over again. It did for me!

Why Roller Coasters

(My Story)

This could be classified as a strange story, but one that I feel I must share with you. It is a classic story of a simple man's journey through his own fear toward overall mental health and enlightenment—a man who, for most of his life, was afraid of roller coasters and other thrill rides. Then at the age of forty, I was able to finally to see things from a different perspective and see the drops and thrills at amusement parks for what they really are—an exciting experience that will always take your breath away and have you craving for more! Let me explain.

When I was around six, my parents put me on one of those kiddy coasters at an amusement park somewhere on the East Coast. My mom gave me the strangest look as she sat me down on this ride. Her expression, a frightened, pained look, instinctively told me that she feared she would never, ever see me again. Taking my cues from mom, I endured the ride, scared and crying and white-knuckling my seat for the duration. I exited, and as you may have guessed, decided that these rides were just not for me. That would be my last ride on a roller coaster for a long while.

Fast forward to my teenage years. Yes, I would go to all the hot carnivals and amusement parks in the area and for the most part, would have a fair time at them. However, that usually changed when someone suggested, "Let's go on that coaster," or "Wow, what a drop on that one," or "That coaster really looks like fun!"

You can guess what came next. "No thanks, that ride looks stupid!" or my other classic reply, "The line is way too long!"

That response was met with the usual retort from my friends. You guessed it. They would tease me, calling out, "Chicken!" or "Wimp!" They would go on the ride and have a fantastic time, leaving me with the pounding shame of their expletives in my ear and I…, well, you get the picture.

The preceding paragraph makes it look like I was afraid of everything under the sun, but if you knew me, you would know that this statement wasn't true. Being cautious by nature never stopped me from participating in varsity baseball and football during my high school and college days. Nor did it dissuade me from earning a private pilot's license and learning how to fly aerobatic maneuvers. You know, like loops! But talk to me about roller coasters or other wild rides at your local amusement park, and that six-year-old would come to the surface of my psyche. My answer was always the same: "No way, man! Not coasters. What, are you crazy?" This proclamation became my friend for many years. After all, I could cling to the notion that "in a car or an airplane I had *control* of my environment. On a roller coaster I didn't have this control, and for anyone who doesn't get what coasters are about, that can be terrifying. Besides, all roller coasters simply weren't safe. End of story!"

That same line from my parents (God, I love them) when I was first introduced to coasters, back when I was five or six, still rang loudly in my ears many years later. If I had known then about the studies showing that a person has a better chance of being struck by lightning several times than of having a fatal injury on a coaster, perhaps things would have been different. In hindsight, I really wish I had done that research sooner.

It was a tough time for my friends, who were real roller coaster enthusiasts. My poor wife suffered the most. She really loved all rides, especially coasters. The crazier they were, the better, and unfortunately, she usually sat on the sidelines, or worse, had to go on the latest coasters and thrill rides all by herself. I felt guilty for making her do that, so neither one of us would have the greatest of times at these amusement parks.

Fast-forward to 1996. We had a beautiful, bouncing baby girl. By 1998, I was ready for my biggest challenge! There was no way that my little girl was going to miss out on coaster fun because of my fear. So I decided to conquer one of my biggest fears, and I put together a battle plan to once and for all get rid of my childhood fear of roller coasters. The battle would begin in the state of New Jersey but wouldn't end there. I would start with medium-sized coasters (I was okay on the really small ones) and work my way up to the top woodies and steel rides all around the nation. That was the plan. I figured with this strategy, it would take around five years to overcome my fear.

But something happened along the way. I grew up! I realized that I was no longer a child but an adult who actually liked to try new experiences. Unfortunately until then, I was stuck with my childhood preconception of what roller coasters were supposed to be like and did not have the ability to move on. It took a very special roller coaster (and let's be honest, any real coaster that you first ride, accept, and enjoy can apply here) to show me that the frightened child in me was gone and the adult, who sometimes acted like a child, had successfully put the past behind him.

You can always tell a coaster fanatic by the way he or she talks about his or her first real experience on a roller coaster. Sure I had ridden the local mine trains every now and then, closed my eyes and hoped for the best, but I did not experience a real coaster until 1998. It was called Rolling Thunder out of Six Flags Great Adventure in New Jersey—a slow, rough, loud, and rickety old coaster by today's standards, but boy, when I finally let go of my fears, what a ride I received that day! I actually don't remember much from the first ride, but the most important thing had been accomplished. *I did it* and lived to tell the tale. That was all that mattered! So I decided to try the ride again, and guess what? It was actually was a lot of fun. I proceeded to spend the rest of the year on rides that I never thought I would ever even go near. I started to ride other wood coasters, and there was another great one in New Jersey called Great White, located at Morey's Pier in Wildwood. From there, I rode such classics as the Cyclone in New York City, Ghost Rider in San Diego, Boulder Dash in Massachusetts, and the Texas Giant and the Comet at Six Flags in Lake George, New York.

It was now time to tackle the big steel coasters the nation had to offer. There were literally hundreds of steel coasters to choose from. A steel coaster ride is extremely different from a wood coaster experience, in that on a steel coaster, the rider receives a much smoother and faster ride then those you will find on their wood counterparts. The reasoning is simple. Steel can be bent into many different shapes, the riders can be dropped down or catapulted up many types of loops and inversions that you can't do on wood.

Steel coasters can be built as high as a thirty-story building. These are called mega-coasters, and you can attain top speeds of almost one hundred miles per hour, as in Superman the Escape at Six Flags Magic Mountain in California does. A wood coaster's appeal is in the "out of control" feeling that you get when riding one. They are generally louder than steel coasters as they clank and plummet down the track at speeds of forty to sixty miles per hour. Even though they are not as fast as steel coasters, in many ways they are as much fun as their steel offspring. Besides, I started this adventure with them, and wood coasters will always hold a special place in my journey.

So wood was conquered, and steel was next on my list. I started my conquest of steel and picked coasters like Batman and a floorless coaster by the name of Medusa at Six Flags Great Adventure in New Jersey to start me off. Not bad, but like a hungry tiger on the prowl and no longer weighed down by my fears, I wanted (and needed) more! So from there I went to Massachusetts and tackled Superman Ride of Steel at Six Flags New England, one of the best and tallest roller coasters in the world! What a ride! After that, I decided to check out the Incredible Hulk and Dueling Dragons at Universal Studios, Florida and since I happened to be in the neighborhood, I progressed to Kraken at SeaWorld and Rock "n"-Roller Coaster at Walt Disney World on my roller coaster adventure. Of course one of the tallest coasters in the world, Millennium Force, had to be included, and the list just kept growing.

What follows is a total of five hundred new and exciting roller coasters, as well as over three dozen top amusement parks to visit around the country. You name me, and chances are, I have been on it. To date, I have ridden forty of the nation's top fifty combined coasters (wood and steel) that *Amusement Park Today*, the amusement park industry's top-rated trade newspaper, lists as top coasters in the country. I also take advantage of all drop towers, water rides, and other high-energy action that you can find at these amusement parks. In the near future, I plan on visiting Europe and riding the best of the best there as well. At this point, there are no boundaries or borders when it comes to riding coasters for me.

And thanks to my efforts without coaxing, well, maybe just a little coaxing from my little girl (at that time) and who by the way is now and adult has ridden hundreds of-four roller coasters around the country as well. Like her dad, she still has a scrapbook at home of all her coaster accomplishments and has the pictures and statistics to back them up. This is truly something that we share, and I am sure we will be able to do this for many years to come. What a big difference from the way I spent my childhood and I am glad for that. It seems to me that the people who invented these rides had us in mind when they created them. And thanks to them and the new wave of safe but exciting thrill rides, we are now in the midst of experiencing a new renaissance in the industry.

So you say, how did this happen? How did a cautious person like me morph into a roller coaster fanatic able to tackle the tallest and fastest coasters this nation has to offer? I really couldn't tell you. But like all of you, I can safely say that screaming loudly on the ride sure seems to help. For it is a proven fact that those who scream really don't feel the drops (something about blood rushing to the head) and usually come off the ride feeling fantastic and ready to tackle the next challenge. Most importantly, I just took the chance, believed in myself, and in doing so was rewarded for my efforts. Every aspect, from the anticipation of riding the new mega marvels, to the rides themselves, not to mention the thrill of watching your child's reaction on these wonderful contraptions, is more than enough enjoyment.

This should also be a lesson to all those who fear coasters. I tell people that your fear of coasters (or anything for that matter) can be erased forever if you are willing to make the commitment to tackle this fear head-on. "Why not just try it?" I ask. If you enjoy it, you just might be forever hooked on them. If you don't enjoy the ride, the worst thing that could happen is that you might feel woozy and maybe a bit disoriented when you get off. Now how bad is that? We all know that the industry has an exemplary safety record and that you are thousands of times more likely to receive personal injury driving to and from an amusement park than you are while riding **a** coaster.

In either scenario, the chances are pretty good that you will be talking about that ride for weeks, maybe even years to come—that is, if you still have a voice left after your adventure. And that, folks, is the main point of my story! A wise person once told me, "To live and encounter for one's self is far better than sitting around watching others experience life firsthand." Take that from me! The former is far more life enriching and gratifying than the latter. Even if you never ride the new mega-roller coasters, there is so much to see and do at these parks (especially at any of the Disney parks, but we will get into that another time) that your trip will be well worth the price of any admission. Take it from me the person voted least likely to write this book. You are never too old nor too young to try something new. Feel the rush and, in doing so, erase your fears!

You might ask, what does my wife think of all this? Well, that's another story for another day. I can tell you that she is in fact a little shocked at my recent strange behavior and has attributed my sudden enjoyment of roller coasters to a midlife crisis. She might be right in that respect, but I might add is also extremely happy that my outside interests lie with these new large behemoths of the midway rather than in the latest blonde or brunette at work.

A Brief History of Roller Coasters Then and Now

So where did the concept of roller coasters come from? You might say it started when mankind decided that it might be fun to roll down hills, with or without some kind of apparatus, just to see what happened. It was not very comfortable, but you can be pretty sure it left a lasting impression on the participants. It is uncontested that the first gravity slides were created in the fifteenth century, when someone had the brilliant idea to create a wooden ramp, freeze the water, and, well, slide down the ice. They were called "ice slides" and were very popular for their time.

And so it went until the French constructed the first wood stock coasters in 1817. Two of these rides, Les Montagnes Russes a Belleville and Promenades Aeriennes, introduced wheels and axles on their cars, grooved tracks, and a primitive cable system to lift people up the slide. They didn't go very fast, but these mechanical contraptions were very popular and seemed to be popping up all the Europe.

Fast forward to America, where the father of all coaster inventors appeared. His name was La Marcus Thompson, and this inventor would forever change the way we look at coasters. Primitive and small, the La Marcus Thompson Switchback Railway opened at New York City's Coney Island beach on June 13, 1884, and officially created the craze we still enjoy today. The ride featured two parallel straight tracks with raised platforms at either end. The rider got on at the top and, after the ride ended, got off at the bottom. With a top speed of about 6 miles per hour, it wasn't very fast but people would wait in lines as long as three hours to ride this innovation. Thompson created many switchback (or scenic) railways over the years, but the 600-foot long wonder at Coney Island was the catalyst which triggered the craze. In 1904, the Philadelphia Toboggan Company was formed, and in 1915, John Miller took over the reins and created new innovations such as anti-rollback and under-wheel devices to make the coasters much safer.

The "golden age" of coasters had begun. And thanks to Miller and other influential coaster designers like Fred Church, Frank Prior, Harry Baker, and Arthur Looff (names familiar to any roller coaster enthusiast) during the first golden age, there were over 1,500 coasters rolling around the country.

Coasters were extremely popular until the Great Depression hit in 1929, when most of the country's great amusement parks either closed or changed names. Usually the parks were destroyed *"accidentally"* by fire or by the hand of a real estate developer. It is amazing to me that even today, some of these coasters still exist, but they do, hanging on to the innovations that keep them in a special place in everyone's heart.

In 1955, Walt Disney took the coaster concept to the next level with the creation of Disneyland in Anaheim, California. Along with Arrow Development Company, he created the first tubular steel coaster with polyurethane-wheeled, rolling stock cars, and he called it the Matterhorn Bobsleds. Well, since that innovation, the rest you might say is history. Thanks to the visionaries in coaster technology, it is not uncommon to see coasters in this millennium that almost seem to touch the clouds at over four hundred feet tall, while sending their passengers traveling around the track at speeds of over 125 miles per hour. Coasters are indeed the craze of the new millennium, and one that I hope you will be able to share with all your loved ones. I know I will!

Is This Ride Really Safe?

In all my travels, one of the things that I have been constantly asked when doing interviews with the media is this: are these rides safe? This is a very common question. One of the biggest fears most people have regarding roller coasters (or any thrill ride) is that they feel that these scream machines are unsafe. They hear the creaking of an old wood coaster or see the sway in the steel of a new fangled impulse ride and—they are done! The truth of the matter is that you will not find an industry more safety conscious than the amusement park industry. After all, this industry lives and breathes on its success or failure. Any major accident and *bang*, you're out of business! We all have heard of incidents happening at these parks and wondered if it could happen to me. Well, I am happy to say that that those odds are astronomical!

The truth of the matter is that going to an amusement park is one of the safest forms of recreation you can find. As a pilot, I can say that flying airplanes is pretty safe. Some may disagree with me, but if you look at the statistics, flying an airplane is much safer than operating a car. So the question arises: is flying safer than riding a roller coaster or any other thrill ride you would find at an amusement park? The answer is no! How about riding a motorcycle or a bike? Are riding these machines safer than coasters? According to the International Association of Amusement Park Attractions, the answer is again… No! According to their study, you are more likely to be injured when you play sports, ride a horse, drive a car, or yes, even ride a bike than when you ride a coaster. Statistics show that the occurrence of death on an amusement park ride is approximately 1 in 250 million.

These statistics are supported by the National Consumer Products Safety Commission, which says that more than 140 million people visit amusement parks yearly. Their findings indicate that only around 8,000 of over 140 million actually end up in an emergency room. These incidents include falls at the local park, restaurant mishaps, and other non-ride incidents. Even when you add these injuries, a mere 0.000259 percent of all amusement park goers will actually get hurt at an amusement park. I will take those percentages every time!

Out of those injuries that do occur at amusement parks, the above reports also state that a great portion of ride injuries happened through no fault of the ride or its manufacturer. It occurred because someone—the ride operator or the rider himself—disregarded the safety rules and took unnecessary chances in order to increase the thrill factor on the ride. We hear stories all the time of children that are too small for the restraints somehow getting on the ride, people undoing their restraints while a ride is in progress or trying to stand up at the most inopportune moments. And finally, let's add to the statistics, the hundreds of passengers who have chronic back or neck injuries, but due to their excitement have forgotten about their medical condition prior to riding.

I will mention that these reports also concluded that, in some very rare cases, the ride was poorly maintained and that better maintenance of the attraction could have prevented injury but this was classified as a rare event. The truth is that unlike the car you drive every day, all rides at an amusement park are inspected on a daily basis. You can rest assured that at every amusement park, experienced mechanics and hi-tech computer personnel watch carefully to ensure that all of the equipments are running at top mechanical and electrical condition. This job needs to be accomplished every day and there can be no cutting corners!

Also in addition to the daily inspections in the off-season (if you live in the east), the entire ride gets a complete overhaul by licensed mechanics, computer specialists, electricians, and carpenters who work at the park full time. In southern parts of the United States, where the weather is mild enough that the park doesn't close down, you might notice that a particular ride might be closed for weeks at a time. This is what they are doing making sure the ride passes all ride safety criteria, so that it is safe for you and thousands of others to ride.

So the next time you climb that lift hill, get shot like a cannon out of a train station, spin uncontrollably, or drop like a rock, please take comfort in the fact that many people are still working hard every day to make sure your ride experience is a safe and enjoyable one.

©2005 Jeff Rogers
www.CoasterGallery.com

Fighting the Fear of Coasters

Family Coasters Are Still the Ticket

So how does one get over their fear of roller coasters and thrill rides? The question has been asked of me before. After all, I had to overcome my fear in order to write these books. The question on the surface seems easy but sometimes the answer can be quite difficult. Every individual is different, but people tend to fall into two categories when it comes to answering this question. There are those, like my wife, who tackle their fear by hitting it head on. They take the fear on and will challenge the biggest and baddest roller coasters out there. The idea behind this is that once you have conquered the biggest and the best there is to offer, you have accomplished your task in one quick swoop. I envy those individuals in that they can have the nerve to accomplish this as quickly as possible. The other group takes a 180-degree or opposite approach to this quandary. I can relate to these individuals in that, like them, I have had to tackle this challenge in stages. I can remember going to the amusement parks when I was younger. I heard the comments from my peers and the way they seemed to want to pressure me or just plain embarrass me so I would relent in riding roller coasters. I don't think it was fully intentional, but by using the peer pressure method, they were actually creating a reverse effect on me, which made it even more difficult for me to ride those crazy contraptions with them.

For those in the second category, I am here to tell you that this approach always fails in the end. Sure, the person in question might ride with you but never, and I mean never, will you see them subject themselves to this kind of peer pressure again. I actually hated to go with them to these parks and came up with excuses all the time not to go. I knew what was going to happen and let's just say the feeling of being put on the spot like that was not very appealing.

The best approach to helping someone overcome his or her fear of roller coasters or anything else for that matter is to take it slow. Don't push them into doing something they don't want to do. Let them make it their choice to say yes or no to the experience. They have to want to do this, and all the teasing, prodding, and name calling won't help them overcome this fear. I can speak for myself that the childhood fear I had was deep, and it would take the birth of my daughter to tackle this childhood nightmare. However, like many people, I needed to do this in stages and not all at once. I would not be hiking the Grand Canyon or climbing the tallest mountain that I could find as my first venture. Nor would I do this when riding roller coasters. For many others as well as myself, it makes sense to start small and build up your confidence before looking to increase the thrill level. Also I like to check the ride out and watch others first before I go. Looking at the track, anticipating the drops, turns, and loops sit easier when you are unfamiliar with the ride. It's sort of like the experience I had when I was going for my FAA check ride as a pilot. I would imagine the maneuvers and go over it in my head several times until I got it right. Well on these thrill rides, you can get yourself mentally (as well as physically) prepared for what lies ahead by watching the track, the riders, and the coaster itself. I found that the best way to go about this was to start with these family coasters that you can easily find at most amusement parks around the country.

A family roller coaster is one that is made for the whole family to enjoy, and they generally are not too wild or intense in nature. The bigger and more extreme coasters will get your pucker factor up and your adrenalin pumping while subjecting you to high g-forces that fighter pilots usually experience. As a pilot, I can tell you it takes a little time and practice to get accustomed to this level of intensity. It is not advisable to start out with this type of ride, especially for those individuals who like to have control in their lives. If they start with these family coasters, however, they can experience the fun of a roller coaster in an enjoyable and nonthreatening way. Once you begin to see roller coasters as fun, even the extreme rides look a little more interesting.

In my mind, one of the best tricks to coaster riding is to slowly acclimate yourself to these ride experiences. Sometimes that means watching the exposed coaster, understanding where the dips, loops, and spins will occur so that you are prepared mentally and physically for them. This is very similar to a student pilot preparing for his check ride. Usually he will go over every aspect of his flight in order to be prepared for what lies ahead. The same can be said for many fainthearted riders of coasters. They want to know everything beforehand. This is why I suggest that if you are new to coastering, but for whatever reason would like to get over this fear, there are things you can do to accomplish this task.

In the beginning of any ride, you might want to keep your lap bar, harness, or straps extremely tight to the body for psychological and physical support. This will also relieve the floating (negative-g) effect that can get to first-time riders. As you get braver, you might want to keep a tad more space between you and the harness to experience more of what that particular ride has to offer. It also makes it easier if you make sure that you breathe properly during the ride, especially during those times when your eyes think they see more than the body can handle.

You'd be surprised how many people hold their breath when going down the most exciting elements of a ride. Do not do this! Not only should you breathe during the ride, especially during the big drops, wild turns, and crazy elements, but also it would be advisable to scream your lungs out. Medically, the effect of this screaming is to keep the blood flow up in your upper body and head, thus decreasing your chances of blacking out or experiencing tunnel vision on a wild ride. In many cases in steep drops. The negative-g effect on a person can be minimized by simply yelling or screaming at that point on the ride. This means less discomfort in your stomach region during this aspect of the ride. The same can be said when being whipped around turns and loops in a high positive-g environment. Relax. You're on a ride, so it is really okay to yell. You will notice everyone else doing it and if it works for them, it will also work for you. Also keep your eyes open at all times. By doing this, you will not become as nauseous or queasy after your ride experience.

If you've not been on a major roller coaster in a while, or it's been some time since you last rode, don't start with the biggest roller coasters around. Rides that are two hundred or three hundred feet in height are not a smart way to start off overcoming your phobia. Instead, start off with family roller coasters, and there are literally hundreds of them around the country. I'm not talking about kiddy coasters, but roller coasters that can accommodate people of all sizes but in no way can be considered an e-ticket top thrill ride at the park.

Lastly, for those people who feel that coasters are unsafe, remember that after you are strapped in, enjoy the ride and don't give in to your fears. Coasters are much safer than just about any other activity. Your chances of receiving bodily injury are hundreds of times greater when you get into your car and drive to the park. In fact, statistics show that you have a better chance of being struck by lightning than receiving a major injury on a roller coaster, so relax and enjoy the ride. Remember, riding a coaster gives the illusion of being unsafe, but in fact, the roller coaster industry is one of the most safety-conscious industries out there. NASA should take as many precautions as they do.

So now that you are ready to start your adventure, how do you go about doing it? Well, earlier I said that a good way to start is to plan your coaster acclimation with some family coasters. Here are some examples of this type of coaster:

Seven Dwarfs Mine Train is a fantastic new ride at the Magic Kingdom in Fantasyland. I like this ride a lot, and it's a great one for the entire family. Although the coloring is very similar to another mine train located in the same park, Seven Dwarfs is all new and different. Manufactured by Vekoma, the roller coaster is situated in the Fantasyland section of Magic Kingdom. It opened to the public on May 28, 2014, as part of a major park expansion called New Fantasyland. The ride is themed around the classic 1937 film *Snow White and the Seven Dwarfs*, which, by the way, was the first animated feature film from Walt Disney. While waiting in line, you can find several interactive activities and plenty to keep the kids busy. One such activity is a gem-sorting game where you match up three jewels of different shape but the same color. The ride is almost forty feet high with a top speed of around thirty five miles per hour. During the middle of the ride, you are treated to the seven animatronics dwarves working in the mine, and this attraction features cars that seem to tilt. This new technology simulates the swaying and tipping that you might find if you were riding an actual mine cart. It's a great ride for the whole family, but unfortunately, the lines are rather long at this time. It's best to obtain a free, fast pass for this attraction so you can ride at an assigned time and skip the wait.

Flight of the Hippogriff at Universal Studios in Orlando, Florida, is located in The Wizarding World of Harry Potter section of the park. It's a mild alternative to the more extreme rides like Dragon Challenge that is located in the near vicinity. This is considered a typical family coaster. At two thousand feet long and reaching speeds of nearly thirty miles per hour, this one is great for the kids as well as their parents. The wooded area really sets the mood in the Jurassic Park section of the park, and the biggest drop on this coaster is only around thirty feet. A standard Vekoma junior "roller skater" coaster, this is a nice ride to try out before you tackle the big-name coasters like the Hulk.

Harry Potter and the Escape from Gringotts located in Islands of Adventure at Universal Studios, is a dark, three-dimensional (3-D) ride and has multiple ride manufacturers attached to the project. It is Gringotts and has has a Wizarding Bank setting from the Harry Potter movies and is themed to the Gringotts Wizarding Bank, a top attraction for the expanded Wizarding World of Harry Potter at Universal Orlando Resort since its opening in July of 2014. It has a track length of two thousand feet and the ride uses many 3D projection screens to set a scene full of surprises, in much the same way as the other 3-D ride. It's a ride you will truly love.

Harley Quinn Crazy Train made by Zierer Company is a junior roller coaster, and if you're at Six Flags Great Adventure in New Jersey, this is one that the whole family can enjoy. It stands twenty-six-feet high with a twenty-five-foot first drop and several twisting turns on what can only be described as one of the longest trains ever created. This single train has a total of twenty cars (sitting two abreast) for a total of forty riders. The train is so long that the whipping action in the back end of the ride is comparable to an intermediate coaster of double its size and often. Because of this, the last several rows are actually closed off to riders. The ride twists around the 1,164-foot track at speeds approaching twenty-five miles per hour. There are ten similar coasters operating in the United States and many more found at parks around the world. You will find this type of ride an excellent fit if you are trying to overcome a fear of roller coasters.

Big Thunder Mountain Railroad, found worldwide by my favorites are at both Disneyland Park in Anaheim, California and the Magic Kingdom at Walt Disney World, Lake Buena Vista, Florida. It is a good family coaster to start off with as well. This is truly a fan favorite and built for family fun. The outdoor mine train type ride. It might be that fast only reaching speeds of around thirty miles per hour. It isn't very long, and there are no steep drops to speak of but we are talking Disney here, so of course, the theming of Thunder Mountain (as with most Disney attractions) is second to none. With slightly different settings in Florida and California, you can compare the two and see which one you like better. At Disneyland, you can fly by snoring inmates, singing gals, rattlesnakes, and dynamite-eating goats. Yes, you heard it right! Disney World's version is set up so you get not one, but two chain lifts during your run, while you race by a pleasant waterfall, around exploding geysers, and through "them there" mountains. One also gets to go through some "trick track" comprised of vertical train movement along the 2,800-foot course. I must say that I prefer the Disney World version, but all in all, both mountains are great rides for the whole family and for that budding coaster enthusiast. Both are popular attractions have inspired similar mine train rides (minus the great Disney effects of course) at many other parks around the country.

Grover's Vapor Trail at Sesame Place in Pennsylvania is a good family coaster to ride. This specially crafted, enhanced Vekoma, roller-skater stands at fifty feet tall and takes riders down a 1,300-foot track at almost thirty miles per hour. This is a junior coaster but can be ridden and enjoyed by adults as well. That is, if you can fit in the train. Just kidding! I would recommend this coaster for any beginner or intermediate coaster enthusiast who also enjoys wet and wild, water parks. Pleasing their guests since 1998, Vapor has enhanced park patrons' experience by bringing an added dimension to what is primarily a water park. Since the track is so small, only one train with accommodations for twenty people, can be utilized at a time. Even so, lines are never too long at this attraction. From the lift hill, you can scan the park area and see blue water from several adjacent water attractions in every direction as you get ready for your ride. But don't blink. You, just might miss it. Grover's Vapor Trail is a fun ride for everyone!

Matterhorn Bobsleds at Disneyland in Anaheim, California was developed by Arrow Corporation in 1959, becoming the world's first, steel track coaster. The ride itself only climbs to around eighty feet with a speed of around eighteen miles per hour. Blissfully devoid of any steep drops, this magnificent coaster allows your imagination to soar, instead of your blood pressure. Despite being quite slow in comparison to others in its class, the beauty is in its design and feeling of illusion. Like the later version, Space Mountain coaster, this one has two tracks as well. They are, in fact, slightly different from each other (one is faster than the other) and weave in and out of this scaled-down version of an actual mountain range that Walt Disney saw while on vacation in Switzerland. Kids just love the abominable snowman. This one is very different than the one that pops out at ya when you ride "Expedition Everest" and ice caves that can be seen inside this manmade mountain marvel ride. Don't close your eyes, or you just might miss the red-eyed bats that frequent these caves. It's Disney magic at its best!

Woody Woodpecker's Nuthouse Coaster at Universal Studios, Florida is a good choice if Space Mountain and Big Thunder Mountain seem too daunting for you. Despite its small, cramped nature and long line, I assure you this Vekoma coaster, with cars shaped like roller skates is well worth the wait. The steepest drop is just around twenty feet, with top speeds at twenty-two miles per hour. Just remember, higher and faster doesn't always mean better.

If you head to Disneyland, California, you can find a similar version of this fun, kiddy coaster.

Gadgets Go Coaster at Disneyland is simply a fun roller coaster. Situated in the ToonTown section of the park, Go Coaster is a colorful edition, surprisingly quick for its size.

The roller-skater coaster is one of Vekoma's most successful, mass-produced creations. They currently boast over fifty of these types, running worldwide as of 2015. However, with the Gadget, Veromi added the additional element of strategically placed water spouts, effectively allowing some passengers to get wet as the cars maneuver the helixes. This is a twenty-eight foot high roller coaster. The Gadget coaster is twenty-eight-feet high and takes kids and nervous parents alike through a maze of small, tight turns and twists, but don't worry, it rarely reaches the double digits on the miles-per-hour meter.

After you've braved the family coasters, you should be ready to move up to coasters that go a bit higher and a little faster. At this point, I wouldn't recommend any inversions (loops or corkscrews) to contend with just yet. For now, try some of the ones listed in this section instead.

Wooden Warrior is the newest wooden roller coaster located at Quassy Amusement Park in Middlebury, Connecticut. The coaster was designed and built by the Gravity Group. Despite the coaster's small size, it has been well received by enthusiasts for its air time. It was one of the first wooden coasters to use Timberliner trains that carry twelve people per load. Standing only thirty-five feet high with a forty-foot drop, this ride is great for the family and those just starting out. The ride has a top speed of thirty five miles per hour and is a lot of fun.

Space Mountain at Disneyland in Anaheim, California, and at the Magic Kingdom at Walt Disney World, in Lake Buena Vista, Florida would be my next choice. Okay, so I realize that some would want me to put this roller coaster in a different section, but to me, this ride has always been built for the family and, in my mind, is the "best of the best" in that category. The special *"space"* effects are great, and because it is indoor and dark, the anticipation adds to the psychological drama. The rides are different from each other in that the Magic Kingdom version emphasizes twists and sharp turns with slight drops, while the Disneyland version emphasizes sheer speed and smoothness throughout the ride. Both Space Mountains are great rides even though they have different soundtracks and subtle differences. They are worth the wait, which can average forty-five minutes, unless you use the fast pass program. Through Disney's magic and ability to create illusion, both rides feel much faster than the reported top speed of just twenty-nine miles per hour. The star-like illusion and brilliant sights and sounds during the wait in line make these two destination coasters a good next step on your roller coaster adventure. Whichever one you prefer, there is no doubt that these two (actually there are four tracks, two for each ride) are classics and ones that you will surely enjoy.

Next up, is Runaway Mountain at Six Flags Over Texas in Arlington, Texas. Created in 1996 by Premier, this ride is similar to Space Mountain without the themes or illusory atmosphere, but don't think it isn't a great ride. It's pitch dark inside and is a slightly modified Windstorm *Production* coaster. It will drop its guests around thirty feet and will reach top speeds of up to forty miles per hour during its 1,500-foot-long track. It's a heart-pounding, mysterious adventure, especially for those who don't like the dark, and is a hidden treasure at this park. Twist and turn through this giant mountain while hidden somewhere in these grounds, it has been said, awaits a bountiful treasure! With its near fifty degree drops, ninety-two degree banked angles, and two high-speed horizontal spirals, it's a good coaster to ride and will set you up for the next level of coasters on your list.

Skull Mountain at Six Flags Great Adventure in Jackson, New Jersey, is a good coaster for those who have graduated from the junior coaster league and want to try something a little more exciting but still family oriented. Built by Interman and Giovanola in 1986, this indoor coaster has just about everyone guessing where it will go next. Starting off in a themed cave-like station, riders negotiate through a darkened cave-like building in order to get to their destination. The ride is darker than Space Mountain, adding to its illusion of speed and danger. When they say Skull Mountain, they aren't kidding. The rocky exterior on the front of the building includes a giant skull-like image with dual waterfalls protruding from the eyes. The actual ride is not very long, and its top speed never goes past forty miles per hour. Also at forty-feet high, you don't really feel that first drop all that much, but you will enjoy the tight turns and total darkness, which definitely confuses your senses during the 1,300-plus-foot trek. Since only one train runs at a time, lines here can get quite long, so you might want to allow yourself some time for this one. I enjoy the front seat for this ride because you can just make out the track and see how close you really come to the exterior of the ride itself. It is also a good warm-up for the biggest and baddest rides (Nitro,

Superman, or Kingda Ka*)* that this park has to offer.

The Comet at Hershey Park in Hershey, Pennsylvania, is a great, classic wood coaster. This ride has a seventy-eight-foot drop and reaches a top speed of fifty miles per hour. The coaster dates back to 1946 and is one of the biggest coasters ever created at that time. Designed by Herbert Schmeck and built by the Philadelphia Toboggan Company, this coaster has a modified double out-and-back design. I especially like the first drop, suspended over the water, followed by a hairpin turn and launch into a nice, but sometimes rough, ride. It creaks, cracks, and looks rickety, but in my mind, it is a gem of a coaster and one that all coaster aficionados should experience.

The Classic Dragon Coaster at Playland Park in Rye, New York, was built in 1929, just after the park's debut. It was built by Fred Church and is one of the last remaining examples of his work in America. This is a very interesting ride with a unique V-shaped layout. Standing at seventy-five feet tall with a sixty-foot drop, the Dragon flies riders down the 3,400-foot long track at speeds reaching forty-five miles per hour. You might notice that this ride seems a little longer than it actually is. This feeling is achieved with a multi-layered, design, so that just when you expect the ride to end, you have another section of track to cover. It's these little surprises that make this coaster nothing less than a classic. The Dragon has been featured in many movies, and one of its more memorable moments occurs when riders get to go through the dragon's mouth and can be seen exiting out its tail section. A classic coaster and one that can help set you up toward the next level of thrill rides. Note: Playland Park is a pay-as-you-go park, so you can ride this one many times without notice of any long lines.

Thunderbolt at Six Flags New England, built in 1941 (just one year after the flyer Comet at Whalon Park), has a surprising element that very few coasters have, a double dip/drop series. This means that as you drop, you stop, level off, then drop again. It is a great ride experience for those who have never tried this type of element before and makes this coaster a classic. It is also a coaster with very few surprises and seems to deliver a consistent ride every time. For new coaster fanatics and families alike, this is one you should ride. Take advantage of Thunderbolt and ride this vintage, family woodie at night. It's a little spooky, but in the end, you will be happy you did.

Finally, you are now ready for the next level in coastering.

Batman: The Dark Knight is located at Six Flags Great Adventure in Jackson, New Jersey. More than just a mouse ride, the Dark Knight coaster features the most world-beloved DC Comic's characters (The Batman Crew) in an adventure that utilizes storytelling, physical movement, video, sound, and special effects to bring guests a one-of-a-kind dark, thrill ride. As part of the experience, park guests will see, hear, and feel the action of the movie, the moment they enter the ride queue line, and are transformed into citizens of Gotham City, caught in the middle of a city under siege and torn apart by the Joker. Guests board a Gotham City railcar and careen through six 180-degree hairpin turns, climb unseen hills, and plunge into pitch darkness. It is said that the Dark Knight Coaster offers guests a one-of-a-kind ride experience that combines the action and excitement of *The Dark Knight* movie with the thrill of a roller coaster. The $7.5–million-roller coaster is located in the Movie Town section at Six Flags Great Adventure, adjacent to Batman: The Ride. Guests can receive up-to-the-minute park news and purchase a season pass online at Sixflags.com.

Congratulations, you're doing great! Now that you're somewhat comfortable with the intermediate coasters described above, it is time to check out progressively bigger ones. On this level, you might try coasters like the crazy, spinning-mouse rides. These coasters spin you around as they traverse the circuit. When you have graduated from that level, you will then be ready for the bigger wood coasters (eighty feet or higher).

After that, you can experience single or double loop and corkscrew coasters that are in the park. There are literally hundreds of these types of coasters in the country, and I am sure there is one near you

Riding a looping coaster is a big step, and for most people when this has been accomplished, the pathway is clear for mass-produced coasters such as boomerangs and shuttle-loop coasters.

If you are like me, you will now start to enjoy new rides and experiences. Rides like X2, drop coasters like Griffon and the classic multi-element, inverted loops (five or more inversions) and spin rides like B&M's Batman, the Ride, along with the many Vekoma (SLC), "Mind Eraser- type coasters found throughout the United States. From there, it's just a short putt to the best coasters built today, there's a smorgasbord of coasters with wacky features (flying, compressed air launch, stand-up, floorless, and impulse coasters) to try until and eventually, you will ride the ultimate, e-ticket two, three and now four hundred-foot hyper-coasters available. Once you've battled your coaster demons, chances are quite good that, like me, you'll be hooked for life on these coasters, and the feeling of overcoming another challenge will subside, paving the way for a new set of obstacles

This completion phase creates a whole new set of challenges. Now that you love to ride, the question is, where do you go to get your next rush? Usually coaster enthusiasts travel together in clubs, and there are many out there to enjoy. I have found that no matter what language one speaks, laugher is universal. With these groups, cultural differences are forgotten and fun and newfound friendships that last a lifetime are made by all. Have fun with that. I know I do.

Types of Roller Coasters

All over the world, there are many different types of roller coasters that have been created for our enjoyment. Although there are many subcategories, these coasters can be put into two distinct categories—coasters made of wood, and coasters made of steel. Wood coasters have been manufactured to fit into basically four different subcategories: out-and- back style marvels; twisters; racers; and all-terrain, or mountain coasters. Each type of coaster brings a different fear factor to the rider.

Steel coasters come in all shapes and sizes too, but again, most are manufactured to fit into a specific subcategory: wild mouse rides; mine train; loop or corkscrew; and stand-up coasters. Also there are inverted, suspended, floorless, flying, and, of course, the new linear induction motor roller coasters as well.

Finally, we have the biggest and baddest coasters every created, the mega (and even taller, giga) coasters. These behemoths seem to lack any limits at all, breaking record after record, pushing the thrill levels beyond anything we've seen before. Heights are now soaring past 300 feet and at the time of this reading, there are several erected at 450 feet. So now that you are aware of the basic types of roller coasters out there, let's get into specifics so that you may be able to make an intelligent decision as to if, or when, a particular coaster would be right for you and your family.

The Mighty Wood Roller Coaster

Out and Back Coasters: Out and back coasters are just that. They are coasters that fly down a track, have a turnaround section, and fly back toward the start, covering a lot of ground in as little time as they can. They are pretty much straightforward or L-shaped in their design and have many small hills, dips, and summits that make the ride very enjoyable. With an out and back, the main element that people are looking for is airtime. That is the time when your backside is flung off your seat and into the air. This gives the feeling of negative gravitation forces and can wake your senses up in a hurry. For those unfamiliar with the feeling of negative- g's, it is sort of like taking a small hill or pump too fast in your car and getting the feeling that you are about to the hit the roof of your vehicle. Not fun in your car, but on a coaster, it can be, quite a different story. Some examples of out and back design coasters are Shivering Timbers at Michigan Adventure, the Phoenix at Knoebels Amusement Resort in Pennsylvania, and there's even an out and back combined with a twister, called Ghostrider, at Knott's Berry Farm in California.

Twister Coasters: Twister coasters are very different from the out and back design in that they usually are more compact and seem to go in and out of their own structure many times. They literally crisscross up and down into their frame to make for many curving drops, whirlpool turns, and head-bumping effects along the course. The best of these coasters are almost impossible to figure out. You will need to ride those several times in order to get a good course layout, so if you don't like surprises, you might just want to watch others ride before you come on board. Some of the most famous twisters around and still in operation today are the Cyclone in Coney Island, New York, and Roar at Six Flags America in Maryland.

Racer Coasters: Racer coasters add the element of competition in that there are dual tracks and trains that go up the lift hill and course together in a mirror image of itself. Coasters of this design can be any combination of out and back/twister designs and can be set up in a figure eight design. On this ride, you see many riders trying to get as streamlined as possible in order to be more aerodynamic in an effort to go faster and have their side of the track win the race. Some of the best racing coasters in the country are Lightning Racer at Hershey Park, Pennsylvania, and Racer at Kennywood in Pennsylvania.

All-Terrain/Mountain Coasters: Yes, terrain coasters have lift hills like most roller coasters, but as those of you who have been to many parks can concur, these parks can have uneven terrain. Hills and valleys seem to split many parks up, and as a result, at the end of the day, your feet can be living proof of this statement. All-terrain coasters adhere to the contours of the landscape. They exploit ravines and mountains by using them as part of the ride structure. The great thing (or the worst thing for some riders) is that usually on these types of coasters, you can never see the course track layout and never know what is really coming next. Foliage is everywhere, and the track is obscured by the mountains, trees, and high grass. You rarely know where you are in relation to the end of the ride unless you've ridden it a few times. That can be a problem for those coaster enthusiasts who like to know where they are and where they are going at all times. If you want to feel like you are going through the wood at full gallop, this type of coaster is for you. Some of the best examples of this type of coaster are the Beast at Kings Island, in Ohio; the Raven at Holiday World in Santa Claus, Indiana; and Boulder Dash at Lake Compounce, in Connecticut, just to name a few.

Steel Marvels
(There are many types out there)

Wild Mouse/Crazy Mouse Rides: These are commonly referred to as family coasters in that these are great for beginners and those who want to have fun without much intensity. Yes, it may feel like you are going to go off the end of the track and plummet fifty to seventy feet onto the ground below, but for the most part, these rides are less intense than the other high-intensity rides at the park. They follow a track that has a series of U-turns that gradually increase tension as the ride progresses. The crazy mouse versions add another element to the experience by making the car continually spin as it treks down the track. An example of a really good wild mouse is found at Hershey Park's Wild Mouse ride in Pennsylvania. One of the best crazy mouse rides, Prime Evil Whirl, can be located at Walt Disney World's Animal Kingdom.

Wild Mine Trains: These rides give you the feeling that you are careening through a mine shaft at breakneck speeds on a runaway train. These were the first steel-production coasters and they still have a place today at almost every big amusement park. Again, these rides can be enjoyed by most people who are afraid of doing loops or inversions of any kind. They are generally themed for the family and give the feeling of being inside a mine in the Old West. However, that being said, some of these mine trains can now reach speeds of sixty miles per hour and have a height of over 125 feet. You can find one that big in Cedar Point in Sandusky, Ohio, named Gemini.

Looping Coasters: Looping coasters (although tried in the early 1900's) were not very successful until a coaster by the name of Revolution, emerged at Six Flags, Magic Mountain. California)–in 1976. Yes, it is true that a year before, another coaster (Knott's Berry Farm's Corkscrew), was created to have a place in the history books as the world's first inversion coaster. But the story belongs to Revolution, which you can still ride today.

You're not really a full member of the "club" until you have experienced this and here is where many people simply "stop the ride!" They think it is too intense or are afraid of the experience. What I usually tell my television and radio audiences and reinforce during my many speaking engagements, is that you should think of this as doing a reverse somersault in your house. If you're in decent shape, all you have to do is go home, get down on the living room rug and roll over backward. It will give you a good idea of what a smaller, looping coaster feels like and will get you used to the sensation. I've been told by many people who have tried this then gone on to actually ride a looping coaster that the fear was in their head. Most have been excited at that point to move on to even more inversions in the future. Just like in real life, they simply conquer their fears and move on.

Suspended Coasters: These were the first roller coasters that had the rider hanging below the track. Unlike inverted coasters, these coasters used centrifugal force to swing riders from side to side. These coasters, created by Arrow Development, were actually created to spin and loop, but unfortunately, the actual design had many problems, limiting their ability to maneuver. If the heavy train was not traveling fast enough, there wouldn't be enough momentum to have its cars loop all the way around the track, resulting in the cars often falling to the side with tremendous force, causing injury to the rider. After many years trying to correct the problem, they concluded it would be too costly to change the design. They left it alone, allowing these suspended coasters to do what gravity does naturally, swing riders from side to side as they negotiate turns around the track. Although not as intense as inverted coasters, they are still a lot of fun to ride. One of the best of these suspended coasters can be found at Six Flags, Magic Mountain named Ninja.

Inverted Coasters: This type of coaster is suspended from the rails above but, unlike a suspended coaster, does not swing freely. Riders are horse-collared in their seats, legs dangling, with literally nothing beneath their feet but the ground below. There is nothing quite like the feeling of being strapped snugly in the chair during a smooth ride full of loops, corkscrews, and other inversions. It is surely a different sensation than being seated in a typical roller coaster car and can be a lot more fun when you get to a point where you can embrace the heavy, positive g's. If you get to this level in your coastering, baby, you have arrived and can handle just about anything that comes next. One of the most well-known rides in this category is Batman the Ride with production models all over North America. The tallest inverted coaster to date is Alpengeist, 200-foot monster located at Busch Gardens in Williamsburg, Virginia.

Stand-Up Coasters: These innovative steel coasters were brought to America in 1984 by the Togo Corporation. What set them apart was their specially designed harness that allowed passengers the new experience of soaring through the air from a standing up position. Being vertical can be a little harder on the knees and feet but they are still worth riding for the unique sensation they produce. There are at less than a dozen stand-up coasters operating currently in the United States with anywhere from one to six inversions, depending on the coaster. One of the best stand-up coasters, maxed out with six inversions, is Riddler's Revenge, located at Six Flags, Magic Mountain, California. A slightly shorter ride with less inversions, the Green Lantern, can be found at Six Flags Great Adventure, New Jersey.

Dive- Style Coasters: This is a steel roller coaster manufactured by Bolliger & Mabillard, includes at least on ninety-degree drop and gives riders a momentary feeling of free-falling through the air. Unlike other roller coasters where the lift hill takes the train directly to the first drop, a Dive Coaster lift hill leads to a flat section of track, followed by a holding brake, which stops the train just as it enters the first vertical drop. After a few seconds pause, the train is released for a three to six second drop. Some of the best out there are the Griffon, at Busch Gardens, Williamsburg, SheiKra at Busch Gardens, Tampa, and one of the originals out there, Oblivion at Alton Towers in the United Kingdom.

Linear Induction/Hydraulic Motor Roller Coasters (LIM): Before linear induction coasters, the coaster world had to be satisfied with going up a lift hill and having gravity drop them back to earth. Sure there were a few innovations that shot a train out of the station, but nothing that could take its passengers from zero to One hundred miles per hour as quickly, as well as shooting them straight up and down efficiently. That was finally achieved through the use of a new propulsion system.

This type of propulsion system is accomplished by using a new concept in motor technology: the linear induction motor (LIM) system. It is really a very innovative concept that propels a coaster forward on waves of electromagnetic energy. The coaster is blasted to remarkable velocity, much like being shot out of a cannon by dozens of linear induction motors strategically placed under the track. This is what makes the LIM coaster different from your typical gravity (lift hill) coaster. It literally *launches* the train and its passengers down the track. This is accomplished by alternating current, which creates an electromagnetic field, generating linear motion. This form of technology was created by Premier Rides in 1996 with their first coaster called the Outer Limits: Flight of Fear. You can still ride this enclosed spaghetti-track ride at King's Dominion and King's Island. In 2005, there are literally dozens of these rides all around the nation. Some of the best can be found under the name Mr. Freeze at both Six Flags Over Texas and Six Flags, Missouri. Disney even has their own version. The Rock 'n' Rollercoaster can be found at Disney's Hollywood Studios in Orlando, Florida. If you're searching for the very best of these, try Top Thrill Dragster at Cedar Point.

Hydraulic Type Launch Coaster: Hydraulic launched roller coasters give the riders high acceleration, yet with improved smoothness, over the electromagnetic and catapult launch mechanisms. The Swiss manufacturer Intamin pioneered this new style of roller coaster. The heart of the system is several (usually eight) powerful hydraulic pumps, each capable of producing around 500 horsepower. The concept is pretty simple. Hydraulic fluid is pumped into several different energy storing devices containing two compartments separated by a piston. As the incompressible hydraulic fluid is pumped into one compartment. A gas in the other compartment is compressed. One of the best known of these types of coasters is Kingda Ka at Six Flags, Great Adventure. The system as a whole can produce a peak power of up to 20,800 horse power for each launch. Now that's a lot of horses running all at once.

Floorless Coasters: In 1999, the ride manufacturer, Bolliger & Mabillard (B&M) came up with a new concept in the roller coaster industry. Why not get the experience of an inverted coaster, but instead of having the tracks above you, rework it so the tracks are below you, and your feet are dangling just inches above these tracks? It is literally like being strapped to your favorite easy chair and flying down a series of twists, turns, and inversions at speeds in excess of sixty miles per hour. This type of ride is for those coaster enthusiasts who like to take their experiences up to the next level. It's not recommended for the faint of heart. The introduction of the floorless wonder, Bizarro at Six Flags Great Adventure in Jackson, New Jersey, is just one of the many innovations that have come along in the thrill ride industry. Right now, B&M-a lock on these coasters and have several throughout the nation.

Flying Coasters: This coaster, among all its other virtues, offers the rider a sense of flight that can be described as intoxicating. This sensation is accomplished using an ingenious track layout and a unique coaster car design to replicate the feeling experienced during flight. It is literally a roller coaster where its passengers ride below and parallel to the tracks. With special harnesses made for the occupant, there is literally nothing but air separating you and the ground below. It is safe to say that no other coaster gives you the same sensation of riding below the tracks and hanging upside down. The inversions on most coasters briefly turn riders upside down, but on most flying coasters, you usually maintain a down position for a large portion of the ride. At first, the urge is to hang on for dear life, but in order to truly experience this ride, you will need to let go, put your hands out in front of you, and "fly." In 2000, Paramount's Great America in Santa Clara, California, put the first flying coaster, The Stealth, into operation. It was created by Vekoma International, and since then, you will find other flying coasters such as Batwing at Six Flags Over America (also created by Vekoma) and Superman Ultimate Flight at Six Flags New Jersey, Great America, and in Georgia.

Hyper/Giga-coasters: "Hyper-coaster" was the original term given to a roller coaster that broke the two hundred -tall mark. The term not only applies to steel coasters, but wooden coasters as well. Most hyper-coasters are non-looping, but one thing they share in common is the fact that they are very tall and extremely fast. The first one of kind was built by Arrow Dynamics and debuted at Cedar Point in Sandusky, Ohio, in May of 1989. It was called Magnum XL-200 and stood two hundred feet above the pavement. Most hyper-coasters, have now evolved into the "giga-coasters", evolved steel versions that mimic the design of wood, but as you may have guessed, are hundreds of feet taller, smoother, and of course faster, forcing the need for a way to distinguish between the latest improvements. The only exception to this statement can be found in a wood coaster at Kings Island, where you will find The Beast, boasting a 214-foot first drop combined with a loop and all while maintaining a top speed of seventy-eight miles per hour. Despite its wooden origins, it gets classified as a giga-coaster because its speed and maneuvering are in line with the newer, steel models going just over seventy-five miles per hour at its fastest point.

As hypercoasters go, if you like the feeling of your stomach in your mouth (negative g's), or the feeling of being pushed into your seat (positive g's), you will love these new monsters of the midway. They are not for the squeamish, and if you want to try these coasters, I suggest you build up your tolerance level before any attempt is ever made.

In the past few years, hyper-coasters are now even taller than two hundred feet. Millennium Force at Cedar Point became the first hyper/giga-coaster to stand over three hundred feet tall when it went into operation in 2000. Since then, other coasters have taken that title away. Today you will find hyper-coasters all over the country. Some of the most notable ones are Titan at Six Flags Over Texas; Nitro at Six Flags Great Adventure New Jersey; Raging Bull at Six Flags Great America in Gurnee, Illinois; and Steel Force at Dorney Park in Allentown, Pennsylvania. If you like to do more than just gamble, you can even find one called Desperado at Buffalo Bill's Resort and Casino, just outside of Las Vegas, Nevada.

Lately, the giga-coaster has begun to spring up all over the country. Cedar Point's latest attraction, Top Thrill Dragster, shoots its passengers down the track at 120 mph and climbs to a height of 420 feet. In New Jersey, you will find the tallest and fastest coaster ever created (at this writing), which races its riders around the track at 125 mph and zooms to the dizzying height of 455 feet. You will find this coaster at Six Flags Great Adventure under the name Kingda Ka.

The Best Mass-Produced Coasters in the Nation

Many people are unaware that some of the best coasters in the country (and in the world) are actually being mass-produced. Yes, the names have been changed, but the ride itself (at other parks) is exactly the same. It is just one more version of a successful thrill ride that has been duplicated for the masses. Below, you will see just a few of the most successful clone roller coasters that are out there and that I have ridden over the years. No matter how old they get, these rides are classics and will be around for many years to come.

Mass-Production Model Coasters

1. **Batman: The Ride (inverted BTR).** There are many out there, but one of my favorites can be found at Six Flags Great Adventure. It may be getting old, but it is still one of the best-loved inverted coasters around. It is true that there are many taller and faster rides in place (especially now) around the world, but when you compare its size to the ride's overall intensity, sometimes bigger isn't always better. Since the Batman ride was created with such a small footprint, the g-forces attained going through a particular element are in fact much higher (due to tighter turns and faster track), and this gives the ride the added punch that makes it feel much more powerful than it looks. The ride sustains heavy g-loading (sometimes as high as five Gs) throughout the ride and has always maintained a constant speed throughout. The best seats for visuals are of course the front four, but if you really want to get knocked around, and most of us do, try the back seats at night. In many cases, this ride is left dark, and with no daylight to see by, you definitely get a different ride experience. For me, it doesn't matter how many times you ride this marvel, it will always keep you second guessing. Bolliger & Mabillard can be very proud of this invention they concocted almost two decades ago. Also worth mentioning, is the queue through Gotham City before you actually get to the ride itself. It is has been nicely done and accurately sets the mood for your adventure. If you can't visit New Jersey, you can find this type of ride in many parks across the country.

2. **Vertigo-Style Coaster.** A coaster named after a character from the Batman comic books. In this case, the name is quite appropriate. The vertigo class coaster is slightly taller than its "boomerang" cousin (125 feet), climbing to a height of about 140 feet, but what makes this coaster different is the seating arrangement. The seats are arranged so that the riders actually face each other, and that makes this shuttle coaster very different than any other. When you reach the top on this ride, you just wait there for what seems like an eternity, and when you least expect it, the train drops at over fifty-five miles per hour past the future riders waiting in line. The first inversion you get to experience is a pretty nifty seventy-foot boomerang, which flips you over not once, but twice. Like Vekoma's smaller cousin, the original boomerang, this element is pretty disorienting, and riders experience almost five g's while entering it, but it's so fast, that you barely even notice the speed. After a loop, you go up slowly the opposite side and a second hill. This is a good time to check out the people staring back at you. After another stop, you go through the course in the opposite direction, but this time, backward, streaking past the station and partially up the first hill. At this point, the train is taken slowly down the hill and back to the station. It's a good ride, but the older style restraints can be a little hard on the neck and

shoulders. Since there is only one train running at any time, the lines will get long as the day goes by. It is best to ride this one early.

3. **Boomerang Style Roller Coasters.** The first of its kind was created by Vekoma Corporation way back in 1984 and can still be found at of Morey's Pier in Wildwood, New Jersey. This standard shuttle rides takes riders in reverse up to a height of 125 feet. At the top of the station, the train is released and drops through the station into a boomerang (or cobra roll) element, where it then goes through a vertical loop and up a second lift hill. Here the train is pulled forward to the highest point then released backward over the same 825-foot course. The best part of this ride is traversing the course backwards. It is quite a different experience, and one that all coaster enthusiasts ought to try. While the ride might be a little rough by today's standards, it is worth trying as long as the lines are short. Unfortunately, since only one train can be dispatched at a time, the lines tend to get pretty long on busy days. At one point, this type of ride was popular around the world and considered one of the best rides out there. Like the Batman-style coaster, they leave a small footprint, making them ideal for smaller parks with little room to spare. The boomerang is still one of the most common shuttle coasters ever produced.

4. **The Standard Suspended Looping Coaster.** This coaster is a standard Vekoma roller coaster, but unique location–gives riders a great ride for their money. There are many of this type out there, but my favorite of the bunch is still the Great "Nor'easter" (suspended looping coaster or SLC) at Morey's Pier in Wildwood, New Jersey. This coaster is built literally out on the pier itself, so when you are at the top of this lift hill, you see nothing but blue sky and ocean in front of you. That is, of course, until you begin to dive to the right toward the pier below **at** speeds of fifty-five miles per hour. You don't always get a smooth ride on these coasters and depending on the day, it's sort of like catching the perfect wave. If you hit it just right, you will get a pretty intense ride. If not, you might need a chiropractor after it's over. This ride seats two abreast in trains that carry the older horse-collar restraints. A few of the struts have been changed on this ride, along with the station itself, and now it wraps itself around one the best water flumes on the East Coast. The clearances are very tight, causing riders to instinctively raise their legs as high as possible as this SLC screams down the track, through five different inversions:-a cobra roll that inverts the riders twice, a twist loop, and two heart line flips. I consider this ride a classic, and one that you will find under different names all over the country and around the world.

5. **The Crazy Mouse (spinning-type coaster).** This coaster, created by Reverchon, takes the standard wild mouse ride to the next level and is still quite popular today. Like the wild mouse, this ride goes up a lift hill then down a track of hairpin turns and small drops that increase in overall size and intensity as you go along the track. The spinning motion gives you a dizzying giving this compact 1,377-foot-long coaster tremendous punch when the cars reach the lower level. One of the most popular coasters of this type can be found at Disney World's Animal Kingdom, but you will find many out there. The crazy mouse is perfect for people who like getting disorientated, although I wouldn't recommend it for anyone that gets nauseous easily.

6. **Zyeklon Loop-Style Coasters.** Like the "Python" at Playland in Ocean City, New Jersey, is just one of a dozen Zyklon loop rides created worldwide by Italian-based, Pinfari Corporation. What I like about this one is that you get a good ride from start to finish. It is definitely the ride to choose if you are just starting and want to try doing a loop or two. Standing at thirty-six-feet high and racing down the 1,200-foot-long track, I have found that you get a pleasant experience all the way. With this ride in particular, it doesn't hurt that you're on the Jersey shore and overlooking the Atlantic Ocean either. Usually this type of model has two four-seat cars attached

to it, but be careful, the lap bars are pretty snug. Unless you have a wiry body frame, you might want to suck in that stomach or even push it in with your hand, when you get in the car.-Even though there is a loop here, this coaster is definitely in the family coaster category, and one that parents should try with their kids.

If you like this one, then you may be ready for the next level of coaster thrills. This coaster is actually a progression from other Pinfari non-looping coasters of the same name, which came before it. In fact, there are only three of these babies left in the United States.

7. **Mine Train-Style.** Like the "Runaway Train" (mine train style) at Six Flags Great Adventure in New Jersey might not be the oldest of this type out there. The oldest mine train can be found at the Mine Train at Six Flags Over Texas circa 1966. The Runaway Train is the first roller coaster to be built at SFGA in 1974 is 2,400 feet long (a mine train standard), utilizes only one lift hill (seventy feet high), and races its guests around the track in excess of thirty-five miles per hour. Its scenic views of the park are spectacular, and that last swooping (and most photographed) turn over a manmade lake is what separates this mine train from all others. Recommended for the advancing beginner coaster aficionado, this is indeed a family coaster with a capital "*F.*"

A mine train coaster is designed to create the feel of an old, runaway train. It usually features sharp turns and short little bunny hops. The train itself looks like a string of coal mining cars, and in most cases, you can find mini-locomotives right up front. Except for the tunnels, Runaway Train has all these elements. On most other rides of this type, you will usually encounter tunnels and mineshafts as you go. In recent years, many mine trains have been produced by Morgan Manufacturing Company to meet the demands of a renewed interest in this classic type of coaster.

8. **Wildcat-Style Coaster.** Created by Anton Schwarzkopf, this coaster might be less than Fifty-feet high, but its figure eight design and high visibility seating arrangement (usually just one car that looks like a German-style automobile) make this a decent ride for your local amusement park. The cars seem to glide at times as they traverse each end of the 1,380-foot structure. But what makes the Wildcat a classic Schwarzkopf coaster is the three steep drops of over forty feet that will treat the rider to some unexpected negative g's and do it at speeds approaching forty miles per hour. A welcome for all those who need to feel the rush, the Wildcat can be a little rough at times for its smaller passengers. Overall, it delivers a good ride experience for its size. There are three versions of the Wildcat that have been produced. The largest ones are fifty feet in height. Overall you will find many around the country (and the world), but many are being replaced by newer family-style coasters that are easier to maintain.

9. **Corkscrew-Style Coaster.** You will only find a handful of these types of coasters left. Standing at seventy feet in height, this ride, sends its riders into a tight right turn followed by a sixty five-foot drop into a double corkscrew. Be careful not to touch the trees as you go through these elements. The ride comes close enough to the foliage that you feel like you can grab a few tree leaves as you go by. Reaching speeds of forty miles per hour, this coaster rides along a 1,250-foot track that you only wish were just a bit longer. But back in late seventies, this coaster was state of the art and one of only a few coasters that took their riders upside down.

In fact, they were the first modern coasters to invert passengers. The first coaster to do this is still in operation. This type of ride will always have a special place in my heart because it was the ride that was the first one to flip me and you never forget you're first! It can still thrill newer-generation riders even today, and is my first choice for those who have braved the family coaster genre and want to experience an inversion in its simplest form.

Overall, there are less than a dozen of these Arrow coasters operating around the world, so I say, if you can find one, ride it!

10. **City Jet-Style Coaster.** A city Jet-style coaster at Gillian's Wonderland Pier in Ocean City, New Jersey, is the only one of its kind in North America. In fact there were only a handful of these coasters ever built around the entire world, but I like the ride it gives. A smaller version of the Jet Star series, coaster City Jet, actually utilizes a spiral lift hill. An electric motor is housed inside the car and takes its passengers up thirty-six feet before it drops them one foot short of the ground along 1,362 feet of track. Built by the Schwarzkopf Industries Company, this coaster is great for those who are just starting out on their coaster careers or for those parents who want to see if they can still ride the rails. It is a pleasant coaster to ride, and one that everyone in the family can enjoy. I say ride it and have some fun in the sun!

11. **The Flitzer Series.** These type of rides were originally created as a portable coaster by Franz Schwarzkopf (Anton's brother) and sold by the Zierer Company, known for their seventy-five Tivoli coasters around the world. The Flitzer at Morey's Pier, first built in 1981, takes its passengers (overlooking the ocean, of course) to a height of twenty-five feet. Passengers are then subjected to a slew of zippy turns and twists all through the 1,200-foot course. Passengers usually sit together in a line, sort of like a log flume arrangement, and the more weight you have in each single car, the faster you will go. This is an excellent starter coaster for anyone who wants to try coasters and is perfect for the kids. If you live in New Jersey, you will find three of six of these coasters right along the Jersey shoreline. They all go under the same name, Flitzer, and are located at Jenkinson's Family Center in Point Pleasant; Keansburg Amusement Park in Keansburg; and Playland in Ocean City, New Jersey. Another notable Flitzer can be found at the Ocean City Pier Rides in Ocean City, Maryland.

12. **The Original Wild Mouse.** If you find yourself in a decent amusement park, chances are there will be a wild mouse ride in the park. They are great for the family and some still pack a kick in them. These rides, in fact, have intense tight turns and give you that out-of-control feeling as you move along the track. Take my word for it, hats and glasses off for these type of rides! I almost don't even want to call this a family coaster even though they are.

The wild mouse concept is a simple but ingenious one. Create a single car train on a track with very, very tight turns. Position the car wheels closer to the rear of the car than on a traditional coaster, causing the front of the car to travel past each turn before suddenly U-turning, making the riders feel that their car is literally going to fall off the track. If you are able to achieve this sensation, then you have been successful. Wild mouse coasters have been popular since the 1950s and '60s, but lately you will find many new ones popping up just about everywhere. Coaster companies like Arrow, Mack, Maurer, Miler, Schiff, and others have thrown their hat in the ring and added these coasters to their lineups. Some are better than others, but they all manage to get you and your family's adrenaline going in a small amount of space. They do mine!

The Best Wood and Steel Roller Coasters Around

There are literally thousands of coasters in the country. So how do you pick the best ones to ride? Well, there are many ways to accomplish this. You can rely on surveys or just go by what the rider attendance has been over a certain time period. When I decided which coasters to ride, I took a simpler approach. I asked myself if I would enjoy the ride, then after the experience, I asked if I would go on it again. If the answer was yes, then to me, it was a great ride and one that I would recommend to others. In the grand scheme of things, the deciding factor on whether a ride is successful or not, is its overall excitement factor and it's re-ride ability to make riders come back for more. I can safely say that if you ask one hundred people what their favorite wood or steel coasters are (and I have), you will surely get dozens upon dozens of different answers swayed by where the rider lives, their level of enthusiasm, and what they were actually looking for in a thrill ride. Some enthusiasts love steep drops from dizzying heights. Others prefer speed but hate inversions. Still others love inversions but hate lengthy drops from high towers. The combinations of criteria can go on and on. One person's thrilling ride experience can be another person's nightmare, so the trick here is to find a ride experience that everyone will enjoy. In my mind, that is the key to building the ultimate roller coaster. Variety is the spice of life, so why would it be any different when it comes to riding roller coasters?

Having said that, I can easily say that my top roller coasters (for both wood and steel) picks are based on my experiences and personal preferences. They are thrill rides that I have personally ridden, and they are mine and mine only. Yours might differ. Please use this guide to help you decide which coasters you would like to experience, but in the end, remember your top picks may differ!

Steel Roller Coasters

1. Millennium Force at Cedar Point, Sandusky, Ohio.
2. Bizarro at Six Flags New England.
3. Banshee at Kings Island amusement park, Mason, Ohio.
4. Apollo's Chariot at Busch Gardens, Williamsburg, Virginia.
5. Kingda Ka at Six Flags Great Adventure, Jackson, New Jersey.
6. Leviathan at Canada's Wonderland (just outside of Toronto Canada).
7. Montu at Busch Gardens, Tampa, Florida.
8. Nitro at Six Flags Great Adventure, Jackson, New Jersey.
9. Top Thrill Dragster at Cedar Point, Sandusky, Ohio.
10. Volcano-The Blast Coaster at Paramount's Kings Dominion, Virginia.
11. The Incredible Hulk at Universal Studio's Islands of Adventure, Florida.
12. Bizarro at Six Flags Great Adventure, Jackson, New Jersey.
13. Griffon at Busch Gardens Williamsburg, Virginia.
14. Phantom's Revenge at Kennywood in West Mifflin, Pennsylvania.
15. Gatekeeper at Cedar Point Sandusky, Ohio.
16. Superman-Ride of Steel at Six Flags America, Largo, Maryland.

17. Raptor at Cedar Point, Sandusky, Ohio.
18. Superman: Ultimate Flight at Six Flags, Atlanta, Georgia.
19. Kumba at Busch Gardens, Tampa, Florida.
20. Titan at Six Flags Over Texas, Arlington, Texas.
21. Dragon Challenge at Universal Studios Islands of Adventure, Florida.
22. X2 at Six Flags Magic Mountain, Valencia, California.
23. Steel Force at Dorney Park, Allentown, Pennsylvania.
24. Diamondback located at Kings Island in Mason, Virginia.
25. Thunderbolt at Lunar Park, Coney Island in Brooklyn, New York.
26. Intimidator 305 at Kings Dominion, Doswell, Virginia.
27. Behemoth at Canada's Wonderland, Vaughan, Ontario, Canada.
28. Raging Bull at Six Flags Great America in Gurnee, Illinois.
29. Iron Rattler at Six Flags Fiesta Texas.
30. Powder Keg at Silver Dollar City Branson, Missouri.
31. Lightening Run at Kentucky Kingdom.
32. Skyrocket at Kennywood, West Mifflin, Pennsylvania.
33. Mamba at Worlds of Fun, Kansas City, Missouri.
34. Manta at SeaWorld, Orlando, Florida.
35. Storm Force Runner at Hershey Park, Hershey, Pennsylvania.
36. Kraken at SeaWorld, Florida.
37. Alpengeist at Busch Gardens, Williamsburg, Virginia.
38. Riddler's Revenge at Six Flags Magic Mountain in Valencia, California.
39. Great Bear at Hershey Park, Pennsylvania.
40. Hollywood Rip Ride Rockit, Universal Studio's Orlando, Florida.
41. Batman the Dark Knight at Six Flags New England, Agawon, Massachusetts.
42. Batwing at Six Flags America, Largo, Maryland.
43. El Loco at the Adventure Dome in Las Vegas, Nevada.
44. Expedition Everest at Disney's Animal Kingdom in Orlando, Florida.
45. Rock 'n' Roller Coaster at Disney's MGM studios, Florida.
46. Maverick at Cedar Point in Sandusky, Ohio.
47. Fire Chaser Express at Pigeon Forge, Tennessee.
48. Flight of Fear at Kings Dominion, Virginia.
49. Montezooma's Revenge at Knott's Berry Farm in California.
50. Shockwave at Six Flags Over Texas, Arlington, Texas.

Bonus Roller Coasters also worth mentioning are Joker's Jinx at Six Flags America, in Largo, Maryland and Loch Ness Monster at Busch Gardens in Williamsburg, Virginia. And now, the list!

1. **Millennium Force** at Cedar Point, Sandusky, Ohio is a sight to see. This steel marvel can be observed for miles in any direction. Every year there are challengers and every year, in my mind, this 310-foot monster with overbanked turns of 122 degrees, still takes first prize. At least for me it does. Built by Interman AG Corporation at a cost of twenty-five million dollars, Millennium Force broke all the record books in 2000 and has one of the fastest lift hills in the world. You travel up this hill at around fourteen miles per hour, reaching the top in seconds instead of the minutes we've become accustomed to on most mega-type coasters. If you hate to linger at great heights, then this feature can be a good thing. From the top, the view is amazing, but the coaster's first drop is–what really makes Millennium a cut above the rest. I assure you, it will take your breath away. Traveling at speeds of over ninety miles per hour and dropping at an eighty-degree angle, you will be moved by the negative gs of this ride. But that will only be the beginning. This ride will take you to dizzying heights on a consistent high-speed trek along a 6,500-foot track, topped off with three of the tallest hills you will ever find. And let's not forget those overbanked turns and dramatic tunnels! Altogether, Millennium Force, gives a great ride on a very sleek, two-across stadium-seat train that gives a smooth but rapid ride throughout. The way I see it, if you like continual drops and a lot of airtime, then Superman-Ride of Steel at Six Flags New England is your top coaster. But if you want the best first drop in the nation along with sheer overall speed and highly banked turns, then Millennium is your choice as the best of the best. I personally love them both.

   It is best to try this ride just as the park opens and stay close with the crowd. You can also get in an hour early if you stay at one of the hotels at Cedar Point. If you attempt to ride during the midday hours, it is almost a foregone conclusion that you will spend most of your day waiting in line for this world-class coaster. One note of caution: Millennium has one of the strictest ride enforcement rules around. Your seatbelt must be securely fastened with at least half an inch leeway in order to experience the force. Those individuals who have over a forty-four inch waist might not be allowed to ride.

2. **Bizarro** at Six Flags New England in Agawam, Massachusetts is a work of art. If any roller coaster had a challenger for the top spot every year, it would seem to be this one. Not even the Millennium Force can boast the amount of airtime (or floating time) that this ride delivers in one sitting. Bizarro also features an incredibly tall lift hill, rising slowly alongside the Connecticut River. This breathtaking view from the top only heightens the level of excitement as the train climbs to just over 208 feet. From here, you can enjoy the view and note that on a clear day, you can see for ten to twelve miles in any direction. However, you will only experience the view for a brief moment before plummeting down the first hill at almost eighty miles per hour. After this, you should be prepared for two and a half minutes of pure, unchecked adrenaline running through your veins. From the seventy-plus-degree, 221-foot first drop to those absolutely amazing 85-foot bunny hops, it's truly a thrill a second. You literally feel like you are going to be ejected out of your seat on almost every hill, but fortunately with those comfortable and very effective waist harnesses, there is no need for a parachute on this ride.

In addition to the negative drops and the feeling of being ejected from your seat, there is so much more to this ride. The rider ends his adventure with an incredible, high g-force dual helix finale. Not bad at all! It's one of the best I have ridden, and I am sure you will think so as well! Note that the lines can be really long on this one, so make this your first stop when entering the park. If, there's a wait, take it from me, the ride is still worth it. Bizarro is truly a coaster that all other mega-coasters must measure themselves against and, in my mind, is truly a cut above the rest. Not recommended for family coastering, but what a ride!

3. **Banshee** is a steel roller at Kings Island amusement park located in Mason, Ohio-was designed by Bolliger & Mabillard (B&M). This is one of the first inverted coasters built in the United States since Patriot came into existence in 2006. This fantastic ride is just one of the many reasons to visit this incredible park. Banshee features over 4,100 feet of track that takes the rider through seven inversions, reaching top speeds of almost seventy miles per hour. This ride is also one of the longest inverted roller coasters on the planet. In fact, it's the first female-inspired theme park ride to ever be created. When Cedar Fair (parent company of Kings Island) announced a new coaster, ears perked up. With the addition of Banshee, there were suddenly fifteen great rollercoasters, all in the same place, making Cedar Point one of the biggest parks in the United States. Banshee is to be experienced, not just ridden, and I guarantee if you have the courage to get on it, you will be happy you did. This monster of the midway cost over twenty-five million dollars to build and is well worth the hour and a half in time that it takes to experience this magnificent ride. If you are ever in the Cincinnati area and love thrill rides, this is definitely one you want to put on your bucket list.

4.   **Apollo's Chariot** at Busch Gardens Williamsburg, in Virginia is still one of my favorite roller coasters of all time. If you have ever ridden this roller coaster, you will ~~quickly~~ have already discovered why this is still a fan favorite. Highlighted by an impressive 210-foot first drop, this ride features great floating time and high negative g's on almost every hill. The out and back design was the first of three mega-coasters created by Bolliger & Mabillard. (Raging Bull at Six Flags Great America and Nitro at Six Flags Great Adventure would complete the package a few years later.) The ride makes excellent use of the park's natural valleys with three drops skimming the "Rhine River." The turning drop to the left on the third hill is one of the best I have seen. It is safe to say that Bolliger & Mabillard really took the time to make this ride stand out.

All told, there are nine drops on this coaster, and if you measured them all together, it would total 825 feet, a world record for coasters at conception in the late 90's. On Apollo's Chariot, every seat is simply enjoyable. This ride is very fast and can be very intense, reaching seventy-five miles per hour at times. You will also experience one of the most comfortable rolling stock trains ever created. If you don't like hyper-coasters (coasters two hundred feet and higher), then Chariot might just change your mind about them altogether. It did for my wife, who absolutely hates long straight drops. All the pieces certainly do fit together in this presentation to create a fantastic, enjoyable, and fun ride experience for all who ride.

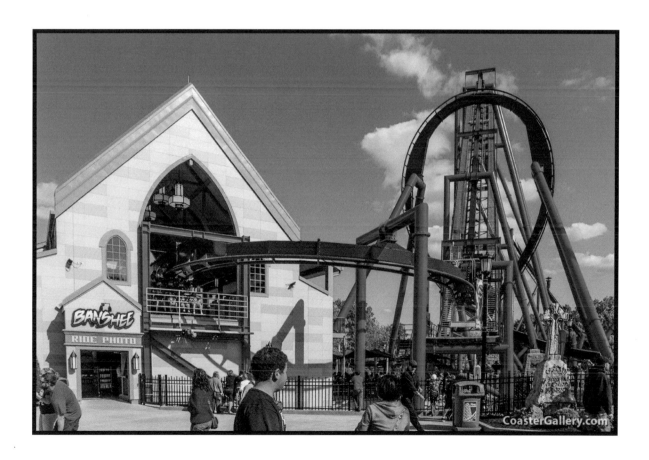

5. **Kingda Ka** at Six Flags Great Adventure in Jackson, New Jersey, is not just the biggest and fastest coaster in the United States. In my mind, it's one of the baddest. Weighing in at a whopping 456 feet, it stands at more than forty-five stories tall. That's roughly three times the height of the Statue of Liberty. It propels riders at speeds of approximately 130 miles per hour and does this in less than four seconds. This is more than fifty-five miles per hour faster than the Batman and Robin roller coaster, and 45 miles per hour faster than my favorite ride at this park—the beloved Nitro. In addition, the ride has an amazing 270-degree-angle spiral. When Kingda Ka opened in 2005, it broke all the records in its class. What if a coaster could be launched at 128 miles per hour in just a few seconds, be catapulted to the dizzying height of 450 feet, plummet down at 120 miles per hour, and still be back to the starting gate in less than thirty seconds? Well, the manufacturer (B&M) came up with a ride that would do all of these things and much more. Kinda Ka is very similar to another powerhouse ride that I love so much called Top Thrill Dragster, but unlike Top Thrill, you never know when you are going to be rocketed down the 3,118-foot-long track and at the end of Kingda Ka; get ready for one last 130-foot hill that will literally pull you out of your seats. At the top of this last hill, you will experience zero gravity and know what it feels like to be in outer space if only for a second or two. All in all, Kingda Ka is an experience you must not miss and make sure you wear some eye protection. At these speeds, you will need it.

6. **Leviathan** at Canada's Wonderland lies just outside of Toronto, Canada. This unforgettable steel coasters the first by Swiss manufacturer, Bollinger & Mabillard. It is one of the first roller coasters to exceed a height of over 300 feet, making it what we call a *giga-roller*-coaster. Built in April of 2012 at a cost of twenty-eight million dollars, this 5,486feetlong track has a top speed of ninety-two miles per hour. Leviathan is currently the tallest and fastest roller coaster and is (at the time of this writing) the seventh-tallest coaster in the world. It was the sixteenth roller coaster to be built at Canada's Wonderland, putting this park in the top five list of most roller coasters rides in a given park. The coaster opened to season pass holders on April 27, 2012, and to the general public on May 6, 2012. After leaving the station, the train turns completely around and starts to climb a chain lift hill. Once at the top of the 306-foot lift, it drops to the ground at an 80-degree angle (that's almost straight down), reaching speeds in excess of ninety miles per hour. Following the first drop, the train goes through a 100-foot tunnel, then curves upwards into a 160-foot-tall overbanked banked turn to the right before dropping again and turning at high speed into a left hand bank at around 75 miles per hour. What comes next is a high-speed turn. It even gets even better from this point on but I will let you experience this yourself. Let me tell you this is one ride that you should not miss. It lives up to its billing and is one of the best rides you will find. The lines on this contraption can get very long so this is a ride you want to experience when first entering the park or just before closing.

7. **Montu** at Busch Gardens, in Tampa, Florida, is one the best inverted coasters I have ever ridden. No matter how old it gets, this ride can still surprise people. Nestled in the Egyptian section of the park, the coaster really does fit well into its environment. Montu was built by B&M and opened back in 1996 for twenty million dollars as the world's tallest inverted coaster at 150 feet. It was also the first inverted coaster to increase the number of inversions to seven. They come very quickly, so try not to close your eyes during the ride. On the first drop, if you can see it, please take note of the crocodile pit that appears directly beneath you. Following that theme, you can expect Montu to take you on a journey into tunnels around temples. And through a few excavation ditches that you swear will leave your body in pieces.

The best part of this ride comes during the second half of Montu's run. Just when you think the best is behind you, you get hit with several tight inversions where you swear you are going to hit the impeccably designed and placed walls around you. This part of the ride is strangely reminiscent of another ride that is now gone but not forgotten from our memories: Big Bad Wolf, at Busch Gardens' sister park in Williamsburg, Virginia. On that ride, you get to maneuver quite closely through a Bavarian village, while Montu takes you through a Middle Eastern setting instead. As in all inverted coasters, I suggest the front seat for the best visuals and the very back for that out-of-control sensation. It's a great ride, but definitely not for beginners or the faint of heart.

©2008 Joel A. Rogers
www.CoasterGallery.com

8. **Nitro** at Six Flags Great Adventure is without a doubt one of the most intense rides I have ever been on, and it seems to get better every year of operation. From its 215-foot steep dive (the tallest B&M coaster to date), to the high g turnaround (helix) section, Bolliger and Mabillard does it again with a coaster that is consistently ranked no less than fifth in the world by *Amusement Today* magazine. I think it's safe to say that Nitro is more than just your average 200-foot-plus hyper-coaster! It's an elite machine in an elite park. Although its L-shaped out-and-back layout looks a lot like Apollo's Chariot, this monster has some different elements up its sleeves. At sixty-six degrees, the angle of the first descent is far from completely vertical, but from this dizzying height, it sure feels like it could be. In addition to its first drop, Nitro has plenty of secondary drops, turns, and high-speed maneuvers that will literally keep you guessing no matter how many times you ride it. Even though Nitro delivers a consistent ride, no two elements are exactly alike. The best seat on this ride is the left front seat. The reason for this occurs on the second drop: A 189-foot plunge to the left leaves the unsuspecting passenger stationed in that seat looking straight down at the ground below, while racing at speeds in excess of eighty miles per hour. On the way up the lift hills, riders will notice signs that show how high you are in comparison to famous structures around the world, such as the Sphinx in Egypt 66 feet), Niagara Falls (176 feet), and the Statue of Liberty (189 feet). Overall, the ride is extremely smooth, fast, and airtime-filled. Clearly it is still one of the best and most intense rides at Great Adventure (along with Kingda Ka), but watch out for those long lines. They can be pretty lengthy. This needs to be your first or second stop as you enter the park.

9. **Top Thrill Dragster** at Cedar Point in Sandusky, Ohio, is a class all by itself and, in my mind, is actually just a tad more enjoyable than its sister coaster, Kingda Ka. Riders begin their journey aboard this whopping forty-two-story screamer by securing themselves into these ultra-cool trains that resemble top fuel dragsters. I absolutely love this ride! The train then moves into a "starting line" position, where it is launched forward, reaching 120 mph in approximately four seconds. The train then zooms straight up the 420-foot-tall hill on track that rotates ninety degrees, crests the coaster's apex and then free falls back to Earth. On the way down you spin like a corkscrew 270 degrees and riders then return to the station to begin regaling their friends with stories of the greatest ride of their lives. Designed by world-renowned coaster manufacturer Intamin AG of Wollerau, Switzerland, Top Thrill Dragster is located directly between two other Cedar Point legends: the Magnum XL-200 and Millennium Force roller coasters. Riders must be at least fifty-two inches tall to ride Top Thrill Dragster and if you're tall enough, this is a must do while at Cedar Point. Lines get very long so plan on getting on this ride early or right before the park closes.

10. **Volcano, The Blast Coaster** at Kings Dominion in Virginia is truly a one-of-a-kind thrill ride contraption! Located in the Congo section of the park between the Avalanche Bobsled coaster and Outer Limits: Flight of Fear, the Volcano rises above a shady pseudo-tropical landscape that is quite interesting to look at. There truly is nothing like this ride where the visuals are concerned. Imagine yourself being on an inverted coaster (like Batman: The Ride) but instead of going up a lift hill, you are literally launched out of the station, going from zero to seventy miles per hour in less than four seconds. Just when you're trying to figure out how they accomplished the speed, without any sort of lift hill to help with propulsion, imagine being shot straight up out the top of this volcano to continue your experience, courtesy of a second set of motors and the Linear Induction Motor System, all while flames shoot out from the top of the mountain!

On this ride, the best place to be is clearly in the front row, where the speed and the small clearances around the volcano's exterior simulate a very fast-moving lava flow. There are usually three trains carrying four cars at a time with riders arranged two across in two rows, for a total of sixteen riders per train. It's a fantastic ride!

11. **The Incredible Hulk** at Universal Studios' Islands of Adventure in Orlando, Florida is just a great ride, period. With an angled, dynamic tire-driven launch, riders burst into daylight (or night light) and are immediately flipped upside down. What comes next are seven very quick and enjoyable inversions. Most of this occurs right over the park walkway, and the speed is clearly felt, not just by those who are riding this coaster, but by those watching it on the ground as well. In addition to the tire catapult over water, which they say feels like a cat shot from an aircraft carrier, the immense cobra roll and vertical loop are quite memorable.

Great visuals are also accented in the Hulk ride experience. The ride features a mist tunnel and a huge airtime section immediately following a deceptive halt, halfway through the ride. This section is designed to make you think the ride is over, but surprise, surprise. It's not! Despite the Hulk's compact size, the ride is incredibly smooth and packs quite a punch. In all the excitement of getting on the ride don't forget to enjoy the great queue while you wait. One thing to remember about the Hulk is that it is best to ride this coaster early. When the park opens, the Hulk is the ride you should head to first. If you can take advantage of the park's Fastpass system or stay at one of the local hotels at the park, you surely will be ahead of the waiting game. If not, please note that crowds will generally form for this ride in the late morning and early afternoon, so get there as soon as possible. However, if you get the chance to experience this coaster at night, where its close proximity to other rides greatly accentuates your view of the park, you won't be sorry. You can find the Hulk to your left, in the superhero section of the park. Or just look up. You won't be able to miss the green track that dangles above you as you enter the land of superheroes. Bolliger & Mabillard really come through with this heroic green monster. Why not take a ride and see for yourself.

12. **Bizarro (formerly Medusa)** at Six Flags Great Adventure in Jackson, New Jersey, is an interesting ride to experience. Have you ever wanted to be strapped in a chair with your feet dangling precariously from fourteen stories up? Better yet, have you ever been strapped to a chair whose sole purpose is to fly through a powerful series of twists, turns, and inversions at speeds that reach over sixty miles per hour? If you've answered yes to both questions, then chances are, you've experienced the unique, exhilarating, unforgettable thrill from the new generation of manmade adrenaline machines created by Bolliger & Mabillard, commonly known as the "floorless" roller coasters. Medusa went into the history books on April 2, 1999, when it streaked down the tracks as the nation's first floorless coaster. This 140-foot monster gives you a great view of the drive-through safari for a brief second before you are dropped at speeds reaching over sixty miles per hour. Since the track is below you and your feet dangle just inches from it, you might want to look anywhere but down at your feet as you speed across the course. Many a rider will try to keep their legs up while traversing the 4000-foot track. This ride is packed with fun and has seven thrilling inversions guaranteed to put a smile on your face. In 2009, Medusa was renamed to Bizarro and the new theming makes it even more interesting to ride. Inversions include a vertical loop, dive loop, the zero-g roll (the best), Cobra roll (two inversions), and two corkscrews. This one is truly a winner.

13. **Griffon** at Busch Gardens in Williamsburg is the biggest and baddest dive coaster on the planet. Once, while hosting live television, I took someone who was afraid to ride roller coasters on this ride. Ever since their reaction, I am convinced that Griffon will always be a real blast even for the terrified. As the name implies, diving coasters climb the lift hill (in this case over 200 feet tall), momentarily hang precariously at the top, and about eight seconds later drops–you, ninety degrees straight down. Mimicking the movement and speed of its mythical counterpart, a creature consisting of part eagle and part lion, Griffon is a coaster experience unique to anything else in the world

Griffon is one of the tallest dive coasters available, but at a top speed of seventy miles per hour, it is also the fastest you will find out there. Not only does it get bragging rights as the world's first floorless dive coaster, it was the first to incorporate two Immelmann loops, a second 130-foot dive, topped off with one water splash-down feature that you need to see to believe. Griffon offers over-the-edge excitement on more than half a mile of steel track and is the centerpiece of the French section at Busch Gardens Europe. The best seat in the house is the front row. Just make sure to keep those eyes open and take in the view when you're hanging there. Sure, there might be taller coasters out there, but this one will surely make your day and is well worth riding, no matter how long the line is.

14. **Phantoms Revenge** at Kennywood in West Mifflin, Pennsylvania, is a ride not to be missed. The coaster was originally named The Steel Phantom. It was the first hyper-coaster in the world to feature inversions, but this accolade would soon prove to be the downfall of the first version of the coaster. After the 2000 season and numerous rider complaints about how rough the coaster was on the head and neck, Morgan manufacturing redesigned the coaster, removing the inversions entirely. The Steel Phantom was reopened for the 2001 season under the new name, Phantom's Revenge. The newer version has a top speed of eighty-five mph, putting it in a tie for seventh place of the world's fastest coasters, alongside the Xcelerator at Knott's Berry Farm. It is currently ranked as the seventh best steel roller coaster in the world according to the editors of *Amusement Today* and is always ranked very high in all major roller coaster surveys. Due to the modifications, both Morgan and Arrow types of track are used in the design now. Although the first hill is only 160 feet high, the second hill drops riders 232 feet into a ravine and through the support structure of Thunderbolt, a completely different coaster in the park. This strategic use of the park's hilly terrain is one of the coaster's most distinguishing features and one of the reasons Phantom's Revenge was able to improve on its predecessor, despite removal of key features. It's even bigger and badder than it was with the inversions. With memorable views of the Pennsylvania countryside, this is one of the best rides you will ever get. The eject action on the bunny hills and the feeling of speed throughout the ride are exceptional. For those that like head chopper action, there's plenty of it as the coaster careens through the nearby Thunderbolt. Roller coaster enthusiasts will agree that the Phantom is one that is here to stay and a ride that will please even the fussiest adrenalin junkie out there.

15. **Gatekeeper** at Cedar Point in Sandusky, Ohio, (B&M) is truly in a league by itself. At its launch in 2013, it quickly emerged as the fifth best coaster overall, while sliding into the number one slot for the best Wing Coaster model in the world. At a cost of over thirty million dollars to make, it has broken many records, most notably its high ranking as one of the tallest inversions in the world. Its hefty price tag and creative design has helped it break Wing Coaster records in height, track length, and drop height too. Gatekeeper is over 170 feet tall and has a fantastic 165foot drop that you will just love to experience firsthand. In addition to the three inversions on this ride, the cars slide tightly through keyhole towers that have been placed around the track, Its innovative design makes you truly feel like your ride is going to smash right though the final towers as your car suddenly turns sideways at top speed, leaving the appearance that it won't clear the opening. When it's over, it feels a little like watching one of the final scenes in the movie *Independence Day*, and you breathe a sigh of relief because somehow you managed to get out unscathed. This sensation happens not once, but twice, and in close proximity to each other as you trek down the 4,164 feet of Gatekeeper's tubular track. Sure there are other winged roller coasters like X-Flight at Six Flags Great America and Wild Eagle at Dollywood out there, but this one takes the cake, giving you a memorable, Wing Coaster experience.

16. **Superman—Ride of Steel** at Six Flags America, Largo, Maryland, places very high on my list of rides to experience. No matter how old this one gets, the ride is, in a word, *fast*. World ranked in the top five of 2004 by *Amusement Park Today*, this coaster created by Interman AG Corporation stands at 209 feet tall and can be clearly seen for miles around the park. It also has one of the steepest first drops (sixty-eight degrees) that there is on such a ride. I will admit, for those who have never ridden mega-coasters before, the sight of this contraption can be very daunting, but be assured, looking at it can be quite exciting as well. If you can brave your first reaction to just run away, then all you have to do is strap yourself in and enjoy what follows. Surely you can hide in your seat and take solace in the sense of security of your enclosed car? Wrong! Like its New England and New York sister coasters, the cars have elevated stadium seating and low-slung sides. Instead of an over-the-shoulder harness (required for inversion coasters), an unobtrusive seat belt and a single ratcheting safety bar add to the car's open, exposed feeling. This was created to better scare the daylights out of you and has gotten many a rider nervous at first. Interman really put in a good effort here with this ride, and until they built the New England version, in my mind, Superman—Ride of Steel was the best version of its kind.

    The difference between this ride and its New England cousin is that, whereas the New England version throws in the best drops and negative-g pullouts you can experience, the Maryland version concentrates on the perception of sheer speed throughout the entire course. The bunny hops at the end are small but exhilarating, and I usually come into the station with a big happy grin on my face. While at this park, try to ride this one last, because after doing Superman—Ride of Steel at Six Flags America, all other rides at the park are great but not as intense as this one.

17. **Raptor** at Cedar Point in Sandusky, Ohio, is in my mind still one of the best inverted coasters ever built. Raptor rules the sky at Cedar Point! Built in 1994 by the world-renowned team of Bolliger & Mabillard out of Monthey, Switzerland, the Raptor roller coaster was voted number eleven in the "Best Steel Roller Coaster in the World" category in a survey conducted by *Amusement Today* in 2005. Guests ride in cars that are suspended from the track above while specially designed seats allow passengers" legs to dangle, providing the sensation of flight. Aiding that is the fact that riders go upside down six amazing times! The highlight is a first-of-its-kind cobra roll, a thrilling element that flips riders over, spirals them upside down into a 180-degree roll, and repeats the twisting motion in reverse. Looming 137 feet above the main midway and reaching a top speed of fifty-seven miles per hour, Raptor is one of the tallest and fastest inverted roller coasters in the world. Nearly twenty-seven million guests have been picked up by the claws of this steel giant since 1994. Will you be next?

18. **Superman; the Ultimate Flight** at Six Flags, Atlanta, Georgia, (and several other locations), is simply like no other ride out there. Superman was the second B&M coaster in the world where you could literally *fly* around the track. This coaster offers the rider a sense of flight that can really be intoxicating. On this ride, you swoop, dive, and race over the treetops with nothing but an inverted open-air car tethering you. It was built upon the idea of taking the first of this type of roller coaster to the next level. Flying coasters use an ingenious track layout and a unique car design to replicate the sensation of flight. With special harnesses, there is literally nothing but air separating you and the ground below. It is an odd, but interesting, sensation to hang upside down for what seems to be a long period of time. (The ride itself is only about 140 seconds long.) The inversions on most coasters briefly turn riders upside down, but Superman maintains a down position for a large portion of the ride. At first, the urge is to hang on for dear life. (I know I did that.) However, as the ride progresses, you realize that you can trust the harnesses, stretch out your arms, and, well, fly like Superman through the corkscrews and

additional elements. Packed with five inversions, the ride literally flies you through the course at almost fifty-five miles per hour. Also on the ride, make note that during the top of the pretzel loop, you enter this element on your back and then fly through the loop in a forward position, making it a sensational one-of-a-kind ride experience. You can find another one of these rides at Six Flags Great Adventure in Jackson, New Jersey.

19. **Kumba** at Busch Gardens in Tampa, Florida, is quite a coaster, and one that was surely created for the masses. At 143-feet high, this was B&M's first traditional sit-down looping coaster, and it has performed that task flawlessly in cars made differently than any other rolling stock. The ride's open airiness and slick design were ahead of their time and one for the record books. In fact, before the notorious Montu came into being, this ride was the main reason why coaster enthusiasts came to the park to begin with and is still considered one of the main attractions there. Even today, Kumba is one of the largest and fastest coasters you will find in the Southeast. Despite its harrowing speed, this one is still considered a great one for the family. Packed with seven inversions and reaching speeds in excess of sixty miles per hour, this one still holds its own against even the newer coasters out there and is well worth the wait that can form around this attraction. It may interest you to know that at one time, Kumba was the tallest inverted coaster in the world. In fact, Kumba still boasts one of the world's largest vertical loops, reaching a height of 108 feet, and is still considered an intense ride, even by today's standards. The 4000-foot track seems to wind seamlessly through the beautiful scenery, passing under walkways, through trenches, and even over water. Its camelback inversion, a tall camel shaped hill, designed to lift riders out of their seats and cobra roll elements were Bolliger & Mallibard's firsts, and these designs are still used today. Kumba blends in with its surroundings and you really get a feel for the park when ascending that first lift hill. As you know, Busch Gardens is renowned for its animal safaris and nature walks, and from the top of this ride, you can take in the park's beauty (if only for a few seconds) before your inevitable

128-foot plunge down the track to start your greatly accelerated African adventure. This ride may be, a little rough by today's standards, but it's still pretty smooth compared to other top coasters I have ridden around the country. I also love the color scheme of aqua blue, yellow, and orange on this ride. It is a colorful way of putting you in the mood for your adventure. It's a good ride to enjoy with your entire family.

20. **Titan** at Six Flags Over Texas is still one of the tallest roller coasters (as of this writing) out there today. I love this ride! For its age, Titan is still a world-class mega-coaster and brings to the table some of the best positive-g ride elements ever created. It is essentially Six Flags Magic Mountain's Goliath with a 255-foot drop, eighty-five miles per hour and a wicked added upward helix at the block brake. The extra helix makes Titan feel like a more complete ride and makes it doubly as intense! It stands ten feet higher than its west coast counterpart, Goliath (also created by Giovanola Corporation of Switzerland) and has a pretty steep drop. As you plunge down 255 feet at eighty-five miles per hour into a small tunnel, you will definitely feel your heart pounding. The drop is good, but what makes this ride experience different from other mega-coasters is the *sustained* positive g's that come into play during the second portion of the ride. Usually a rider receives high g-forces for very short time periods. This is not the case with Titan! The g-forces on this one can last much longer than on most other rides. These forces are also sustained. I have found that a lot of grunting and groaning helps counteract the effect and keeps the rider more alert and focused on the ride. This is one coaster you have to actually experience in order to enjoy. As a frustrated pilot who loves aerobatics, this one's for me.

At the top of the lift hill, don't forget to look to your left, As an added surprise, what you will see is the ball park in Arlington where the Major League Texas Rangers play their home games. The ballpark is less than a quarter of a mile away. From where you are sitting, the stadium actually looks dwarfed, making this ride even more impressive! Overall, I found Titan to be a pretty intense and enjoyable ride, but make sure you are ready for those intense positive-g helixes before you attempt this ride.

21. **Dragon Challenge** at Universal Studios Islands of Adventure in Orlando, Florida, is a very different and extremely exciting inverted coaster. Originally opened in 1999 as Dueling Dragons, the ride was refurbished to fit the Harry Potter theme in 2010. Your interest in this ride starts as soon as you pass under two menacing statues at the entrance. Once you enter the castle itself, you experience the best queue area ever designed for a coaster ride. When first entering the queue, guests are taken past a number of banners for the Tri-Wizard Tournament showing support for the four contestants. After passing the "Weasleys" crashed flying Ford Anglia, they enter the Champions Tent. From there, guests pass a large pedestal with the Tri-Wizard Cup glowing at the top and several dark tunnels, which lead to both coaster stations. Just before entering the station guests must choose which coaster they want to ride: Chinese Fireball to the left or Hungarian Horntail to the right. When you finally make your choice, please note that each ride is very unique, so you want to set aside enough time to experience both sides while you are there. The ride is timed by computer the best seats for this experience are the front four so you can look directly into the widening eyes of those individuals on the opposite train as they head directly toward you. Dragon Challenge is a series of rides you don't want to miss. Both tracks are approximately 3,200 feet in length and take its riders over fifty-five miles per hour while reaching heights in excess of 120 feet. You will love it!

22. **X2** at Six Flags Magic Mountain in Valencia, California, is, in a word, "revolutionary!" It is truly one of the most highly complex and technically advanced attractions to debut in quite some time. You might not have heard the term *"four-dimensional" coaster*, but after riding X, I am here to tell you, that term truly fits. Created by Arrow Dynamics Corporation in 2002, this incredible ride stands at 190 feet tall, and the revamp in 2007 cost over forty-six million dollars. X2 was a prototype coaster (originally costing twenty million) and when built (and for the first time ever), riders sit on the edge of a massive twenty-two-foot-wide vehicle that actually spins independently 360 degrees forward and backward during the ride. Plummeting over two hundred feet face first down a near-vertical first drop at seventy-six miles per hour, riders will experience an unprecedented "don't know what to expect" sensation that you just won't find anywhere else. The rotation occurs throughout the ride, so you literally have no idea where you will end up, and if you think you will be able the figure it out, I would think again. There is literally nothing else like it on the planet! X2 is truly different and incomparable to any traditional coaster you have experienced. Honestly, words cannot justly describe the sensation or rush you get on this ride. The secret of X2 can be found in the ride's third rail, which increases and decreases in width, causing the ride vehicle to flip unexpectedly, depending on the space between the rails. Sounds simple, but I am sure the Arrow experts will disagree with you on that one. Unfortunately with prototypes, this ride (like other newer rides out there) has had some mechanical problems. Having the technology to create a first-of-its-kind ride also means that it takes time to get all the bugs out. This has meant closing the ride and adjusting the ride vehicle at times. But in my mind, that is the price you pay for innovation, and in X2, you get just that with its new and innovative coaster technology. X2 is quite simply several minutes of steel mind games over 3,610 feet of track that tinkers with your senses, delivering a disorienting experience of fear and joy all at the same time. It is a ride that most everyone will love. I know I did!

23. **Steel Force** at Dorney Park is one of the main reasons why you want to come to this incredible Cedar Fair Park. Ranked sixth in the world in 2002 by *Amusement Today*, this ride really describes what mega-coasters are all about. Although very similar to Morgan Manufacturing's, Mamba at Missouri Worlds of Fun and Wild Thing at Minnesota's Valley Fair, this fast, smooth coaster is near the top of everyone's list. Often compared to Magnum XL-200 at its sister park in Sandusky Point, Ohio, it measures up and even surpasses Magnum in overall thrills. Morgan created an exciting but not too intense ride that drops its riders 205 feet through a long tunnel, managing to give you some unexpected float time on the second hill. After the third hill, the rider is subjected to a descending turnaround helix that shoves you in your seat for some medium g's as you enter the bunny hop section of the ride. Now I don't like to use the term *"bunny hop"* because it indicates an element that this ride definitely does not have. These "hops" range from fifteen to twenty feet high and make you feel like you are literally riding a bucking bronco at the local rodeo. They should not be lightly compared to watching a bunny rabbit scampering around a knoll around Easter time. There is a lot of ejection and float time in this section of the ride that makes it a true gem. When you think you're at the end, the last element sends you through a horizontal double uphill, which you swear is going to send you flying out of your seat. Ride times can vary, but again, try to get to Steel Force as early as possible and make this the first ride when you enter the park.

24. **Diamondback** located at Kings Island in Mason, Ohio, is a Bolliger & Mabillard masterpiece and it's loved by many roller coaster enthusiasts. At 5,282 feet, the expansive track spans from International Street and the Eiffel Tower over the Rivertown area, continues into a wooded area of the park. It features a splashdown element near the end of the ride that only a half dozen coasters around the world can boast about. The price tag on this ride was twenty-two million dollars and makes it one of the most expensive rides in the park The money was well worth it, Diamondback has a nice 230-foot lift hill with a 215-foot first drop, followed by nine more drops at speeds up to eighty miles an hour before it's all said and done. I find that this ride is very similar to Behemoth at Canada's Wonderland in dimensions, statistics, and like Behemoth has a staggered seating arrangements. When this ride opened in 2009, it became the park's first ever Bolliger & Mabillard roller coaster. It was also the first new roller coaster to be installed after Kings Island was bought by the Cedar Fair Corporation.

You know you're on a great ride experience when you rise 230 feet and descend quickly, only to shoot straight up the second hill before dropping into a ravine. The ride then ascends another hill and drops straight into a crazy turn. Along the way, you will encounter a 280-degree counter-clockwise helix, several bunny hills, and another helix with that final splashdown before re-entering the station. Diamondback is one that you have got to try if you're at King's Island.

25. **Thunderbolt** at Lunar Park, Coney Island in Brooklyn, New York. Only a few of us out there remember a wooden roller coaster of the same name. It was great woodie created in 1922 and was featured in Woody Allen's movie *Annie Hall* (1977) and along with another roller coaster at the park called the Cyclone packed an amazing one-two punch for roller coaster enthusiasts. Eventually the ride was removed and replaced by a minor league ballpark. The new Thunderbolt was created in honor of this legendary roller coaster. In fact, the new Thunderbolt designed by Zamperla is the first custom-made roller coaster on Coney Island since the Cyclone debuted in 1927. The new Thunderbolt is a steel marvel and flies through 2,233 feet of track in under two minutes. Top speed for this ride is around fifty-five miles per hour and, even though it has a small footprint (at 800 feet long and 48 feet wide, the new Thunderbolt is one of the skinniest and longest roller coasters ever built) and sure does pack a punch. Standing at 110 feet tall with a 100-foot vertical (and I mean straight down) drop, this is a great ride even though it may not be a woodie. One of the most unique features that this ride has is that it has a vertical lift tower that allows the cars to go ballistic (straight up) to the top of the tower before sending riders straight down on the first hill. The new Thunderbolt incorporates a 100-foot loop, a ninety-degree vertical ascent, five crazy inversions, and a zero-gravity roll. It's a great new ride and one that every coaster junkie should try.

26. **Intimidator 305** at Kings Dominion in Doswell, Virginia-is a twenty-five million dollar, three hundred foot drop coaster ride that never seems to let up. Nicknamed for the late NASCAR driver, Dale Earnhardt, this 2010, Intamin built, steel marvel reaches speeds up to ninety-four miles per hour. To date, it is the tallest, fastest roller coaster at Kings Dominion. During its creation, there were some issues arising from excessive g-forces the ride's original design. I will tell you it was kind of rough back then, but Kings Dominion installed what they call trim brakes on the first drop in order to reduce the speed. Eventually, the radius of the first high-speed turn was widened as to reduce friction and g-force impact on riders, creating a much smoother experience. It is the fifteenth roller coaster installed at the park and has become one of only a handful of roller coasters that surpasses the 300-foot level. Other roller coaster created by Intamin in this category are Millennium Force and Top Thrill Dragster at Cedar Point in Ohio. What sets Intimidator apart, is not just its height; it's the first drop angle that surpasses eighty-five degrees. That's almost straight down! Intimidator 305 uses Intamin's double-spine track, allowing for longer spans with fewer supports, beams needed to sustain the cars. If you like the feeling of ejecting out of your seat, this is the one. There are three near-ground level, high-speed turns, and five airtime humps that produce a feeling in the pit of your stomach that feels a little like waves of butterflies flying toward your throat and back again. Despite its 1600 riders per hour capacity, lines are long here. On the other hand if you're not afraid of heights, love speed, and don't mind feeling out of control for three and a half minutes, then this contraption is well worth the wait.

27. **Behemoth** at Canada's Wonderland, in Vaughan, Ontario Canada is another out of this world hyper-coaster designed and developed by the Swiss manufacturer, Bolliger & Mabillard. Behemoth is currently the tallest and fastest roller coaster in Canada with an amazing 200 plus foot first drop. The ride is similar to Diamondback (at Kings Island), Goliath (La Ronde), and Nitro (Six Flags Great Adventure). Behemoth premiered in May 2008 and has been one of the biggest rides in this park since its creation. With its high speeds, tall heights, and rapid changes in both direction and elevation, the attraction is one of the most aggressive thrill rides that I have ever experienced. Behemoth can also accommodate many people, making for quick lines and happy riders. The ride also features a special prototype seating arrangement to ensure that you get the best view of the park. The Behemoth experience lasts three minutes and races around the track at seventy-seven miles per hour. It has five airtime hills, a hammerhead turn, and two helixes during its circuit. Behemoth has been praised by roller coaster enthusiasts everywhere and, along with Leviathan (a 300-foot wonder at this park), is a ride you must experience firsthand.

28. **Raging Bull** at Six Flags Great America in Gurnee, Illinois, The Raging Bull is a Bolliger & Mabillard hyper-twister steel roller coaster located at Six Flags Great America in Gurnee, Illinois. This is a big ride with a small footprint and that's what makes Raging Bull so special. The Bull features a 208-foot first drop at sixty-five degrees and a top speed of seventy-three miles per hour that seems to be sustained throughout the ride. Track length is 5,057 feet and is the longest roller coaster at Six Flags Great America. Created in 1999, Raging Bull is the world's second "hyper-twister." It is also B&M's second hyper-coaster ever built. Before the main drop, this ride teases the passengers by having what's known as a pre-drop. This helps get the momentum going and is a good setup for its memorable first decent. After a quick tunnel, the train then ascends into a hammerhead turn to the right, passing over Viper's queue line not

once but twice. After the turn, there is a nice little hill and several overbanked turns, which you will just love. The thing about this ride is that unlike Nitro (a similar ride by B&M), this ride twists and turns inside itself so the g-forces on this ride are sustained much longer than most rides of this type. You will literally feel like you are riding a bull on this one. That is riding a bull for not just eight seconds but for, in fact, several minutes. The only question you have to ask yourself when riding this monster is "are you ready for that?"

29. **Iron Rattler** at Six Flags Fiesta Texas, in San Antonio, Texas. Now this is one incredible roller coaster and one I highly recommend if you're lucky enough to visit this park. The ride originally opened in 2013, replacing a wood coaster classic called Rattler. It was built in the same location using pretty much the same support structure from the original but with steel improvements. The original version, although large, wasn't so hot and I was not a very big fan of it. However, being redesigned with ride manufacturer, Rocky Mountain Construction, coming into play here, this ride has done a complete 180 from the original. At a height of 180 feet and a first drop of 170 feet falling at eighty degrees, you feel like you're careening straight down.

If you like the feeling of falling, then this one's definitely for you. The speed of this ride remains pretty constant over the 3,266 feet of track, reaching top speeds in excess of sixty-five miles per hour. It was, in fact, the first "hybrid" wood and steel roller coaster to feature an inversion, in which riders are completely upside down in what is known as a barrel roll element. The train seats two across and the cars are comfortable, but with only a small lap bar separating you from the air, you might be inclined to wonder if going up that chain lift hill was a bad idea. Well, I'm here to assure you, that's not the case. You and all your thrill ride maniac friends will love the experience. The best seats in the house for me on this ride are in the back of this monster, and hold on to your hats and glasses, folks, because unless you secure them, you're destined to buy new ones.

30. **Powder Keg: A Blast Into The Wilderness** sits at Silver Dollar City in the entertainment capital of the Midwest, Branson, Missouri, This steel coaster was built from a former attraction called Buzzsaw Falls and reopened in 2005. It is also the longest and one of the fastest roller coasters in Silver Dollar City. I really liked the 110-foot first drop, and the ride seems to maintain speeds of sixty-five miles per hour.

Since there was already a roller coaster/water ride on this spot, the park borrowed elements of the former ride, mainly the lift hill structure, in order to keep costs down. They also used an old Buzz Saw Falls car and piece of the old track, then stuck it out of the roof of the first building in the queue line The ride itself is memorable for many reason. Mainly, it launches you up a small hill before dropping you like a rock. Riders go up and down many hills, careening through several tight turns before slowly traveling up a chain lift hill equipped with audio speakers playing bluegrass music. Several pretty cool elements come to being here, and the final leg of your trek travels through a large helix that literally slams you into your seat and feels like you might be flung from the train at any moment. It truly has an Old West feel to it and, like the city of Branson itself, leaves you wanting more. Talk about a typical mine train, and this one acts like one on steroids. Ya gonna love it for sure. I did!

31. **Lighting Run** at Kentucky Kingdom in Louisville, Kentucky is a GT-X hyper-coaster (the name we are using for really tall roller coasters) from the Chance Morgan Corporation. Lightning Run first opened officially on May 24, 2014, and since then has become an instant hit with roller coaster enthusiasts as well as the general public. The coaster was the first of its kind and cost seven million dollars to complete. This new coaster features a 100-foot lift hill, an eighty-degree drop with a very compact and twisted layout. The ride hits a top speed of fifty-five miles per hour and really keeps you guessing along the 2,500-foot track. This roller coaster fits perfectly into the size of the park and offers quite a ride for those who like to try something different.

This ride is literally a thrill a minute. It can accommodate eight hundred riders per hour. The ride has two trains with five cars. Riders are arranged two across in two rows for a total of twenty riders per train. It is, in my mind, one of the best rides out there and by far the best one you will find at this park.

32. **Skyrocket** at Kennywood, in West Mifflin, Pennsylvania is one of their newest roller coasters and is one of the best of its kind out there. Riders literally go from zero to fifty miles per hour in less than three seconds up a 95-foot vertical hill and straight down (at a ninety-degree angle) in a drop that seems to last forever. By the time you reach the upside-down loop, you're really flying down the track. These inversions, by the way, are the first to be added in this park since the Steel Phantom. Next up is a cool cork screw, barrel roll, and second vertical drop. It may be a short ride at just a little over a minute in length, but there's never a dull moment over the 2,400 feet of track. The coaster itself is small in scale but don't let that fool you. It reaches speeds of over fifty miles per hour and has the best aspects of a high-tech state-of-the-art ride that just happens to be a good fit for the family as well. The Sky Rocket was built by Premier Rides, and uses Linear Synchronous Motor (LSM) technology to catapult riders forward, giving a rocket-launch feeling. Other coasters that use this same LSM technology can be found at Disney's Hollywood Studios with Rock 'n' Roller Coaster and Superman: Escape from Krypton located at Six Flags Magic Mountain. Kennywood has definitely added a winner here and one that should be around for many years to come.

33. **Mamba** at Worlds of Fun, in Kansas City, Missouri is a steel hyper-coaster. Designed by Steve Okamoto and built by D. H. Morgan Manufacturing, the ten million dollar price tag in 1998, would be considered cheap by today's standards. But back then, that kind of money built Worlds of Fun one of the first mega-coasters in existence. Despite its age, Mamba is formidable, even now, standing over 200 feet tall with a 208-foot drop that is sure to wake you up. Mamba has a second drop of over 180 feet that even in today's standards, is still pretty exhilarating. At its peak, this ride hits speeds in excess of seventy-five miles per hour. I would compare it to Steel Force at Dorney Park and Magnum XL at Cedar Point. Custom made for Worlds of Fun, Mamba is one of the fastest, longest, and tallest roller coasters in the world. Spanning out more than a mile, it follows a traditional "out and back" layout, Mamba delivers a mighty bite for those adventurous enough to ride it. From start to finish, Mamba keeps riders on the edge of their seats, no matter which one they are sitting in. There are three trains, with six cars sitting three across in two rows, for a total of thirty-six riders at a time. Riders are arranged three across in two rows for a total of thirty-six riders per train. It is recommended that you stay alert or Mamba (named after Africa's deadliest snake) or it may just get the best of you.

34. **Manta** at SeaWorld in Orlando, Florida-amazed us with a great addition to a park that, in fact, vastly benefited by adding such an appropriately themed and tailored roller coaster. Even before you get on this ride, Manta allows guests to encounter numerous species of live marine rays before boarding what looks like a manta-shaped train. This attraction officially opened to the public on May 22, 2009. Manta is intended to be much more than just a roller coaster. The experience begins upon entering the attraction's queue, designed to resemble a seaside village. Manta is a flying roller coaster that defiantly simulates the sensation of flight as the ride takes you soaring above this beautifully landscaped theme park. Guests board and are seated upright on the trains. These trains are situated with eight rows of seats that hold four passengers, for a total of thirty-two riders per ride. The roller coaster has 3,359 feet of track and reaches a height of over 140 feet. It includes four inversions and reaches speeds in excess of fifty-six miles per hour. Statistically, this makes Manta one of the longest, tallest, and fastest flying roller coasters in the world. In order to control noise, some sections of the track are filled with sand. Manta (which is very similar to the Superman: Ultimate Flight rides at Six Flags amusement parks) will put a smile on your face as you head towards one of the best elements on this ride. It's a 98-foot-tall pretzel loop that is, without a doubt, the best thrill ride you will find at any SeaWorld park. Don't miss this one!

35. **Storm Force Runner (SFR)** at Hershey Park in Hershey, Pennsylvania is a powerful, steel-launched, Intamin contraption. Hershey Park has always been known to be the sweetest place on earth, but it is also known as the thrill ride capital of the east. It first opened in 2004, and it was (at the time) the third Intamin Accelerator Coaster put into service. Standing at a height of 150 feet, it may not be the tallest ride at the park, but it is perhaps the most memorable. Riders catapult-from zero to seventy-two miles per hour in just about two seconds. It features what is

known at a top hat element as well as three inversions. SFR boasts a magnetic braking system that is state of the art as well.

What I like about this particular ride is that the creators built it to interact with three other Hershey Park rides like the Dry Gulch Railroad, the Monorail, and the Trailblazer. Storm Force Runner is also one of the first accelerator-style coasters to utilize an over-the-shoulder restraint system and the first to have a dual-loading station with switch tracks. It is also the first coaster of this type to have several inversions incorporated throughout. The innovative propulsion system launches the trains using hydraulics that have now become the gold standard for propulsion on these types of coasters. The launch track also features magnetic brake fins, which, as you might have guessed, is pretty important. These fins will actually slow down the car if the launch is unsuccessful (also known as a rollback). During Halloween, Storm Force is decorated in a Hershey Park in the Dark theme and playfully dubbed Ghost Runner. It's still the same ride but with a different name, but believe me, no matter what time of year you ride it, it's still one of the best out there.

36. **Kraken** at SeaWorld in Orlando, Florida, is a very pleasant surprise for all roller coaster enthusiasts tired of the Disney and Universal parks in the area. This ride, along with Manta and SeaWorld's water ride, "Journey into Atlantis," makes this park stand out among its counterparts around the nation. This 151 foot coaster by Bollinger & Mabillard cost forty-two million dollars to create the views overlooking the lake and a good portion of the park. This aqua blue, floorless marvel seems to keep your feet just inches from the track as you sizzle along. If you have long legs, try to touch the seat in front of you with your feet as you enter the oversized loop because doing that is only possible on a few floorless coasters around the world, and it's a real treat if you can manage it on the Kraken. SeaWorld took a standard design, then increased the thrill factor by straightening out the first drop in order to add more negative g's to the mix. What comes next is a series of seven memorable loops at speeds in excess of sixty miles per hour. Three low clearance tunnels highlight the ride, including an unexpected dive and dip through a lagoon. There you will encounter a serpent's underwater lair, complete with live eels. Don't blink, or you will surely miss it! The ride has three trains that have a total of eight cars. Riders are arranged four across in a single row for a total of thirty-two riders per train, so the lines do move pretty quickly. All in all, there are seven beautiful inversion you are sure to love. This is one coaster worth riding over and over again.

37. **Alpengeist** at Busch Gardens in Williamsburg, Virginia, is a smooth, and graceful inverted coaster. Did I also mention it is one of the tallest inverted coasters in the world? If you thought Montu was all you could handle (once the tallest coaster on the planet), stay away from this monster. Alpengeist adds roughly forty-five feet to that former record holder's 150-foot lift hill. Once you've crested the 195-foot lift hill, a 170-foot drop to the right awaits you and at speeds reaching sixty-seven miles per hour this one truly gets your blood flowing. Alpengeist has a great alpine setting, and from the ski lift design of the cars themselves to the blizzard conditions you notice on the ride, you are about to experience something just a little bit different and unusual. This ride is pretty intense, but since it is much larger than other inverted coasters, there's a welcome break between ride elements, giving a much more enjoyable, and smoother ride overall.

True, it does have its moments, especially the ski lift that has gone amok as it races around the six decent inversions, as well as a distinctive, record-holding 106-foot-high vertical loop. If you can keep your eyes peeled as you streak down the track, you might also spot the poor unfortunate skier who smashed through the top of a house on his way down the hill. You know, the house that you are heading for, directly ahead of you! Also, let's not forget that zero-g roll, the element that B&M is famous for. They are all here wrapped elegantly together in a coaster that is simply a pure joy to ride. Note: since all seats have literally closed off any front views, the best visuals occur in the front row only. If you are looking to see it all, you must experience it there. If you want to be surprised, then sit in the back. No matter how you add it up, Alpengeist is a destination coaster located at one of the best amusement parks ever created. If you love your coasters, you will cherish this one.

38. **Riddler's Revenge** at Six Flags Magic Mountain in Valencia, California, even today, is undoubtedly one of the best stand-up coasters you will find anywhere in the country. Built by Bolliger & Mabillard in 1998, Riddler's Revenge is the world's largest stand-up coaster in existence. Themed after Batman villain, Edward Nygma, also known as "the Riddler," this coaster has continued the Six Flags tradition of designing rides around comic book characters. The adventure begins as guests are drawn into the attraction by a glowing green neon entrance, which is disguised as a question mark. Once inside and prior to boarding, guests witness mysterious and chaotic experiments of mind-bending proportions in the confines of the Riddler's laboratory-Once seated in one of the Riddler's latest creation of sleek green trains, riders are carried up the 156-foot-tall lift hill. Within seconds of reaching the top, the train makes a quick 180-degree turn and then dives 146 feet into a vertical loop, the first of six inversions. The Riddler continues to twist the rider's mind with two consecutive dive loops followed by an inclined loop while traveling at speeds of up to sixty-five miles per hour. As the train accelerates, riders travel through a barrel roll over a bunny hop and into a gravity-defying upward spiral. But wait, it's not over, there remains one more brain-tossing barrel roll left in its 4,370-foot track. As the train finally returns to the laboratory some three minutes later, you will find that compared to its rougher counterparts, this is an ultra-smooth stand-up ride that the coaster enthusiast will love. If you're not crazy about stand-up coasters, this one could be the one that changes your mind about them. It just also happens to be the biggest and best of them all!

39. **Great Bear** at Hershey Park in Pennsylvania, is an excellent ride and one that, when built in 1998, had taken the inverted coaster concept to the next level. Most B&M inverted coasters seem to have similar pacing, but this one clearly breaks that mold. Great Bear starts out differently in that instead of plunging from a height of 124 feet straight down to start the ride, it actually helixes into a double dip before the expected plummet. That's when you know you are in for a far different experience. The four inversions you encounter along the way are pretty intense. One of these inversions actually goes through one of the supports of the ride, giving the rider an "eye of the needle" effect, while the ones over the pond are beautiful and exciting. Great Bear also finds itself (and you) wrapped around one of the first looping coasters ever built, Sooper Dooper Looper, which makes for an amazing photo opportunity for your friends watching as you race through this section of track. Great Bear can definitely be rated high as one of the favorite steel coasters out there. The lines for this ride can get long, however, so I suggest you ride this one early.

40. **Hollywood Rip Ride Rockit.** Now for those of you that visit Universal Studios in Orlando, Florida, there is one ride you for sure can't pass up. From the distance, it looks like a carnival ride, but with closer inspection, you can see that this baby really packs a punch. Thus, it's actually one of the largest X-Coaster types ever built by German manufacture, Maurer Sohne. The track is 3,800 feet long filled with many tight turns and speeds reaching in excess of sixty-five miles per hour. The ride officially opened in March of 2009 and continues to gain popularity even today. Some of the special features of Hollywood Rip Ride Rockit are that riders can choose one of thirty songs to listen to and are recorded during the one-minute and thirty-seven-second ride. Another interesting feature on this ride is that there is a moving sidewalk on both sides of the station that move at the same speed, so rides have to load and unload while this platform is moving. Even though Rockit can accommodate 1,850 rides per hour, the lines for this beauty can be long but once you get moving, you won't care. Once the train departs the station, riders head straight up ninety degrees of track (no kidding) in something called a vertical chain lift system. You have to experience this to believe that physics actually allows for it. It is right out of the gate on this ride that one knows this will be a memorable ride like no other. If you choose one moving attraction at this park (and love roller coasters), this is the one that I would definitely choose.

41. **Batman, The Dark Knight** at Six Flags New England might appear to be a short ride but, in my mind, is *still* one of the most intense and unique floorless coasters I have ever experienced! Standing at 117feet high, this Bolliger & Mabillard concoction debuted in April of 2002. It might not be the tallest floorless coaster around, but it doesn't need to be. Like the original Batman, The Ride, counterpart Dark Knight maintains a small footprint in its 2,600 feet of track, and, like Batman, travels at sustained top speeds of fifty-five miles per hour. This makes all turns sharp and the g-forces high during a good portion of the ride. Inversions include a dive loop, vertical loop, a sweet zero-g roll, and two interlocking flat spins. Unlike traditional roller coasters, Batman: Dark Knight utilizes floorless trains. Once the passenger is strapped into the

pedestal-style seats, the floor drops away, providing the floorless effect we all have heard about. What this means is that riders get–to sit in an open "flying chair" and watch the track below speeding just inches under their feet. On floorless coasters, all seats are pretty good, but I prefer the back row on this ride. The purple and black paint scheme sets the mood for this innovative coaster, which is guaranteed to be a crowd pleaser, especially for those who would like to experience the next level of coaster enthusiasm.

42. **Batwing** at Six Flags America is a really interesting and innovative ride. This ride was actually only the second of its kind to be built that situates passengers in a flying position. Since then, there are many others out there, but this was my first experience with such a ride. On Batwing, you swoop, dive, and race over the treetops with nothing but an inverted open-air car tethering you. Flying coasters, like this one use an ingenious track layout and a unique coaster car design to replicate the sensation of flight and Vekoma didn't disappoint with their design. Special harnesses were designed so there is literally nothing but air separating you and the ground below. While the ride is only about 140 seconds long, it's an odd, but interstation sensation to hang upside down, for what feels like much longer. The inversions on most coasters briefly turn riders upside down, but Batwing maintains a down position for a large portion of the ride creating an overwhelming urge to hang on for dear life at first. However, as the ride progresses, you realize that you can trust the harnesses, stretch out your arms, and fly like Superman through the corkscrews and additional elements on this ride. At 3,340 feet long and 115feet high, Batwing delivers some sensational stuff for anyone who likes to try new things. Packed with five inversions, you find yourself flying through the course at almost fifty miles per hour and during the loop, riders enter on their back then fly through the loop in a forward position. This unique feature makes Batwing a sensational one-of-a-kind rind experience you don't want to miss. Also, on this ride, make note that during the loop, the rider enters on his/her back and then flies through the loop in a forward position making Batwing a sensational one of a kind ride.

43. **El Loco** at the Adventure Dome is one of two great rollercoasters at Circus Circus Hotel in Las Vegas, Nevada. In addition to the legionary Canyon Blaster, Adventure Dome is one of six El Loco models that are out there and the only indoor, El Locostyle coaster in the United States. Filling the space formerly occupied by another ride (the Rim Runner flume ride), this thriller packs a lot of action into its swift minute-and-ten-second runtime. Its 1,300 feet of bright yellow track that includes a rapid ninety-foot ascent followed by a high lateral G hairpin turn and a steep diving drop. Riders experience many twists two inversions, and several tight turns and drops that are pretty unique in the coaster world. The ride is built by S&S Worldwide and officially opened in 2014. Adventure Dome is yet another intense ride, with a tiny footprint, reaching a top speed of only forty-five miles per hour. El Loco's innovative, four-person cars feature a custom soundtrack with individual speakers for each rider. The open car design-gives riders the feeling of flying. The best seat in the house is in the very front and when you're in Vegas, you should come to Circus Circus and experience this one for yourself.

44. **Expedition Everest** at Disney's Animal Kingdom in Orlando is an addition with a hefty, hundred million dollar price tag, ensuring a luxury, one of kind ride experience. As you walk past the mountain and get a glimpse of one of the ride's drops and turnaround, you can see that any resemblance to the Matterhorn in Disneyland is practically nonexistent. Sure you are entering a mountain, and yes, you will see a fierce yeti inside the structure, but from that point on, the similarities end. Quickly after leaving the gate, Expedition Everest riders are shocked to find that a piece of switch tracks flips over, forcing them to retrace their route through the mountain. As the track banks, the positive g-forces push the lap bars into riders and the riders into their seats. It's a strange and disorienting sensation to be blindly racing in the wrong direction, simultaneously experiencing strong, gravitational pull all the way. A projected shadow image of the yeti is seen ripping up another section of the track, before the train takes off and plunges you down the front of the mountain (smile, this is where your photo is snapped), and with the track destroyed, the yeti sends riders freefalling to their apparent doom. The train proceeds forward, plunges down the front of the mountain. This is where your photo is snapped and with the destroyed track, it than sends riders freefalling to their apparent doom. Instead of actually dying, the coaster careens in and out of the mountain for some high-speed, banked curve action. Before heading back to the station, the coaster makes one last pass through the mountain, and the enormous yeti takes a convincing swipe at riders with his oversized paw. With the coaster flying past, the encounter only lasts a mere second or two, but the effect is wild!

The yeti is Disney's most sophisticated animatronics figure thus far, and be advised, it will definitely scare younger passengers. Despite that, Animal Kingdom opened the ride anyway, in answer to low attendance numbers and much criticism that the park had with few attractions worth experiencing. With Everest, they essentially acknowledged that people wanted more thrilling rides, even at Walt Disney World. Attendance at Animal Kingdom rose steadily after the opening of Everest in 2006, and not only did they make an exciting attraction, but they put an overlooked park, back on the map.

45. **Rock n' Roller Coaster** at Disney's Hollywood Studios in Florida takes you through southern California on what can best be described as a real long *limousine*. Situated at the end of the park's Sunset Boulevard and conveniently located next to The Twilight Zone's Tower of Terror, this is the first place you should head when you get through the turnstiles. This Vekoma creation shoots you (LSM style) out of the gate doing zero to fifty miles per hour in less than three seconds. It then carries you through three inversions on your way to an Aerosmith concert that, of course, you are really late for. Your only warning to the start of the ride is Aerosmith's lead singer, Steven Tyler, saying, "Are you ready *to rock*? Then, *let's get it on*!" At that point, the light turns green, and you are catapulted out of the station, up a double-inverting B&M cobra roll, all while twisting and turning, flipping and rising, falling and charging through the dark of a simulated night sky. After this eye-opening element, you peel around banked curves, flying past palm trees, Randy's Donuts, interstate freeway markers, and through the "*O*" of the famous Hollywood sign. You are literally traffic "jamming" down L.A. Boulevard, pedal to the metal, all the way to the concert. Finally, you set up for the last inversion, a corkscrew maneuver that seems much smaller and tighter than this same element anywhere else in the world, all while five synchronized audio scores by Aerosmith blast out of nine hundred speakers built right into your limo. Even if you don't love the music of Aerosmith, you will become a fan on this ride. This is one ride that will make you suddenly want to be a rock star, more than you've ever wanted to be in your life. Or at least it will make you feel like one for a while.

Overall, this roller coaster is jam packed with everything you'd want in a ride. From the twenty minute pre-show that only Disney magic can create, to a memorable queue, adept at turning an ordinary ride into an experience, you just really can't go wrong with this one. Since Disney has Fastpass options for this, you don't even have to contend with really long wait times. If you only have time for one attraction at Hollywood Studios, then this is unequivocally the one you just can't miss".

46. **Maverick** at Cedar Point in Sandusky, Ohio. Get ready to experience the best new ride out there. This one will make you realize that imagination is all you need to succeed.-Maverick, Cedar Point's seventeenth amazing roller coaster first introduced in 2007 was voted the Best New Ride of 2007 by *Amusement Today's* panel of experts in the newspaper's annual Golden Ticket Awards but is still a top pick today. Located in Frontier town, this twenty-one million-dollar marvel is a coaster unlike any other at the park and does something that very few coasters can boast. It not only drops straight down, but at ninety -five degrees, you are actually heading past that mark. First you board Maverick in a cool train that has an ultra-sleek profile that carry them along the 4,450-foot-long course. Linear motors will lift the train to the top of a 105-foot-tall first hill. From there, as explained earlier, it's not straight down! Maverick takes its passengers down to past the ninety-five-degree angle at speeds of up to fifty-seven miles per hour. Only at about five feet from the ground do you pull out of this hair-raising dive. From there, the train hugs the terrain as it twists and banks around hairpin turns with quick but smooth changes in direction. Throughout the two-minute thirty-second ride, passengers also experience eight "airtime-filled hills," two inversions and a second launch through a dark tunnel that leaves riders wanting for more as you race across the 4,450 foot track at speeds of 70 mph. With an initial drop of a mere 100 feet, it looks like you are about to ride a coaster in the family coaster class. Especially when right next door you have the 300 and 400-foot profiles of the park's Millennium Force and Top Thrill Dragster. However, stats and looks can be deceiving, and this is so true when talking about this ride. This bucking bronco got the goods, and even though it never lets up, the ride is smooth and quick. The sleek and zippy ride positively screams, and its screaming riders invariably sport ten-gallon grins as they enter the loading station. I was truly one of them. The seating of ten riders across is also a first for the industry, and for the best seat, the front row is the ticket. Don't pass this one up if you are in this park.

47. **Fire Chaser Express** in Pigeon Forge, Tennessee, is a steel, family-launched roller coaster currently running at the Dollywood amusement park located in Pigeon Forge, Tennessee. It officially opened in March 2014. The ride is themed around the fictional Volunteer Fire Station 7 and its fictional fire chief. Fire chaser is the first, custom duel-launched (forward and backward) coaster in the nation. Built by the Ride Entertainment Group for ride manufacturer Gerstlauer it-may not be that tall (less than 40 feet) or that fast (around thirty-five miles per hour, but it still packs a punch for you and your family. Riders are arranged two across in a single row for a total of fourteen riders per train. This 2,340 foot powerhouse launches from zero to around twenty miles per hour and then travels across the tracks at over 110 feet above the Wilderness Pass area of the park. Near the end of the ride, cars experience a fire explosion, which causes an abrupt switch in direction, lurching the cars backward at twenty miles per hour and returning riders to the station they left from. Passengers encounter two helices (circular turns) and six zero-gravity moments on the two-minute and nineteen-second ride, proving this journey is not just for children. This one made my list because it's fun without being too overpowering. If you're at Dollywood, this is a must do!"

48. **Flight of Fear** at Kings Dominion is comparable to Disney's Space Mountain, just with more steroids. With a four-and-a-half g liftoff into a dark and strange world, you also might be tempted to compare this ride to Rock 'n' Roller Coaster (Disney, Hollywood Studios) in its overall presentation. The difference here is that this particular ride made the history books as the first LIM/LSM catapult ride when it debuted in June of 1996. The ride was originally themed to the television show, The Other Limits, and **was** called just that. But due to expired licensing, the theme and name underwent a change in 2001. You will also find that this is the same premier ride that you can find at many different parks nationwide (like Joker's Jinx at SFA), but unlike the others, this one is set in the dark for overall effect.

Flight of Fear may be old (and it gets older every year), but coaster enthusiasts will find it to be in great shape for its age. I found it to be a great ride with the newer lap bars (replacing the old horse-collar configuration), are much more comfortable on the head and neck area and the best seats are clearly the front two, folks. Since King's Dominion offers many heavy-hitter thrill rides, I've found there isn't much of a wait on this one, allowing you to experience it several times throughout the day if you're inclined. I'd recommend this to coaster enthusiasts looking for a little something different, and to others that need a warm up before going to the bigger, scarier rides at the park.

49. **Montezooma's Revenge** at Knott's Berry Farm in California is a classic ride for just about everyone. It is one of the last Schwarzkopf shuttle loop coasters to operate in the US, and at just 600 feet long, it maintains one of the smallest footprints in the park. Small imprint, yes, but long on intensity for a ride that was built before most coaster enthusiasts were even born. The coaster train is launched out of the station, attaining speeds of just over fifty-five miles per hour in only four and a half seconds. It then races up a loop, down the other side, and to the top of the seventy-degree incline spike on the opposite side, where it reaches a height of around 150 feet. There it loses its inertia and freefalls backward through the loop toward and through the station, and back up another spike (angled at seventy degrees), then finally dropping back toward the station where it stops on a dime. It is amazing to be sitting, stopping, then dropping at a seventy-degree angle in that last element while the ground is quickly rushing toward you.

There are two variations of the catapult system. They are weight drop and flywheel versions. The weight drop system uses a forty-ton weight in a tower at the end of the ride. The weight connects to a pulley system, which triples the speed of the drop, placing over thirteen tons of force on the train. The flywheel utilizes a six-ton flywheel in front of the loop. The flywheel spins to over 1000 rpm's and then engages a four-to-one ratio speed reducer. This turns a drive pulley and propels the train via a cable system. Montezooma uses the flywheel method to propel its riders down the track and makes the ride much quicker than its predecessor's system. The flywheel launch, although not as impressive as today's LIM/LSM type launches, still gets your attention because this launch technique is much louder on the ears than a standard LIM/LSM launch. The return trip of this marvel back through the station and up the opposite spike is almost deafening for those waiting to ride. The presence of Jaguar's track (another coaster at the park) within the loop adds to the pucker factor. Those who want to move to a more advanced level of coasters should try this one. Back in 1978, this coaster was it! Today, the ride is still a contender in my books.

50. **Shockwave** at Six Flags over Texas is 1976 Anton Schwarzkopf design that all roller coaster buffs will enjoy. Formidable at 116-feet high, Shockwave reaches speeds of sixty miles per hour and is one of the largest steel coasters of this type around. The design combines powerful positive gs in its back-to-back seventy-foot loops, while also giving the rider surprisingly strong negative-g drops. And unlike other compact portable-type coasters of this genre, at 3,600 feet long, this coaster covers a lot of ground. Enjoyed by many, this ride is a classic and still highly ranked in all coaster polls I have seen. With no horse-collar restraints to get in the way, there's nothing but a lap bar between you and the ground, and that, my friends, makes this ride something special. When at Six Flags Over Texas, make this coaster one of your first stops (after Titan and Texas Giant) as lines can get quite long at this Six Flags Park.

My Bonus Roller Coasters

1. **Joker's Jinx** at Six Flags America, in Largo, Maryland may be old, but it's perfect for those who like something a little bit different. At the time of this writing, there were only four of these premier-built LIM spaghetti track rides in North America. (Two were put indoors, Flight of Fear at Paramount's Kings Dominion and Kings Island theme parks, and Poltergeist at Six Flags Fiesta Texas.) When you enter this ride, queue, you'll notice that everything is painted in neon ~~lime~~ green, pink, yellow, and purple and the colorful warehouse has been converted to a fun house, with colorful trains ready to take you on a fast trip. At this point, you can't help but wonder how you are going to navigate the spaghetti-type track sprawled out before you. With a linear induction motor sendoff that goes zero to sixty miles per hour in three seconds, and purple columns flying closely by your head, the next four inversions are quite fun. All you can see at times is a lot of twisting and turning metal as you navigate the course, but I assure you, it's fun to experience being a very large mouse in an even larger maze. I noticed only one dead spot, where the car slows down just so the rider can really get a handle on his bearings. Joker's Jinx, originally equipped with horse-collar (over the shoulder) harnesses, became a much more comfortable and exciting ride when the harnesses were replaced with a simple hugging lap bar arrangement. The technology (linear induction process) created here was a first of its kind, and I am told that even NASA had an interest in this ride when it first opened in 1999. Overall, you will have a good ride experience on Joker's Jinx. It will not feel too intense, but no way can it be compared to any family coaster you have ridden. It's simply a blast to ride, and one that I highly recommend!

2. **Loch Ness Monster** at Busch Gardens in Williamsburg, Virginia, often called Nessie like its namesake, is one of the most unique designs ever created by the Arrow Corporation. No matter how old this ride is, I still adore this classic. Looking over the edge of this coaster, 130-feet high, you can really appreciate its beauty as you plummet 115 feet down the fifty-five-degree first drop into the interlocking loops. The interlocking loops look much more imposing than they actually are, but they are still the main reason you want to ride this puppy. Created in 1978 and the first of its kind, this coaster streaks along the 3,240-foot track at speeds of up to sixty miles per hour. Although not as intense as other rides in the park, the Loch Ness Monster features tunnels, two lift hills, and great use of the local terrain to give you one great ride. The only thing I found lacking here was the horse-collar harness. They are quite old and seem not to fit very well on the car itself. I'd speculate that they will need to be replaced sometime in the future. On busy days, the ride is timed so that both trains enter the interlocking loops at the same time, making for a real unique experience. The best seats for visuals are the front two seats, but if you really want an unbelievable ride, then the back car is for you. After my experience in the back, I was more than ready to make that appointment with my local chiropractor!

My Favorite
Wooden Roller Coasters
Around the Nation

1. The Voyage at Holiday World, in Santa Claus, Indiana.

2. Thunderhead at Dollywood in Pigeon Forge, Tennessee.

3. Boulder Dash at Lake Compounce in Bristol, Connecticut.

4. The Raven at Holiday World, in Santa Claus, Indiana.

5. Goliath at Six Flags Great America in Gurnee, Illinois.

6. Ghostrider at Knott's Berry Farm in Buena Park, California.

7. El Toro at Six Flags Great Adventure, in Jackson, New Jersey.

8. Thunderbird at Holiday World in Santa Claus Indiana

9. The Phoenix at Knoebels in Elysburg, Pennsylvania.

10. Shivering Timbers at Michigan Adventures in Muskegon, Michigan.

11. The Beast at Paramount's Kings Island in Kings Mills, Ohio.

12. The New Texas Giant at Six Flags Over Texas.

13. Outlaw Run at Silver Dollar City in Branson, Missouri.

14. Lightning Racer at Hershey Park in Pennsylvania.

15. Raven Flyer II at Waldemeer, in Erie, Pennsylvania.

16. Gold Striker at California's Great America, in Santa Clara, California.

17. Zipping Pippin at Bay Beach Amusement Park in Green Bay, Wisconsin.

18. Hades 360 at Mt. Olympus Water &Theme Park, in Wisconsin Dells, Wisconsin

19. Prowler at Worlds of Fun, in Kansas City, Missouri.

20. Boardwalk Bullit at Kemah Boardwalk in Kemah, Texas.

21. American Thunder at Six Flags St. Louis in Eureka, Missouri.

22. Kentucky Rumbler at Beech Bend, in Bowling Green, Kentucky

23. Cornball Express at Indiana Beach, in Monticello, Indiana.

24. Giant Dipper at Santa Cruz Boardwalk, in Santa Cruz, California.

25. Tremors at Silverwood in Athol, Idaho.

26. Blue Streak at Conneaut Lake Park in Conneaut Lake.

27. The Cyclone at Luna Park in Coney Island, New York.

28. Rampage at Visionland in Bessemer, Alabama.

29. The Comet at Six Flags Great Escape Fun Park, in Lake George, New York.

30. Twister at Knoebels in Elysburg, Pennsylvania.

31. Le Monstre (The Monster) at LaRonde Amusement Park, in Montreal, Canada.

32. Great White at Morey's Pier in Wildwood, New Jersey.

33. Giant Dipper at Belmont Park in San Diego, California.

34. The Wild One at Six Flags America, in Largo, Maryland.

35. Roar at Six Flags America, in Largo, Maryland.

36. Hellcat at Clementon Park, in Clementon, New Jersey.

37. The Wooden Warrior at Quassy Amusement Park in Middlebury, Connecticut.

38. The Wildcat at Hershey Park in Hershey, Pennsylvania.

39. Rebel Yell at Kings Dominion, in Virginia.

40. The Cyclone at Lakeside Park in Denver, Colorado.

41. Thunderhawk at Dorney Park in Allentown, Pennsylvania.

42. Thunderbolt at Six Flags New England, in Agawam, Massachusetts.

43. The Comet at Hershey Park, in Hershey, Pennsylvania.

44. The Dragon Coaster at Playland Park, in Rye, New York.

45. Jack Rabbit at Kennywood Park, in West Mifflin, Pennsylvania.

1.   **The Voyage** at Holiday World in Santa Claus, Indiana, is a hybrid type of wooden roller coaster, which opened in recently. A hybrid consists of a steel structure with a wood track. In my mind, there aren't many better than the Voyage, which has a lift hill of 163 feet, followed by several, cool drops of 154 feet, 107 feet, and 100 feet. It travels underground through tunnels over a half dozen times and features three ninety degree banked turns. Even with speeds reaching sixty-seven miles per hour, Voyage has the most airtime of any wooden roller coaster currently available. In 2006, the Voyage won the Best New Ride Award at the Golden Ticket that is given out by *Amusement Today* magazine ranks high in the coaster world. I would still rank this roller coaster as one of my top five woodies that you will find in the United States. It's a ride and a half and one of my favorite coasters on this list.

2.   **Thunderhead** at Dollywood in Pigeon Forge, Tennessee, is a ride that you will find has few peers in the thrill ride circuit. One of the most noticeable features of the ride is just how twisted the layout is. For example, the cars cross over and under the track eight times in just the first thirty seconds, finishing with a total of thirty, before it's all said and done. It's impossible to get the track in your head, at least until you have ridden it a few times. Thunderhead is Great Coasters International's tallest coaster so far with a one-hundred-foot lift hill and many unique features like seventy-eight-degree banked turns and the first ever station fly-through element. These turns are very similar to another great coaster by the name of Millennium Force and fall short of their bank by just two degrees. The best seat on this ride, given its twists and turns, is in the back. You're sure to get knocked around a bit but still have a lot of fun. You'll find the airtime to be similar to the Legend and the turnaround comparable to Millennium, both coasters I've covered in these lists. What you will find to differentiate them from the others, is a unique, station fly-through. This maneuver is designed to make it look like you're going to hit the roof when you get close to the station and to inevitably scare the bejesus out of you. I have experienced something similar on the Cyclone at Coney Island, but Thunderhead makes that one look like a kiddy ride. If you need a good wake up during the day, just stand at the station and experience the cars flying past you at forty miles an hour for a while. Then, if you get brave enough to actually ride it, Thunderhead won't disappoint and you'll surely feel moved by the experience and want to ride it again and again.

3. **Boulder Dash** at Lake Compounce in Bristol, Connecticut, is, in my mind, one of the very best, wooden coasters ever created, and even though this is no longer a new coaster, it's still one of the longest and fastest wooden coasters I have ridden to date. Upon boarding one of the two spacious Philadelphia Toboggan Company trains, your journey begins with a serene and picturesque trip up the lift hill. Cresting into a scenic ninety-degree turn, riders are given just enough time to relax before the first drop and launch into a ride you will not soon forget! This coaster has it all. At 4,500 feet long, Boulder Dash is, to date, the *only* coaster that literally was built along the side of a real mountain. At 155feet high and reaching speeds of sixty miles per hour, all the pieces come together in a presentation that constantly gives you a fun-filled thrill ride experience. It is a smooth and great family coaster, set up in one of the most family-oriented amusement parks I have been to. I consistently get off this ride feeling like I really got my money's worth. The trick, I think, is that since most of the course is wooded, you never do know what's up ahead. The ride literally dashes through trees and around rocks, and, unlike most wooden coasters, has a consistent feel to it throughout. The majestic mountain setting also makes this ride a one-of-a-kind experience. Ranked by *Amusement Today* as one of the top five best coasters on the planet (and after riding it, I can see why), there really isn't a bad seat anywhere. However, I will tell you that I prefer the front row on this one. A great ride for everyone, this is a coaster well worth waiting in line for, and the best news is that there are very rarely long lines at this top attraction.

4. **The Raven** at Holiday World opened in 1995 to rave reviews by most coaster enthusiasts. Great Coasters International (GCI) put together a gem when they laid out the course for this. The thing I really like about this ride is that it maintains its speed and power throughout the 2,800-foot track, something that very few coasters around the country have been successfully able to achieve. The Raven is indeed a world class roller coaster which features massive airtime, and lateral sideways) forces driving both positive and negative g's. During the course, the U-turn to the lift hill is a-typically fast and the first drop, boasts lengthy airtime in both the back and the middle of the train. If you prefer visuals to aerobatics, then the front of this train is the place to be. The specialized terrain begins with an 86-foot first drop where at the bottom, riders are rewarded with a cool tunnel and two more drops. After that, the trains take you over what can be called the lake turn, a lateral maneuver with an extremely fast whip. This is by far, my favorite part of the ride. Once you get through that, the second half is comprised of hairpin turns, multiple direction changes, and small hops that take your breath away. This is by far one of the best-designed and most powerful wooden coasters that I have ridden, with a well-hidden layout and multiple surprises along the way. A night ride on the Raven is coaster riding at its very best, an experience to be savored by any enthusiast. I would recommend this woodie any day of the week, but remember, the lines in this park can get long for this ride especially, so keep that in mind when planning your adventure.

5. **Goliath** at Six Flags Great America in Gurnee, Illinois, opened in the summer of 2014 and is **a** triple-record-breaking wooden coaster that has now set the bar even higher and has pushed the envelope for roller coaster manufacturers everywhere. This addition of Goliath resulted in Six Flags Great America claiming it holds the record for the park containing the most wooden track in the world. Goliath is Rocky Mountain Construction's second wooden roller coaster, following the opening of Silver Dollar City's Outlaw Run. This giant is the tallest, steepest, and fastest wood roller coaster on the planet and is one sweet ride. Riders are subjected to a 180-foot drop that sends you down the track at almost seventy three miles per hour. Its 3,100 feet of track that can take about one thousand riders per hour, ensuring that even the most seasoned of them will wake up and enjoy coastering all over again. It has its two trains have six cars with riders arranged two across-for a total of twenty four riders per train. What I like about this ride is not just the speed, height, and intensity, it's the thrilling maneuvers. You'll face three, intense, overbanked turns, a 180-degree zero g roll twist, and two wild inversions, flipping upside down through a winding drop and a spiraling inverted zero g stall. This is indeed truly the one to beat, folks, and one that will be thrilling enthusiasts like myself for many years to come.

6. **Ghostrider** at Knott's Berry Farm in Buena Park, California, is an extremely fast and exciting twister that, even today, fits beautifully in the Western-themed, Ghost Town section of the park. After a couple of twists and turns through the mine shaft, you emerge onto a woodsy path that takes you past the first maneuver, a dipping spiral that drops out of the station and turns the train around toward the base of the lift hill. It sets you up for what is surely going to be a great ride. As you ascend the lift hill, there are a few moments left for you to twist around and check out the view of some of Knott's vertical icons: the Parachute Drop, the Supreme Scream tower, and Timber Mountain. The view is pretty spectacular as you hit the steep 110-foot drop, before racing around the course at over fifty-five miles per hour. This is another ride that provides that careening, out-of-control feeling as you enter and re-enter the structure, wondering if your head will be chopped off during the especially low clearance maneuvers.

Since this ride is located in an earthquake zone, additional wood was needed in order to fit California state guidelines. This makes for an impressive hidden superstructure that ensures the rider can't be sure where their track is really taking them. At 4,500 feet long, this monster track has you just turning around at a point when most coasters are heading back into the station and finishing up. Ranked second only to Millennium Force in Sandusky, Ohio, in an A&E poll of the top ten rides, it's in very good company. I can see why it made the list. Countless rides later, I'm still impressed with this fast and lengthy coaster. When you combine speed with the extreme airtime on every hill, you can see why Ghostrider is so popular for yourself!

7. **El Toro** at Six Flags Great Adventure in Jackson, New Jersey, is–something any coaster enthusiast should put on their list of coasters to conquer. This Northeast dominate certainly made mine. With one of the world's steepest drop and the feeling of full speed ahead throughout the ride, this woodie is unmatched for its tenacity and, most importantly a word I'd like to call, its re-ridability The trains are themed somewhat like mine train cars and have a very comfortable, next-generation look and feel. Loading can be slow, but the trains are longer than normal, holding thirty-six riders compared to twenty-four on Thunderhead and the twenty-eight stowed on the Voyage. The height of El Toro (176 feet) may not be the tallest around, but that first drop is a memorable one, and I have to say one of the best first drops that I have experienced on a wooden coaster. The overall out and back (with a twist) style of this ride reminded me a lot of Shivering Timbers at Michigan Adventure but with a lot more get up and go. What I found most interesting, even though this is a very intense ride, was how smooth it was. You would think you were riding a steel coaster (like Nitro), but you are, in fact, on wood. The airtime of El Toro is sensational, and Intiman's prefabricated wooden coaster in my mind really delivers a real bang for the buck. This is the type of coaster you seek out and, along with Nitro and Kingda Ka, are the main reasons why you come to this Six Flags Park.

8. **Thunderbird** at Holiday World in Santa Claus Indiana. This is a great addition to the park and, flying down the track at sixty-six miles per hour, this wing coaster from B&M is already a classic and a must ride for the masses. The cost of this ride comes in at 22 million dollars and is America's first launched wooden style roller coaster. The ride is over three-thousand feet long and has many inversions and two crazy overbanked turns. You don't need a holiday to celebrate this marvel and is one that makes a good amusement park into one of the best in the country.

9. **The Phoenix** at Knoebels in Elysburg, Pennsylvania, is a classic that continues to stand alone, no matter how many they try to build. Built in 1940 by PTC/Herb Schmeck and named Rocket when it resided at Playland Park in San Antonio, Texas, it was relocated to its present site in 1985. Coaster designer, Charles Dinn, who also created the Beast, was asked to reconstruct this gem of a ride in the Pennsylvania Mountains, and he nailed it. Phoenix is the coaster lover's perfect combination of a classic out-and-back with some unique elements. INSERT LINE

This ride begins with a dark, narrow tunnel, so long, that it actually disorients your perception of the field ahead before expertly emerging you behind the station and right into a seventy-eight-foot climb up that famous lift topped with a stylish cupola. Once you maneuver the drop, the Phoenix traverses mind-numbing hill after hill, screaming you through a three-thousand foot course at forty-five miles per hour. The single lap bar only goes so far down on your body, so no matter who you are, you will feel intense airtime on this one, especially during its double up/double down element. All in all, there are plenty of bigger, faster coasters around but this one packs a heck of a punch for its size. The sheer genius of its design, consistently puts Phoenix on many national top ten lists, and so it should. If you're looking to make a list of your own, then Phoenix should go right at the top of your to-do list.

10. **Shivering Timbers** is a wild, woodie located at Michigan Adventures in Muskegon, Michigan. Created at a cost of $4.5 million by Great Coasters International (GCI) in 1998, this coaster is the main reason why you should visit Muskegon. Standing at 125 feet with a 120-foot, fifty-seven-degree drop, this coaster Shivering Timbers redefines the standard for the out-and-back concept. At 5,384 feet long, this is one of the longest coasters I have ridden and, at a top speed of fifty-seven miles per hour, is surely one of my most memorable. In a word, this coaster is *big* and impressive to look at. The whopping first drop is followed by two more massive hills, creating an almost out-of-your-seat, standing airtime. There are six hills on the out run and six on the back run, and all twelve produce some of the best airtime and negative-g effects there are. If that wasn't enough to convince you, the final helix will certainly drive home the point with its side-slamming intensity. When planning your day, try to find time to do this coaster twice. It provides distinctly different experiences depending on whether you sit in the front or rear. Up front, you'll experience-a whole lot of what I like to call "seat ejection" going over the top of just about every hill, especially on the first three mega-hills. The back seat doesn't have as much airtime over the small hills, but that is more than made up for when you experience those three huge negative-g drops and the whipping action that you will experience from this position. All in all, it's a fabulous coaster and one that you will surely see on everyone's top ten lists for many years to come.

11. **The Beast** at Kings Island in Kings Mills, Ohio, was the first extraordinary coaster built at the Kings Island complex. Created in 1979 by the Dinn Corporation, it might be old but don't count it out. The Beast stands at 105-feet high but delivers a 135-foot first drop at a forty-five-degree angle, reaching a speed in excess of sixty miles per hour. If the first hill isn't enough for you, it has a second, powered hill at 141 feet high that leads to a wicked double helix inside a tunnel, which seems to catch everyone's attention. It is here where the ride achieves its rated top speed of seventy miles per hour. From the sound of the screams, this ride is one of the best traditional wood coasters that you will find, and the top twenty, national coaster surveys seem to concur. At 7,400 feet long, The Beast takes advantage of the natural forest terrain as the ride plunges down 7,400 feet of track, into a tunnel and through the woods at consistently high speeds. I will tell you that this ride, at times, can be a rough one. I guess age has crept up on this wooden marvel a tad, but rough or not, the adrenaline charge is worth the trade-off. A must ride for the serious roller coaster enthusiast, the Beast is one you just shouldn't pass up.

12. **The New Texas Giant** at Six Flags over Texas was revamped in 2011 by Rocky Mountain Construction Company, and has made this wood coaster even bigger and badder than it already was. This renovated oversized, wooden monster features a steeper and longer first drop, as well as several overbanked turns up to 115 degrees. Standing at 143-feet high, this woodie was the tallest in the world when it debuted (from Dinn and Summers) in 1990. The view from the top is exquisite, and the ride itself can be compared to riding a wild bronco, as it streaks down the track at speeds in excess of sixty-five miles per hour. -This twister style coaster, constantly goes back into its structure, so you are not really able to see the next turn and you will find

many head-chopping effects during its two-and-a-half minute ride cycle. Although several other oversized woodies (like Hercules at Dorney Park) have been quite disappointing, this coaster continues to perform like the champ it really is. As with most wooden coasters, depending on the time of day and weather conditions at the park, this ride can be temperamental, varying in its overall intensity. I like riding this monster right at sunset, overlooking the big ole Texas horizon. Clearly the Texas Giant is why you should come to this park.

13. **Outlaw Run** located at the Silver Dollar City amusement park in Branson, Missouri, is currently the first wooden roller coaster manufactured by Rocky Mountain Construction, and the first wooden roller coaster with multiple (yes, you heard it right) inversions. This means that riders are turned upside down in multiples, as in more than any other wooden roller coaster, to date. At top speeds of sixty-eight miles per hour! On wood, this exciting twist, officially makes Outlaw Run the second-fastest wooden roller coaster in the world, and at 162 feet tall with an eighty--degree down angle, it has one of the steepest drops too. Outlaw Run was Rocky Mountain Construction's first "run" into the wooden roller genre. And if this is any indication what they have in store for the public in the near future then look out, because this is one *fine* ride! This stagecoach themed attraction opened in March of 2013 at a cost of ten million dollars to produce. If you ask me, it was money well spent. In its first year, Outlaw Run ranked highly in *Amusement Today*'s Golden Ticket Awards and won the Golden Ticket Award for Best New Ride. I really enjoyed it, and I believe you will also!

14. **Lighting Racer** at Hershey Park in Pennsylvania, is-still a thrill-a-minute wooden coaster and one that I highly recommend. Hershey Park, known for their outstanding chocolate products, factory tour, and three-dimensional rides, also boasts one heck of an amusement park, if you didn't already know this. Their marquee coaster is a year 2000, woodie created by Great Coasters International (GCI). GCI took a traditional out-and-back coaster then combined it with a racing concept, creating something fresh and unique at Hershey Park. The coaster stands ninety-feet high with two, separate, mirrored tracks. Trains race one another down a course clocked by computer proximity sensors. During the two and a half minute race, riders

encounter fifteen drops, a seventy mile an hour near head-on collision, and a near miss with a waterfall. No matter which position you're in when you hit the checkered flag back at the station, everyone is winner on Lightning Racer

15. **Ravine Flyer II** is a hybrid steel and wood coaster) situated at Waldameer Park in Erie, Pennsylvania. It launched at a cost of six million dollars and ranked best new ride in 2008. Today, it's still ranked in the top ten at *Amusement Today* magazine. Ravine Flyer II is a replacement for the original Ravine Flyer that sadly, had to be removed in 1938, due to a tragic accident resulting in a man's death. Initial concepts for the replacement were developed by Custom Coasters International in the early 1990s, further developed by Dennis McNulty several years later, then finalized and constructed by the Gravity Group. Ravine Flyer II won best new ride at the 2008 Golden Ticket Awards (Amusement Today) and was voted in the top 12 as one of the best wooden roller coasters that year.

It still has one of the tallest drops around (as wooden roller coasters go) and is still the tallest (at 115 feet) in the state of Pennsylvania. I really like this 120 foot first drop that can reach speeds of sixty miles per hour. Like its predecessor, Ravine Flyer II actually travels out of the park and over State Route 832. The trains were created by Philadelphia Toboggan Coasters and I've noticed they really provide a consistent ride in all types of weather. For safety, they have a seatbelt and lap bar, carry twenty-four passenger at a time, and can be enjoyed by most everyone.

16. **Gold Striker,** built by Great Coasters International, opened to the public on June 1, 2013, at Great America in Santa Clara, California. At the time of this writing, it's currently the tallest (118 feet) and fastest Fifty-four miles per hour wooden coaster in Northern California. This ride has a unique 103 foot, fifty-degree drop tunnel, follows by the sensation of being pushed into your seat during several tight turns, ejector bunny hops, and a memorable, eighty-degree, banked turn towards the end.

The ride and its name are a reference to the gold prospectors that went to California, seeking their fortunes, back in 1849. Coincidentally, this is the same group of prospectors that inspired the name of the San Francisco 49ers, the pro football team that built their new stadium adjacent to the park. In fact, on the Gold Striker lift hill, you can see the inside the 49er's Levi Stadium, right to the fifty-yard line. The ride is able to accommodate almost ninety people per hour, lines never really get too long. If you're looking for something to accommodate just about anyone in your party, Gold Striker is a solid choice. This is truly a great ride to be experienced for just about everyone in the family.

17. **Zippin Pippin** at Bay Beach Amusement Park in Green Bay Wisconsin, is one of the United States oldest wooden roller coasters still in existence. This design by John A. Miller and Harry Baker, formally called the Pippin, was originally built in 1912 at East End Park in Memphis, Tennessee, but that's just where the story begins. In the 1970s, the city of Memphis made plans to take the Pippin, build a second ride called the Grand Carousel, and theme a park around both of them. Libertyland Amusement Park opened in 1976, and the newly relocated and renamed, Zippin Pippin, opened with it. Libertyland billed Zippin as the most prominent and historic ride in the park, and it reportedly became Elvis Presley's favorite roller coaster over the subsequent years. Sadly, Libertyland closed in 2005, and sadder still, the century old Zippin, sat alone, exposed to the elements, resulting in a partial collapse in 2010. After its collapse, the city of Green Bay made arrangement to buy the rights and the coaster, eventually dismantling what was left. They gently moved the pieces to Green Bay and reconstructed Zippin Pippin at Bay Beach Amusement Park.

For a hundred year old woodie, Zippin is every bit as rough as you might expect, but that's just part of the charm. Besides, it can still reach speeds over 40 miles per hour and it contains a nice, 70 foot drop along its 2,685 feet of track. This is definitely a "must do" coaster, if for no other reason than the nostalgia of a time long forgotten.

18. **Hades 360**, formally Hades, at Mt. Olympus Water &Theme Park, in Wisconsin Dells. Hades is a wooden rarity due to its steep sixty-five-degree drop and ninety-degree banked turns. You don't usually get these steep angles on wood coasters although the new crop of coasters being built actually are starting to incorporate these elements, (like Goliath). In actuality, Hades 360 was one of the newer roller coasters that brought in this new banking-type system. Built by the Gravity Group and voted Best New Ride by Amusement Today magazine in 2005, Hades is still a fan favorite, even today. This is one big roller coaster, as rides go, but in a smaller sized park, it just seems like a monster! Kudos to Mount Olympic for such an effective use of perspective in a small space.

Hades first drop is over 130 feet, but the memorable part of the ride is a unique trip out of the park, twice, where the track winds you underneath the parking lot full of cars. It was renamed Hades 360 in 2013, when they had the manufacturer remove a small hill then add new Timberliner trains and a 360-degree, inverted roll (yes, you heard me right) in its place. Overall, the track is 4,726 feet in length, and the rides has a duration of almost three and a half minutes. It is the largest roller coaster in this park and its unique nature, makes it one you don't want to miss.

©2005 Joel Rogers
www.CoasterGallery.com

19. **Prowler** at Worlds of Fun, in Kansas, City, Missouri–is the park's second wooden roller coaster, and the third ride to occupy its present location in the Africa section of the park. Its predecessors just weren't exciting enough to make good anchors. When Prowler launched in 2009, it won the Golden Ticket Award for Best New Ride, and it looked like Worlds of Fun had finally found a keeper. Prowler tops out at 100 feet high and only lasts a minute and a half, but as it spirals through a ravine and the surrounding woods at speeds reaching fifty-miles per hour, you'll soon forget all about its stature problems. At only a little over 3,000 feet of track, it's rough, but it doesn't even compare to some of the other Cedar Fair coasters around the county. Still, I find Prowler to be a great fit for this section and worth riding, Prowler is one of my favorites and was recently voted Best New Ride of 2009 from Amusement Today's Golden Ticket Awards. If for nothing other than the layout, I say come to Kansas City and give the Prowler a whirl!

20. **Boardwalk Bullet** at Kemah Boardwalk in Kemah, Texas is an interesting, lesser known woodie. This high-speed bullet was created in 2007 by the Gravity Group at a cost of three million dollars. I accidentally stumbled over this little gem while I was interviewing astronauts at NASA one year. I was told that Boardwalk Bullet was the only roller coaster in Houston. So naturally, I had to run right over and see for myself what kind of roller coaster that a town famous for space exploration would build. To my surprise, while lacking the space theme I had envisioned, Bullet more than made up for it with a clever, compact design that would have made the NASA engineers proud. Gravity group crammed almost 3000 feet of crisscrossed track and a whole lot of fun into a very tiny space. It's actually one of the most compact wooden coasters in the world and a very good reason why you should pop over to Kemah Boardwalk if you're ever in the Houston area.

21. **American Thunder** opened on June 20, 2008, at Six Flags St. Louis in Eureka, Missouri. Many might remember that this fine ride was originally named after and themed to around the famous motorcycle daredevil. Evel Knievel. It was renamed American Thunder for the 2011 season. This seven million-dollar GCI creation sports a 2,700 foot course at speeds up to forty-eight miles per hour. This ride features an eighty foot drop, sixteen hills, and multiple high banked turns that can be slanted up to sixty-seven degrees during the entire run. The layout crosses over and under itself seventeen times. This ride also features two twenty-four-passenger Millennium Flyer trains for better cornering and, for the most part, is pretty smooth. There are two trains in the loading area with twelve cars per train. I like the fact that this coaster crosses over itself a total of fourteen times during its two-and-a-half-minute run. There are two trains in the loading area with twelve cars per train. Riders are arranged two across for a total of twenty-four riders at a time. American thunder is never very crowded, and it's not too intense, making it a wise choice for families or for those people looking for a good starter coaster.

22. **Kentucky Rumbler** at Beech Bend Park in Warren County, Kentucky, is another good fit for the whole family. The first drop is 96 feet even through the height of this structure only rises to a height of 80 feet This four million dollar, GCI, was a much needed addition at Beech Bend, who at the time, didn't have a signature ride that guests could get excited about. Since then, it's consistently ranked in the top twenty-five, year after year. Its twisted course layout where the coaster spirals in and out of its own frame over 3,000 feet of track and at speeds up to forty-five miles an hour, is fresh and exciting compared to many others in its class. It incorporates three station fly-bys, and a record setting thirty crossovers with twelve airtime moments that are hard to forget. Rumbler accommodates five hundred guests per hour and it's located in a smaller amusement park, so there is never much of a wait for this one. Which is good, because odds are that it will leave the entire family wanting to ride it over and over again.

23. **Cornball Express** at Indiana Beach in Monticello, Indiana. If you ever get the chance to visit Indiana Beach in Monticello, Indiana, make sure you head on over to check out Cornball Express, one of my favorite rides anywhere in the country. It is a great wood coaster and, in my book, a real hit for the entire family. The ride was created and manufactured by Custom Coasters International at a cost of twelve million dollars. It opened in May of 2001. Since its creation, this roller coaster has been a favorite and is ranked in the top fifty year after year and later gained critical acclaim among coaster enthusiasts, as it was named one of the best roller coasters by *Amusement Today* several years in a row. Cornball Express was one of the last roller coasters designed before closing their doors in 2002. The ride weaves through several other rides like Hoosier Hurricane) as well as over the Kiddieland section of the park. At a height of only 55 feet, the ride is not very tall and only flies down the track 2,100 feet of track at forty-five miles per hour, but don't let that fool you. Cornball Express is still a lot of fun with plenty of air hills that make you feel like you are going to be ejected from your seat. Overall, it's not too intense a ride and one that I have no problem recommending for the whole family.

24. **Giant Dipper** at the Santa Cruz Boardwalk is a historic wooden roller coaster located at the Santa Cruz Beach Boardwalk, an amusement park in Santa Cruz, California. It opened on May 17, 1924. Okay now, you are talking classic rides here. This one is a marvel and is the fifth oldest roller coaster in the United States. It is truly a classic and one that the entire family can ride. It's a great place to put a coaster overlooking the water and on a classic boardwalk like the one they have here. In fact it has been stated that over fifty five million coaster enthusiasts have ridden it since its opening. One thing for sure, the United States National Park Service recognized the Giant Dipper as part of a National Historic Landmark also covering the nearby Looff carousel back in 1987. It was named an American Coaster Enthusiasts Coaster Landmark on May 5, 2007. The ride appeared in many television commercials and movies, including *The Lost Boys*, *Sudden Impact*, and *Dangerous Minds* just to name a few.

The Giant Dipper was designed by Frank Prior and Fredrick Church (1878–1938), with a double out-and-back layout and was actually built by Arthur Looff. One fact you might not know about is that it actually took less than fifty days to build. Total cost of the project, a whopping fifty thousand dollars. You can't build a coaster like this one for less than a couple of million these days. It is interesting to know that it replaced a miniature railway ride designed by (the father of modern-day roller coasters). LaMarcus Thompson. The ride stands at 70 feet tall, has a nice 65-foot drop, and can reach fifty-five miles per hour during your 2,650-feet trek down this track. However, height and speed is not what makes this ride a winner. It's the history behind this ride, its location, and its beauty on the Santa Cruz Boardwalk that makes it so very special.

25. **Tremors** at Silverwood theme park in Athol, Idaho is a Custom Coasters International, created and themed around the popular 1990 movie, Tremors, starring Kevin Bacon. This concept ride features an underground tunnel that dips down below the ride's gift shop, then in and out of several more underground tunnels before it's over. At the time Tremors was built in the late 90's, an underground coaster, where it's dark and cold and tricky to maneuver around obstacles like gift shops, probably seemed like a logistics nightmare for maintenance purposes. After a decade of labor intensive upkeep, a little company called Rocky Mountain Construction, went and put their thinking caps on and invented the "topper track" system.

This unique track was designed to cut down on maintenance and daily wear and tear, a perfect fit, for the hard to maintain, underground Tremors. It was the first to install and use the "topper track" in 2010. With a 103-foot first drop and top speeds of sixty miles per hour, the 3,000 feet of topper track makes the maneuvers feel like a glider's dream. Since its grand opening, this design has consistently ranked at the top of the wood coasters around the country. All in all, I'd say, with elevation changes, helixes, and tight tunnel maneuvers, Tremors really works its magic as much underground as it does terra firma.

26. **Blue Streak** is a wooden roller coaster built in May of 1938 at Conneaut Lake Park in Pennsylvania. This classic, out-and-back sports a 79 foot first drop and is officially, the only wooden coaster in the park. Designed by Ed Vettel and the last of his shallow design still in operation, Blue Streak has long straight-a-ways and minimal turning, allowing the ride to reach speeds over fifty miles per hour, despite a relatively short 2.900 feet of track. Over the years, the Blue Streak has undergone major renovations and still manages to consistently rank in the top fifty best wooden coasters by *Amusement Today,* through even with all the changes. This ride has always been ranked in the top fifty best wood coasters around. Also, it is good to know that the park is never that crowded and the ride can accommodate 1,600 riders per hour, so there is never a long wait for this beauty.

27. **The Cyclone** at Luna Park in Coney Island, is the wooden coaster that set the standard for all others, as far as I'm concerned. Despite lagging behind today's technology by almost a century, this 1927, $175,000 dollar coaster ranks in the top fifteen worldwide, right now. I can only imagine what kind of imposing force it was considered by 1920 standards.

According to the New York Times, aviation legend, Charles Lindberg, said that riding the Cyclone was "greater than flying an airplane at top speed." If that isn't enough to convince you, than how about a legend? In 1989, a story was published in *Popular Mechanics,* boasting facetiously that the Cyclone could make the mute speak. The article detailed the 1948 ride of Emilio Franco, a West Virginia coal miner, who had in fact had a nervous disorder, and been mute since 1942. The story went on to chronicle Emilio's screams beginning at the 2nd dip, eventually ending with him safely on the ground and miraculously uttering his first words in six years. What does a mute man say after six years of silence and two minutes on the Cyclone? "I feel sick," was his fitting response. One can only speculate as to how much of that double entendre was due to the ride.

As if the old school lap bars and original bench seats weren't daunting enough, the creaks, groans, and perceived possibility of advanced wood rot, are sure to reduce a grown man to tears just making his way through the line. As an added bonus, this coaster hasn't been modified in effort to tame the original, as so many have done over the years. With Cyclone, you're getting an original, and one that every enthusiast should ride at least once, and as soon as possible. You just never know when they might retire this coastal classic.

28. **Rampage** at Visionland in Bessemer, Alabama, is without a doubt the highlight of what this park has to offer I am told that this coaster was modeled after Megafobia in Wales, but since I never had the pleasure of riding that coaster, I will just have to take their word for it. Built by CCI (who else?) in 1998, Rampage is a superb wooden coaster that races around a 3,500-foot track at top speeds of fifty-five miles per hour. A few years back, this ride was also ranked as one of the top five wooden coasters in the world, according to a Discovery Channel program on top coasters that year. I think the accolades are definitely well deserved here. The ride is visually stunning, with a hillside location that can be seen from just about anywhere in the park. One of the best aspects of the ride is that there seems to be no braking other than at the end of this ride, so you get the feeling that you are literally out of control most of the time and accruing mounds and mounds of airtime as you go along. From what I hear, Rampage can be very temperamental to some people. I myself loved the ride experience, but if you ask five other people about Rampage, at least one person would not share my opinion regarding this woodie. Also, I like visuals when I am riding wooden coasters, but oddly enough, the better ride on Rampage seems to be found more in the back section than up front where I like it. Airtime is good, but it's the lateral movement of this coaster that most people, including myself, seem to remember. A must ride if you ever find yourself in the hills of Alabama.

29. **The Comet** at Six Flags Great Escape Fun Park in Lake George, New York, is, in a word, fantastic. The Comet was first constructed in 1927 by legendary coaster builder, Harry Traver. Back then it was called the Cyclone, and it was thought by many to be the most intense coaster ever. It had a laminated wood track with a steel superstructure, but it was considered to be a wooden coaster by definition. At ninety-five-feet high with a pretty fair eighty-seven-foot drop, Comet seems to get faster and wilder as it rushes down the tracks at over fifty-five miles per hour. A bunny hop heaven with a double out-and-back setup, the Philadelphia Toboggan Company can be proud of their work here. As you continue through your run, the turns seem to get tighter and there are several unexpected and venomous little side twists en route that will take your breath away. The final turnaround is where this coaster really shines. You seem to be, again, picking up speed as you enter the final turnaround, and you truly feel like you are about to be ejected out of your seat. This ride packs a punch, and if you love negative gs, you will truly love this ride. It has been my experience that the lines are never really too long here, and at this park on most days, you will be able to ride again and again to your heart's content. Enjoy!

30. **Twister** at Knoebels in Elysburg, Pennsylvania, never grows old in my mind. Using the drawings of John Allen's and the old Mr. Twister from Elitch Gardens, at a cost of three million dollars, Knoebels has built a fun, exuberating ride that is relentless from start to finish. An instant classic, I guarantee you have not ridden a twister that can compare to this one. With few lateral slams, this one is designed for fun thrills, not fear. Riders race around the 3,900-foot track at over fifty miles per hour, but in this tight space, you get the feeling you are actually moving much faster than that. At 192 feet with a first drop of ninety feet, Twister also has an awesome double helix as you go down the second drop. Since the coaster has many of these drops and twists, I believe Twister successfully combines two roller coasters into one, and the head-chopper effect on this classic is absolutely magnificent. This one is a good example of a woodie that gets it right with consistent pacing throughout your journey. I also enjoyed the placement of this ride in the park. Nestled in a beautifully wooded area, the coaster looks like it is truly part of the landscape. As with most wood coasters, your experience on this one can vary from day to day, but overall I found it to be an exciting adventure every time I rode it. This is also a classic coaster to ride at night.

31 **Le Monstre (The Monster)** is a racing style ride built by William M. Cobb & Associates, and located at La Ronde in Montreal, Canada. It's quite the Canadian record holder, the most significant of which, is the record for the tallest dual-track wooden coaster in the World. This isn't the standard for a dual track racing coaster, since track one and two opened a year apart and have a 25 foot difference in total length. The tracks don't run parallel to one another so it's a unique experience, but technically, not a race since they don't run the same path. At 130 feet high and speeds up to sixty miles per hour, I can see why it can't be unseated from the top record slot.

La Ronde created this classic with lap bars and seat belts in the Toboggan Company trains, making it a more comfortable fit for riders that vary in size. With lots of float time and that feeling of being ejected from the seat on every hill, Le Monstre is long on intensity and short on stability. It can get a little rough as you're flying around the corners. If you're looking to challenge your senses, and your stomach, Le Monstre might be just the beast you're looking for and when you riding it, try looking around at the people sharing this ride experience with you. In any language (English or French) you will find that Laughter and fun are universal

32. **Great White** at Morey's Pier in Wildwood, New Jersey, is another one of those stunning shore-line coasters you have to check out for the views of the Atlantic Ocean. Yes, I'm referring to the same Atlantic that destroyed much of that same shoreline during Hurricane Sandy. Thankfully, that little act of nature, left this fifty mile-per-hour, seaside treasure, right where they built it, over the ocean and through the floor of the neighboring pier.

This twister, out-and-back design has drops up to a hundred feet. Combine those with high speed turns and the salt air blasting you in the face, and Great White can leave you feeling like you've been through a hurricane yourself. The turnaround elements alone are something of an art form, leaving you feeling a little like you've been literally ejected out of your seat and might plunge directly into the ocean below. The best part? It's a pay as you go coaster, so you can literally spend the entire day doing nothing else but riding this Jersey Shore marvel if you and your wallet are inclined to do so.   It is a must ride experience when you are at the New Jersey shore. One of the two things that enjoy most is that when you are sitting at the top of the 110 foot list hill, you get a bird's eye view of the Atlantic Ocean. This is the same ocean that destroyed much of the New Jersey shoreline during Superstorm Sandy. The second thing I love about this ride is that after you complete the fifty- mile per-hour 100-foot plus first drop you will literally feel your body ejecting out of your seat as you enter the turnaround element that gives a great view of the ocean below. All through this ride, there are amazing drops and high speed turns and twists making this 3,300 foot marvel very popular among roller coaster enthusiasts.

You will just love the negative gs experienced on this ride. Another fun part of this ride is as you leave the station, you will go through the floor (and under the boardwalk) before starting the climb up the lift hill. This combination twister and double out and back is a destination roller coaster and is a top attraction at this pay as you go park. It is most definitely worth the trip to the Jersey shore.

33. **Giant Dipper** at Belmont Park in San Diego, California, is one of those happy testimonials to the preservation of a proven classic. Standing, but not operating for years (closed in the early seventies and reopened in 1990), this marvel was refurbished by the town so that future generations would be able to enjoy this one-of-a-kind ride. This coaster is one of the last remaining Frank Prior & Fred Church coasters ever to be created. Built in 1925, this coaster survived three fires, avoided demolition by the city, and later became a National Historic Landmark. This wooden coaster stands a mere 73-feet high, but don't let the size of this ride fool you. Equipped with flanged wheels, the trains on this wonderful seaside coaster negotiate some remarkable turns and twists over very little straight track all through their 2,600-foot run. Reaching speeds as high as fifty-five miles per hour, this coaster is a joy to behold. Like many coasters, the Giant Dipper has many different personalities. If it seems a little slow in the morning, go back in the afternoon, and you will be positively be surprised. Along with the Giant Dipper in Santa Cruz and the Cyclone in Brooklyn, this coaster is a must ride for any roller coaster enthusiast looking to experience the classic innovation of these early twister coasters. There is something to be said for wooden coasters built around the ocean that just makes them a cut above the rest. Enjoy and don't forget to check out the open-air market all around this quaint coaster park.

©2009 Joel A. Rogers
www.CoasterGallery.com

34. **The Wild One** at Six Flags America, built by John Miller and the Dinn Corporation, stands at ninety-eight feet high and throws its riders off the edge at fifty-three miles per hour. This traditional ride qualifies as a living piece of 1917 history that almost didn't make it past the 1990's. Wild One originally circled along one side of Paragon Park in Hull, Massachusetts, south of Boston, where it was known simply as the Giant Coaster. When the seaside park closed (along with so many other vintage amusement parks) in 1985, Six Flags saved it from the wrecking ball, relocating to its current location in Maryland. The Wild One stirs the senses with its nostalgic appeal. The look of the rickety, white-painted support beams, the sound of the clickety-clack-as the train climbs the lift hill; and the out-of-control feel as riders get tossed from side to side. Even the smell of the grease seems to come from another era. Airtime abounds throughout the ride, and many times you feel like this ride is going to catapult you out of your seat (but of course, you are safely attached to the car's lap bar system, so that won't happen). I defy anyone to emerge from this ride without an ear-to-ear grin. Six Flags America has undergone many changes in recent years, and the Wild One has had to conform to those changes. Slightly modified in its ride intensity, this coaster now runs through the skull of the park's water flume and lasts approximately two and a half minutes. There really doesn't seem to be much of a line for this-but don't mistake that the ride isn't interesting enough to have a long lines. Trust me, this piece of history is a must if you're looking for a quick ride on a classic woodie.

35. **Roar** at Six Flags America was the second wooden coaster created by Great Coasters International. It has a sister coater called Roar West at Six Flags Discovery Kingdom as well. Both are fantastic, but my favorite is at SFA. Roar debuted in May of 1998 and whisks around the twister track at a good fifty miles per hour. What I really like about this coaster is that there are no straight-aways anywhere on this track. The rider is constantly turning, banking, and diving throughout the entire 2,300-foot course. Once Roar's Philadelphia Toboggan trains are loaded and the lap bars secured, the wooden coaster comes to life and three ninety-degree curves lead riders to the lift hill. The chain lift carries the train slowly up to the top of the ninety feet of lift, up and over a twisting, turning layout down below. Once the clickety-clack ceases, the train heads straight toward the impossibly tight curvature of a very steep, twisting first drop, and Roar wastes no time in navigating the curving drop to the bottom. The track next wraps around the layout's fan curve (a 270-degree inclined spiral), which sends the train into its first camelback hump. After coasting over this element, Roar dives back down and takes the passengers up and around another fan-type curve. Diving down and curving to the left, the coaster speeds over a quick hill and sweeps through a 270-degree banked turn leading into the ride's tunneled section, where the train encounters the layout's steepest banked turn. Exiting the tunnel, there is another curve, and you are now ready for the finale. The trains start their furious run to the brake area with a high-speed curving hop, a complete 180-degree turnaround, and one last surprising hop. All told, ten banked curves and twenty-one crisscrosses (under and over) occur on this ride. You can see that after creating the Wildcat at Hershey Park, GCI took this concept to the next level. I might add that they succeeded famously here. This is my wife's favorite ride, and I am pretty keen on this one as well. Lines are never that long, so you can ride Roar as many times as you like during the day. Try the front row. You will love that first drop.

36. **Hellcat** at Clementon Park in Clementon, New Jersey, is the best kept secret in the roller coaster industry. This monster is a wooden roller coaster designed by S&S Power and built by Philadelphia Toboggan Coasters and located at Clementon Amusement Park just outside of Philadelphia. Opened in 2004, its first drop is 110 feet and can take its riders up to fifty-six miles per hour. The ride costs $4 million to make, and its ride time is one minute and thirty seconds and is 2,602 feet long. Originally named Tsunami in 2005, its name has changed several times, but the ride experience has always remained the same. This ride replaced the Jack Rabbit (and one of my favorites), which was, at the time, the seconds oldest roller coaster in operation in the country. Hellcat, in a word, is for real thrill seekers and not recommended for those who do not wish to experience positive and negative gs on their person. When this ride opened, it was a little rough to say the least, but that problem was remedied when parts of the coaster's track was replaced by Great Coasters International to provide a smoother ride. If you're ever in the Philadelphia area, don't miss this one. It is definitely worth the trip to this fabulous little amusement park, and a ride that is New Jersey's best kept secret.

©2007 Joel A. Rogers
www.CoasterGallery.com

37. **Wooden Warrior** is the newest wooden roller coaster located at Quassy Amusement Park in Middlebury, Connecticut. It's not very big, but I really do like this ride. It's also a great coaster for starting your adventure and becoming a thrill ride maniac. The coaster was designed and built by the Gravity Group, so despite its small size, it's still been well received by roller coaster enthusiasts.-The coaster features Timberliner trains that carry twelve people per load. It was one of the first wooden coasters to use such trains. With speeds just over thirty-five miles per hour, and never going over forty feet at the tallest drop, this is perfect for those just starting out and for whole families as well. Riders are arranged two across in a single row (six cars) for a total of twelve riders per train. I also like the turnaround of this ride where riders are lucky enough to head through a very dark tunnel and when you add that to the amount of airtime you get on the new attraction, you can see why this has become such a favorite to many. It may be classified as a junior roller coaster, but flying down the track at almost forty miles per hour, it is in a class by itself for a roller coaster this size. I would give this a shot when you're in this park. The airtime and smaller elements make it more fun than frightening, and a perfect choice for just about anyone.

38. **The Wildcat** at Hershey Park in Hershey, Pennsylvania, was the first creation for Great Coasters International. It opened in May of 1996 and cost $5 million to complete. Perched at the top of this 90-foot coaster, you will experience swooping curves and directional changes not experienced on many wood coasters. On Wildcat, you will also reach top speeds of fifty miles per hour and will wonder where the next turn is. The ride is situated on two acres of land and is 3,183 feet of pure adrenaline. Wildcat reaches a top speed of fifty miles per hour while it crosses its path twenty times. During this ride, you get the feeling of constant acceleration and relentless curves throughout the course. On Wildcat, you enter the course at pretty much the same speed as when you started. You come into the last turn at a startling forty miles per hour. The ride provides great airtime, but the unusual layout is what makes this a great coaster. There are literally no straight portions on this track. Its layout is a throwback to earlier times and like its successor, Roar at Six Flags America, it gives a stunning nostalgic experience.

Riding Wildcat is about as close as you can come to experiencing what it was like to ride the old classics from another age. The ride cars built by the Philadelphia Toboggan Company are comfortable and feature individual ratcheting, lap bars and a headrest. As on most twisters, ride the front and after the first hill, watch the actual frame of this ride sway as you enter the next element. You will truly believe this *CAT* is alive. Since day one, this has been a popular ride with many roller coaster enthusiasts.

39. **Rebel Yell** at Kings Dominion has been featured in many movies in the late 'seventies and eighties. It also is the site where American Coaster Enthusiasts (ACE) was originally formed. Rebel Yell might be a standard out and back racing coaster, but it does have a twist. It has sole claim to the fact that the trains on one side of Rebel Yell were turned to face backward from 1992 until 2007. Eventually it was changed back to meet manufacturer's standards. Even today, these trains seem to rush headlong to the finish, and you never do know until the end which car is going to win the race. Built in 1975 by the Philadelphia Toboggan Company, the train speeds around the dual course at fifty-five miles per hour along a 3,368-foot track. The view at the top of the eighty-five-foot lift hill is splendid, and the coaster still performs like a trooper. Lines are never really long, and I recommend that you ride the cars forward and backward for your own comparison. If you like a consistent, old-style wooden race coaster, this ride is for you.

40. **The Cyclone** at Lakeside Park in Denver, Colorado, is 90-feet tall with a top speed of fifty miles per hour. This traditional wooden roller coaster has been operating at Lakeside Amusement Park for nearly seventy years. It is recognized as coaster classic, and it is indeed one of the best roller coasters of its era. This historic attraction was designed and built by Edward A. Vettel back in1940. The ride was based on one he saw in New Orleans. The Cyclone has an out–and-back layout that features a curve drop that rolls into a helix before the out-and-back portion during your two-minute and 2,800-feet trek down memory lane. Also of note is the Art Deco style station, which you will find along the way. The ride capacity is around 1,100 passengers per hour and each train has five cars with two rows each. The best place to sit on this ride is in the back although it might be a little rough for some.

41. **Thunderhawk** at Dorney Park in Allentown, Pennsylvania, is one ride you will not soon forget. Built in 1923, this wooden coaster is one of the oldest in the country and races down the track at speeds reaching forty-five miles per hour. Thunderhawk is a classic crowd pleaser, once known simply as the Coaster. An initial sixty-five-foot plunge launches riders on a high-speed journey complemented by unpredictable twists and incredible airtime all through its 2,700-foot run. It provides tons of lateral gs, great head-chopper effects, and some very nice airtime. One thing I did notice was the trim on the second-to-last bunny hill coming in to the station. It slows the ride down way too quickly and spoils what could be a great ending. The Thunderhawk was designed and built with pressure-treated Southern pine by the Philadelphia Toboggan Company. The design of the coaster today is a bit different from when the out-and-back coaster was first created. It was designed by the legendary Herb Schmeck (who worked for none other than John Miller) and was converted to a figure eight design in 1930. On some days, this ride can wreak havoc on your body, and yet on other days, you will truly get the ride of your life. This is one coaster where sitting in the back seat is equivalent to going fifteen rounds with a heavyweight boxer. I loved it anyway.

42. **Thunderbolt** at Six Flags New England was built in 1941, just one year after the Flyer Comet at Whalom Park. The Thunderbolt has a surprising element that very few coasters have-a double- dip-drop series. This means that as you drop, you stop, level off, and then drop again. It is a great experience for those who have never tried this type of element before. The coaster is a classic and one that delivers a consistent ride every time. For new coaster fanatics and families alike, this is the one you should ride. Take advantage of Thunderbolt and ride this vintage family woodie at night. You will be happy you did, so will your sons or daughters.

43. **The Comet** at Hershey Park in Hershey, Pennsylvania, is a spitfire. With a seventy-eight-foot drop and a top speeds of fifty miles per hour, the slinky wasn't the only cool thing to come out of the 1940's. Designed by Herbert Schmeck in 1946, and built by Philadelphia Toboggan Coasters, this modified, double out-and-back was one of the biggest coasters ever created. The first drop, suspended over water, launches riders into a hairpin turn, followed by a well done, secondary drop. It's by far my favorite element. If you've got a bad neck or back, I'd recommend avoiding this one. It can get pretty rough. For the healthiest of you, sure it creaks, cracks, and looks rickety, but it's a gem that all aficionados need to put on the list. One note. If you have a bad back or neck injury, you might want to avoid this one because at times, it can get a little rough.

44. **The Dragon Coaster** at Playland Park in Rye, New York, was built in 1929, just after the park debuted. It's truly a classic ride and one that the whole family will enjoy.-This actually one of last remaining examples of work done by Fred Church, and it really shouldn't be missed for that reason alone. This is a very interesting ride with a unique V-shaped layout. Standing at 75 feet tall with a 60-foot drop, riders fly down the 3,400-foot track at speeds reaching forty-five miles per hour. You might notice that the ride seems a little longer than it actually is. This is achieved by making the coaster multilayered and intentionally designed so that just when you think the ride is ending, there's another section of track to cover. This coaster has been featured in many movies, and one of its more memorable moments occur when you get to go through the dragon's mouth and out through its tail. Lines are never a problem with the Dragon, as Playland Park is a pay-as-you-go park. However, with no lines to be seen, you better bring some extra cash so you can ride over and over!

45. **Jack Rabbit** at Kennywood Park in West Mifflin, Pennsylvania. This ride is a classic and one of my favorite oldies out there. Designed and built by John A. Miller and Harry C. Baker in 1920 (for only $20,000), it is one of the oldest running roller coasters in the world. Jack Rabbit's trains were manufactured by Edward Vettel Sr. in 1951 and contains three cars of six seats each. One of the things most loved about this ride is that these cars have not been replaced, and the aging cars are considered a part of the ride's nostalgic experience. Since there are only small lap bars and a double dip drop, riders literally feel like they are going to be ejected out of the car. I caution against this one for younger riders because they aren't always real comfortable with that sensation.-In addition to the double dip on the first drop, another feature of the ride was a tunnel that covered the turnaround section after the first drop. It was removed, but recently, the tunnel was restored at a slightly shorter length.

The Jack Rabbit was built shortly after Miller patented a new track design in 1920 (which all wooden coasters subsequently used). This design involved the use of wheels both under and over the track, which allowed Miller to create a pretty cool 70-foot drop. The speed of this classic ride stays consistent and reaches speeds in excess of forty five miles per hour. This terrain-filled out-and-back is a great ride for those who like adventure. There are very few double dip experiences out there. Some will love it, and others will be frightened out of their minds. If you fall in the latter category, I'd recommend trying to get past that fear, just to say you did the double dip. Try riding in the back seat to get the full effect, and just hanging on for dear life until it's over. On this ride, one thing I would mention is make due to the limited lap bar restraint system make sure you children are a minimum of thirty six inches tall to ride this puppy.

My Favorite Late Addition Roller Coaster List

Some of my favorite newest rides that you will find out there can be found below. They are definitely the top rides in the Country but due to the lateness of their addition to this book, made it to this special section. I am sure you will love them as much as I did

1. **Batman: The Ride** at Six Flags Fiesta Texas. Yes, it does have the Batman name, but this is a very different roller coaster from anything you will find out there. This is an S&S 4-D Fee Spin Caster, and you can find this attraction in the Rockville section of the park. It's 120 feet tall, and loaded with surprises. If you're looking for the next new thing in this industry you have truly found it on this ride. Most of the time you don't even know which end is up and that's an amazing thing. Lines do get long for this so try to ride it as soon as you enter the park or towards closing time.

2. **Cannibal at Lagoon Park** – Farmington, Utah is a 200-foot mega mega-coaster (actually 208 feet tall) that rides the rails at seventy miles per hour with 2,735 feet of track. The first drop is beyond vertical (at 116 degrees) and there are water elements to boot. When you're on these type of roller coasters it's always best to scream your head off and enjoy the view. You get almost 5 g's on this ride, maintain 70 miles per hour and it is one worth experiencing. This ride singlehandedly puts Lagoon Park on the map and a destination location.

3. **Fury 325** at Carowinds. This was a B&M's major addition to the coaster world. What can you say about the tallest gravity drop roller coaster on the planet? This is the tallest non-launched coaster in the world and it is amazing. It is 325 feet tall and flies down the track at over ninety miles per hour. The track is long as well. At 6,600 feet long, this coaster is about twice as long as most rides out there and boasts an eighty-degree first drop, so hold on to your glasses as you head down this beauty. I have talked about this ride many times in the media and it is one ride that should simply not be missed.

4. **Impulse** at Knoebels Amusement Park created by Zierer. This "euro fighter-style" coaster will make your ride experience very different. It may be only ninety eight feet tall, but it really does pack a punch. With over 2000 feet of track and several inversions this is the first ride at this park that actually flips guests upside down since 3010. Arranged seats four across and eight cars in length, makes this ride seem to be going faster than the fifty-six miles per hour it has been clocked at. You will love this ride and it is a welcome addition at to one of my favorite amusement parks… Knoebels.

5. **Justice League: Battle for Metropolis** at Six Flags Over Texas. This is an epic battle between good and evil, and they need your help. If you like 3D rides, then this is one of the newer "must dos." Lines can be long, so make this one of your priorities when in this park.

6. **Laff Trakk** at Hershey Park is the first indoor, spinning roller coaster (that glows mind you) in the country. It's like going through a funhouse/dark ride in excess of 40 miles per hour. . Passengers themselves can influence the spin of the ride and there are loops and high banked turns and hills to negotiate as well. I love it and so will you. As a new addition to the park, you and the whole family will have a great time together.

7. **Star Liner** at Miracle Strip Pier Park. This is a 1963 John Allen classic, and it's getting another lease on life. Glad it found a home and I can't think of a better park to put this old/new woodie at then Miracle Strip.

8. **Thunderbird** at Holiday World in Santa Claus Indiana. This is a great addition to the park and, flying down the track at sixty-six miles per hour, this NEW wing coaster from B&M is already a classic and a must ride for the masses. The cost of this ride comes in at 22 million dollars and is America's first launched wooden style roller coaster. The ride is over three-thousand feet long and has many inversions and two crazy overbanked turns. You don't need a holiday to celebrate this marvel and is one that makes a good amusement park become one of the best in the country.

9. **Twisted Colossus** at Six Flags Magic Mountain, the iconic Colossus (wood roller coaster) is now solid steel. People did wonder when this project would finally get completed, and after long delays and a publicized fire the end result was a great revamp of a classic ride. It's not a racing roller coaster anymore, but at 128 feet tall and 5,000-foot long, this single track marvel also throws a couple of inversions in the mix as well. I have ridden this ride before but now, it has reinvented itself and become not just a classic ride but one that you can't miss hen in this park.

My Top Amusement Parks
(In North America)

Like the roller coasters they house, there are literally hundreds of amusement parks around the country. They all provide a service in family entertainment that is extremely important to all who enter their gates. There are, however, some amusement parks that are simply better than the rest. At these parks, you are not only entering a place of escape, but you are also preparing for an experience that you will not soon forget. When I chose the following locations, I took into account many different aspects. Thrills and top water rides are important but not the entire picture. Food, overall price, the park's accessibility, shows, and many other aspects go into making a great park. I also tried to make sure that for those who want to experience the best amusement parks the nation has to offer, you could find one that was local to your area. Please remember these are my picks for the top amusement parks. In the end, your own personal opinion should always be the sole reason why you visit a park in the first place. Enjoy my top forty list (they have been listed alphabetically) and compare it to yours!

1. Adventureland, in Altoona, Iowa.

2. Alabama Splash Adventure, in Bessemer, Alabama.

3. Bay Beach Amusement Park, in Green Bay Wisconsin.

4. Beech Bend, in Bowling Green, Kentucky.

5. Busch Gardens (Europe), in Williamsburg Virginia.

6. Busch Gardens (Africa), in Tampa, Florida.

7. Carowinds, in Charlotte, North Carolina.

8. Cedar Point, in Sandusky, Ohio.

9. Conneaut Lake Park, in Conneaut Lake, Pennsylvania.

10. Clementon Park, in Clementon, New Jersey.

11. Disneyland/California Adventure, in Anaheim, California.

12. Dorney Park and Wildwater Kingdom, in Allentown, Pennsylvania.

13. Elitch Gardens, in Denver, Colorado.

14. Hershey Park, in Hershey, Pennsylvania.

15. Holiday World, in Evansville, Indiana.

16. Knott's Berry Farm, in Anaheim, California.

17. Kings Dominion, in Doswell, Virginia.

18. Kings Island, in Cincinnati, Ohio.

19. Knoebels Amusement Park, in Elysburg, Pennsylvania.

20. Lake Compounce, in Bristol, Connecticut.

21. Luna Park, in Brooklyn, New York.

22. Michigan Adventure, in Muskegon, Michigan.

23. Morey's Piers, in Wildwood, New Jersey.

24. Nickelodeon Universe, in Bloomington, Minnesota.

25. Quassy Amusement Park, in Middleberry, Connecticut.

26. Santa Cruz Boardwalk, in Santa Cruz, California.

27. SeaWorld Florida, in Orlando, Florida.

28. Silverwood, in Athol, Idaho.

29. Six Flags America, in Largo Maryland.

30. Six Flags Great Adventure, in Jackson, New Jersey.

31. Six Flags—Great Escape, in Lake George, New York.

32. Six Flags Magic Mountain, in Valencia, California.

33. Six Flags New England, in Agawam, Massachusetts.

34. Six Flags Over Texas, in Arlington, Texas.

35. Universal Studios Florida, in Orlando, Florida.

36. Universal Studio's Islands of Adventure, in, Orlando, Florida.

37. Valley Fair, in Shakopee, Minnesota.

38. Walt Disney World, in Orlando, Florida.

39. Worlds of Fun, in Kansas City, Missouri.

40. Wonderland Park, in Toronto, Canada.

1. **Adventureland** in Altoona, Iowa is simply a great park. What you have here are four roller coasters, three wood and one steel types to choose from. Adventureland is a family-owned amusement park in Altoona, Iowa, and is located just northeast of Des Moines. It features over one hundred rides, shows, and attractions, as well as four roller coaster mentioned. Adventureland's largest wooden roller coaster is the Tornado, which opened in 1978. That same year, this ride was listed in the top ten wooden roller coasters around the world. It's safe to say that even today, this ride **packs** a lot of punch and will challenge the most avid amusement park enthusiast.

    There are also plenty of rides for the family as well. This includes some great water rides and many children's rides spread throughout the park. But rides are not the only thing this park offers. Adventureland has a full array of shows in the park-from live music to magic shows to song and dance, this park has it all. In 2010. Adventureland completed its new water park Adventure Bay. This water park includes almost two dozen waterslides and Iowa's longest Lazy River. They also have rental cabanas, a large swimming pool with a swim-up bar, kids' splash pad, food, and much more! In 2012, a twenty-five-thousand-square-foot wave pool and a kids' activity pool were completed. If you really like tall towers, you will love Storm Chaser. This 250-foot-tall swing ride will test the bravery of the most daring riders! All in all, like in the movie *"Field of Dreams"*, it can be said there is a little bit of heaven right here in Iowa, and it's called Adventureland.

2. **Alabama Splash Adventure** in Bessemer, Alabama. Alabama Adventure is a great little amusement park (even though it is over two hundred acres of fun) and is located in Bessemer Alabama, west of Birmingham and east of Tuscaloosa. It is currently owned by Adrenaline Family Entertainment, which also operates the Clementon Amusement Park in my home state of New Jersey. It is home of not just one amusement park, but also a pretty cool water park as well. The Alabama theme park was visited by approximately 345,000 people, making the park Alabama's second-most popular tourist destination according to the Bureau of Tourism. In 2007, it was the winner of Alabama's 2007 "Attraction of the Year."

Alabama Adventure was previously known as VisionLand and Alabama Adventure before it became what it is today. It is the home of one of the best roller coaster around and it's called Rampage. The ride reopened at this park in 2015. It was built largely as a result of efforts by Fairfield mayor Larry Langford, who later became the mayor of Birmingham. With help from the Alabama Legislature, the group borrowed sixty five million dollars to build the park. Construction began in March 1997, and the park opened in May 1998. The park originally opened with four major areas, including Celebration City Theme Park, Steel Waters Water Park, a children's area called Marvel City, and a shopping/dining area known as Main Street. In 2014 the park was purchased by Koch Family Parks. They added a new kid's roller coaster called Centi-SPEED and some new kiddy rides as well. It may be a small park, but it's a fun one for the kids, and the family will just love it.

3. **Bay Beach Amusement Park** in Green Bay Wisconsin. Bay Beach is a municipal amusement park. The park is situated near the mouth of the Fox River as it flows into the city of Green Bay. Bay Beach Amusement Park is the center of the commercial outdoor recreational area. The park really isn't that big, but it's a fun place to check out when you're along the shores of Green Bay. This park is actually one of the oldest out there, dating back to 1892. From the site's earliest days as a private park, a public beach was available for those who visited the park. Unfortunately, pollution of the bay caused the swimming beach to close. From the 1930s to the early 1970s, Bay Beach's pavilion hosted many concerts, political rallies, and many other special events. In 1934, President Franklin Delano Roosevelt visited Bay Beach in celebration of Green Bay's tri-centennial. Today the park is a family place with scenic views and rides for children, including bumper cars, a small-scale passenger train ride, a large slide, and a new Ferris wheel.

Boasting over twenty rides for the family and the roller coaster enthusiast, this is also the home of the Zippin Pippin (the fourth oldest roller coaster in the world). They also recently added the Sea Dragon and a variety of fun activities for the entire family. This park features batting cages (love that), paintball, bumper boats, go-carts, and mini-golf. In addition to the park, the Bay Beach Wildlife Sanctuary is considered to be part of the park and is just down the road from the amusement park itself. In January 2006, it was announced that up to forty six additional acres of land, west of the current Bay Beach boundary, had been purchased and would be used to upgrade and expand the park. On March 2, 2010, the city of Green Bay put this park on the map when they approved the purchase of the Zippin Pippin rollercoaster. At the time, this ride was located in Memphis, Tennessee. A groundbreaking took place in August 2010, and construction on the Zippin Pippin began in September of that same year. Construction was completed in May 2011 and the Zippin Pippin is now open for your enjoyment. One more cool thing right now, is that you can ride this classic for just a dollar a ride. Some rides can be ridden for a quarter. Now where else can you do that?

4. **Beech Bend Park** at Bowling Green, Kentucky. Beech Bend Park was recently named the Fifth Friendliest Park in the World for six straight years by *Amusement Today*'s Golden Ticket Awards! In 2010, the park was also named the "Publisher's Pick Park of the Year." You gotta love this park! Beech Bend Park is family fun at its best. They offer great thrill rides, including three roller coasters; one of which is the wood marvel the "Kentucky Rumbler." For the whole family to enjoy, there's the go-carts, Whitewater Express, and the Grand Carousel; and for the children, the Super Slide and Crazy Bus, just to name a few. Beech Bend offers great entertainment as well. The food here will put you into the right mood and let's not forget several water slides, mini-golf, go-carts, and games of skill for everyone. There is also a petting farm as well. Beech Bend is not just an amusement park, but if you like drag and stock car racing, you also have come to the right place. Beech Bend also offers first-class camping facilities within walking distance of the park. Plus, if you like camping, they got that here to. Bring your own tent or RV or rent one of theirs! It may be a local park, but it sure is very enjoyable and the park is always kept clean and the staff is just so nice. Season passes are available for the park and Splash Lagoon and, overall, the park is very affordable. When in Kentucky, this is a great place to visit with the family.

5. **Busch Gardens Williamsburg** in Virginia is not only a theme park, but also a unique experience for the entire family. The Williamsburg location has 2.5 million visitors come through its doors every year. It is an action-packed, European-themed park combining seventeenth-century charm and twenty-first-century technology. It boasts more than one hundred acres of unparalleled fun and adventure for the entire family. This is also one of the most aesthetic parks in the country. With more than forty thrilling rides and attractions, eight main stage shows, a wide variety of authentic foods and shops, plus an enchanting children's area this park rocks. Busch Gardens Williamsburg is the ticket to a world-class adventure. This park has been voted the world's "Most Beautiful Theme Park" for the twelfth consecutive year by the National Amusement Park Historical Association (NAPHA), and that, in itself, is a feat. In the past, NAPHA has named Busch Gardens Williamsburg the world's most "Favorite Theme Park" as well. If that isn't enough, Busch Gardens has also received (and continued to do so) many *Amusement Today* accolades in the categories of "Best Landscape," "Best Food," and "Cleanest" in the nation. Also the park recently received the prestigious Applause Award from the International Association of Amusement Parks & Attractions (IAAPA) and *Amusement Business* magazine. If you're a coaster enthusiast, you'll love this park because it also holds seven great roller coasters, including their latest, an LSM launch marvel called Verbolten. You also get two of which are the best of their type around the country. They are Alpengeist, the tallest suspended coaster in the world, and of course, the world-famous Apollo's Chariot, a thrill a minute, two hundred-foot hyper-coaster. Guests can also enjoy a variety of options with two, three, and four-day bounce tickets. This means that visitors can enjoy Busch Gardens, bounce over to Water Country USA, and then bounce back to the park. And you can do this all day long, a great feature if you have really small kids. The great thing about Busch Gardens is that you don't need to be a coaster lover to really enjoy this park. True, the rides are first-class, but with your one-price ticket, you get shows that are absolutely spectacular. The staff is always friendly, and the food is also pretty good. This is one of my top picks for just about everyone in the family.

6. **Busch Gardens Tampa**, Florida, is an African theme park. It offers a small but pretty thrilling selection of coasters with a large selection of animals that you and your kids will just love. In fact, it features one of the country's premier zoos (the sixth largest in the world) with more than two thousand animals, as well as a good variety of live shows, exhibits, restaurants, and shops. The park is divided into several themed areas based on countries from the African continent. The themes are very convincing and interesting. Among the park's non-coaster attractions is the Serengeti Plain, a twenty-nine-acre nature reserve that everyone in your family will really enjoy. Also taking a trip on Busch Garden's latest attraction, Rhino Rally lets you get real close to the numerous elephants, rhinos zebras, antelope, and hundreds of other species in the park. Here, man is the visitor, and the animals roam free. The reserve can also be experienced free via the train or skyride, or by a guided truck tour for an additional cost. This is a park with plenty to do for everyone, including a very limited selection of nicely themed flat rides, which include three water rides, a log flume, and a fairly tame river rapid ride. All this and a great educational experience for those who love animals (and let's not forget the great shops). Overall, the park is very clean, like its sister park in Virginia, and is well-maintained. The staff is friendly and, for the most part, knowledgeable. Prices are competitive with the nearby parks, and the crowds are usually lighter than the ones you will find an hour to the east at Florida's Orlando parks. Over four million come to this park yearly.

   Along with the newer Islands of Adventure, Busch Gardens Tampa (a SeaWorld company) has some great coasters. There are eight in all, including one of the world's biggest dive casters in Sheikra, as well as their newest ride Cheetah Hunt. Let's not forget Kumba and Montu. All four of these rides have been rated as the best steel coasters in the world, and I can tell you they truly are. These coasters are the main reason why coaster aficionados come to this park. But **let's** not forget that most patrons also visit this park to see the animals, birds, reptiles, and mammals that you won't find anywhere else. This park also has one of the tallest freestanding drop towers with Falcon's Fury, where rider pivot ninety degrees in midair before diving 335 feet at sixty miles per hour. I really like this park. So will you.

7. **Carowinds** in Charlotte, North Carolina. Carowinds is a spacious 398-acre amusement park, located adjacent to Interstate 77 on the state line between North and South Carolina, in Charlotte and Fort Mill, respectively. This is a great park that boasts some of the best roller coaster around the country. The park opened on March 31, 1973, at a cost of seventy million dollars and after a four-year planning period spearheaded by Charlotte businessman Earl Patterson Hall, who was inspired to build the park from a 1956 trip to Disneyland and a dream of bringing the two states closer together. They have over sixty five total rides and fourteen different roller coasters to choose from and great steel coasters like Vortex, Nighthawk, Afterburner, and, of course, the Intimidator. The Intimidator is a Bolliger and Mabillard roller coaster that opened on March 27, 2010, and put this park on the map. Inspired by the famous stock car racing driver Dale Earnhardt, Intimidator is one of the longest, tallest, and fastest roller coasters you will find. This thrill ride is 232 feet tall and reaches speed of up to eighty miles per hour. If you love wooden roller coasters, then look no further than the Hurler. The rides at Carowinds are based loosely around eight themed areas. Recently, another mega mega-coaster coaster at Carowinds was added and is called Fury 325. This one is the world's tallest and fastest giga-coaster to date. The park has new entertainment offerings and many more new dining options. There is also a dining plan available as well. In 2000, the park first introduced Scarowinds, an annual Halloween attraction. Scarowinds is one heck of a Halloween treat. It is presented on select nights in September and October when the facility is transformed into a haunted theme park. The experience includes numerous haunted attractions and incorporates

most of the existing park rides into a nightmarish experience. If you're looking for a great place to make some memories and get to experience the best thrill rides on the planet, this is truly the place to go.

8.   **Cedar Point** in Sandusky, Ohio, is America's second-oldest remaining amusement park and is, without a doubt, the largest single-standing park that you will find in America. Latest attendance put this park at around 3.4 million visitors yearly. Having opened to the public back in 1870, it is located on a picturesque peninsula jutting out onto Lake Erie and is approximately halfway between Toledo and Cleveland, Ohio. Millions of people flock religiously to this park every year. Cedar Point is a park that has been literally handmade for the coaster enthusiast. With sixteen world-class roller coasters (most of them the best in their particular categories), Cedar Point can take the average coaster fanatic days to experience every ride that this park has to offer. My advice is to take your time and enjoy the sixty plus rides in the park.

In addition to the award-winning rides, you will find some of the best shows and food that you can find at an amusement park. With all this going on, make it a point not to rush. Besides, the Point now has a ride reservation system, utilizing hand stamps called the "Freeway,' where you can ride the hot attractions without paying an extra fee. It is available on Millennium Force, Magnum, Mantis, Raptor and Wicked Twister. All you have to do is go to the Freeway hand stamp booth located near the ride entrance and get your hand stamped with a boarding time. Your boarding time is good for one ride anytime within the one hour stamped on your hand. When you're ready to ride, just show your hand stamp to the ride host at the entrance to the ride, and you will enter the freeway queue, which merges with the regular ride queue just minutes before entering any station. At this point, a ride host will stamp "ride" on your hand to indicate that you have used your boarding time. It's that easy!

Cedar Point, is well known for its world-record-breaking roller coasters and has one of the tallest roller coaster in Top Thrill Dragster. On this ride, you literally get shot out of the station, climb 420 feet, and ascend at speeds of over 120 mph. The pucker factor, ladies and gentlemen, on this ride has now made it the one that all other rides must match, and I tell you, folks, that isn't easy. It has literally taken the thrill experience up to a new level. Top Thrill Dragster is not for the faint of heart, nor is it for the average coaster enthusiast, so beware. Cedar Point's latest is Gatekeeper. A twenty-five-million-dollar thrill ride that will simply amaze you. And then there is Millennium Force, the ride that all others try to emulate.

Adjacent to Cedar Point is Soak City, a gigantic eighteen-acre water park featuring action-packed body and inner tube slides, including the mammoth Zoom Flume, two meandering inner tube rivers, and a fun-filled play area for kids. It also has an enormous 500,000-gallon wave pool. So all in all, you get top coasters, fantastic views of Lake Erie, great shows, and so much more at the #1 park in the country. It is without a doubt the Mecca of all coaster parks and one not to be missed. You haven't experienced the best until you visit this park.

9.   **Conneaut Lake Park** in Conneaut Lake, Pennsylvania. Conneaut Lake Park is a great summer amusement resort for the whole family. Located in Conneaut Lake, Pennsylvania, USA, this park has long served as a regional tourist destination for many years and is the home of the classic Blue Streak roller coaster, which was only recently classified as "historic" by the group American Coaster Enthusiasts. You might not have known this, but Conneaut Lake is Pennsylvania's largest natural (glacier) lake and is a popular summer resort for recreational

boaters. This lake is lined with vacation homes and condos, and you can also find several hotels in the area as well. One such hotel that I recommend is the Hotel Conneaut, which has been in operation since 1903. The size of this park is over two hundred acres in size. The park itself maybe small, but overall has twenty-four total rides and several roller coasters with three unique water rides. This is a great park to just relax and have some fun. To sit in the old wooden rocking chairs on the porch of the hotel overlooking the lake is a breathtaking sight. What I truly love about this park is it's not just for those who love rides and attractions. It's one of those parks that is simply timeless. It's a way to remember your childhood, reacquaint yourself with the family, and just forget about your problems.

10. **Clementon Park** in Clementon, New Jersey. Clementon Park and Splash World is a small amusement park located in Clementon, New Jersey, but it is one that you will surely love. It is also close to the Pine Valley Golf Club. Also known as Clementon Lake Park, it is one of the world's oldest operating amusement parks. It is now owned by Premier Attractions Management. With over two dozen rides and animal shows to boot, this park is pretty special. It was also known as having one of the oldest roller coasters at this park called the "Jack Rabbit." It was unfortunately removed a few years back. Now the most popular ride is still the log flume called King Neptune's Revenge. However, even though the name has changed on their new roller coaster several times, "Hell Cat: is a ride for the ages. It replaced the Jack rabbit and is ranked among the best roller coasters around the world. Being situated just outside of Philadelphia, Clementon Park and Splash World Water Park is open Memorial Day weekend through Labor Day. And the park has been revitalized in recent years, becoming bigger with the addition of several new attractions. The one thing I really love about this park is its reputation for friendliness, cleanliness, and affordability. It's a park you go to on the weekends and one that the whole family will love.

11. **Disneyland and California Adventure** in Anaheim, California, really needs no introduction. Walt Disney really revolutionized the amusement park industry when he opened Disneyland in 1955 and at sixteen million visitors per year (second only to Disney World), holds many records in overall attendance. Walt Disney wanted to create a themed place "where parents and children could have fun together," and he certainly achieved that goal. Disneyland and Walt Disney World in Florida simply obliterated the nearest competition in terms of popularity and overall attendance. Not only that, these Disney parks have set many standards, which all other parks shoot for and very few ever achieve.

The park might be small compared to its counterpart in Florida, but don't let that fool you. It still manages to captivate people and draw over twelve million park visitors a year. The key to Disneyland's success is its staff, customer service program, and total quality management strategy. The rides and shows for the kids are in a league of their own, using the latest technology and animatronics that even today look realistic. There is so much to do and see here. If you are a coaster fanatic, you might not find the most thrilling rides here, but you will be very impressed by the extraordinary themes and outstanding illusion. Space Mountain is still one of the best enclosed coasters to date, not for its intensity, but as an end result of the overall package, and I have never met a person who didn't enjoy this ride. Another attraction worth riding is the new and improved Runaway Mine Train. Family coaster enthusiasts will like this one. The new Alice in Wonderland ride is great for the entire family.

Also because of its size, Disneyland makes you really feel like you're a part of the action. It is much smaller than the World in Florida and is very quaint. The original Matterhorn Bobsleds, the first steel track coaster, created in 1959, can be found here and is a scaled-down version of the actual Matterhorn mountain located in Switzerland. Kids, as well as adults, love this ride, and over the years, a new generation (including my daughter) feels the same way. And let's not forget Splash Mountain. Maybe not quite as intense as Splash Mountain in Florida but still an e-ticket ride in my book.

California Adventure. Until recently, Disneyland stood alone on a seventy-five-acre lot in Anaheim, but now you can find many more attractions with its neighbor, California Adventures, and this park has certainly brought the Land into the new millennium. As in Florida, you now have another amazing park and a slew of new rides to choose from. These include the top coaster, California Screaming, a ride that will take your breath away as well as a drop tower that will scare the daylights out of you. Other great attractions you will find at California Adventure are as follow. Radio Springs Racers, Soaring Over California, Toy Story Midway Mania, Sun Wheel, ElecTRONica and Monsters Inc. just to name few. If you haven't visited Disneyland or California Adventures in California, now would definitely be the time to do so. At last count, over eight million people from all over the world will go to this park yearly.

12. **Dorney Park** in Allentown, Pennsylvania (Cedar Point's sister park), has some of the best rides and attractions that you will find on the East Coast. Dorney Park & Wildwater Kingdom's two-hundred acres are home to more than one hundred rides and attractions, including eight roller coasters and dozens of state-of-the-art thrill machines, as well as a water park that are second to none. It is here you will find one of the tallest and fastest coasters in the world right here at Dorney. The two-hundred-foot-plus mega mega-coaster (and one of my favorites) Steel Force glistens in the sky, and if you like loops and spins, then why not take a ride on the tallest inverted coaster on the East Coast called Talon? Another superride in Hydra and, let's not forget, Possessed a crazy LIM launch that will leave you breathless. For all you wooden coaster enthusiasts, there is the 1923 classic called Thunderhawk that you will love. For the kids, there are wild mouse rides and Woodstock Express to name just a few. This is a Cedar Fair park not t be missed, and it keeps growing every year.

All Dorney coasters are built to thrill you whether you are seven or seventy. Also at Dorney Park, you will find an authentic 1921 carousel ride and an old-fashioned steam engine that takes you around the park. If you like heights, why not ride the Dominator, a tall monstrosity combining a 170-foot drop and ejection tower. What I really like about this park is that there is action happening everywhere, and the hilly terrain gives the visitor some really nice views of the park. At Whitewater Rapids, you will find a state-of-the-art wave pool, some steep, fast water tube rides that start your descent from as high as seventy feet above the tarmac. When you get hungry (and you will), you can choose from more than forty food locations throughout the park. The park also has live shows for everyone. Their staff might not be the friendliest people you will find, but overall, the rides, shows, and water attractions are well worth the price of your admission.

13. **Elitch Gardens,** in Denver Colorado. This is truly America's only downtown theme and amusement park. For more than 120 years, it has been a must-see destination right in the heart of downtown Denver. Open May through October with over fifty rides and attractions, six great roller coasters, and an entire water park to experience, there's literally something for everyone. There are also over a dozen Kiddie attractions and the view from the 20-story observation tower is breathtaking. There's Blazin Buckaroo, Boomerang, Half Pipe, the classic Mind Eraser, Sidewinder, and Twister II. However, you don't just come here for the rides and attractions. The shows here are fantastic too, and I love the food here as well. Being right smack dab in the city, Elitch Gardens is easily accessible to visitors by foot or car. There is also a dedicated light rail station and right off of I-25 exit 212A Speer Blvd. South. Visit Elitch Gardens.com for more information and to purchase discount tickets.

14. **Hershey Park** in Hershey, Pennsylvania, is an amusement park (with over three million visitors yearly) that combines wild roller coasters, exciting shows, and the best candy your taste buds will ever experience. It all started in 1903 when chocolate magnate Milton Hershey founded the town which today has not only a world-class chocolate factory and amusement park, but also several professional sports teams as well (soccer and hockey). Also you will find just outside the park, Hershey has a sensational chocolate factory ride, a Muppet-style 3D show for the kids, and a trolley ride that let you see chocolate city up close and personal. In Hershey, Pennsylvania, you will find street lamps shaped like Hershey kisses down on Main Street, a fine five-star hotel, a golf course or two, and, of course, the award-winning park itself.

When you enter the gates of this nicely laid out (but pretty hilly) park, you'll surely know that you have come to one of the sweetest places on earth. There is literally candy everywhere! Also you just might find several of the nation's top roller coasters in the country right here. You should start your trip by visiting Chocolate World, the gift shop, and, while there, checking out the 3D movie. After your chocolate tour, burn off those candy bars with a trip to the park itself. At Hershey Park, you will find over twenty kiddy rides and eight stellar roller coasters to choose from.

For wooden coaster lovers, there are three winners to choose from. If you like to race, then your best choice is Lightning Racer, a coaster that really brings out the competitiveness in everyone. The Wildcat will also amaze you with countless twists and turns through the course. And if you're looking for a wooden classic, then the Comet is your choice.

If steel is your deal, they don't come any better or intense than SkyRush, Fahrenheit, Storm Runner, and Great Bear among others. You will also find the classic Sooper Dooper Looper still in action here, and if you want to ride a real Wild Mouse, you can do so here. Also there is an eleven-acre walkthrough zoo that was once Milton Hershey's personal animal collection. The park is clean and well maintained. It is logically laid out with just about the right mixture of attractions, food courts, shops, and displays throughout the park. If you have the time, and you should make some, then Hershey is truly one great vacation hotspot for you the entire family.

15. **Holiday World,** in Evansville, Indiana. To me this is a very special park. It's not the biggest around, but what it has to offer is truly unique and special. This park has five world class roller coasters to choose from. The history of the nation's first theme park is the story of a family, which has, for seven decades, dedicated themselves to providing millions of guests with good, old-fashioned family fun. Louis J. Koch created the world's first theme park as a retirement project. He was troubled that the tiny hamlet of Santa Claus, Indiana, was visited by children who were disappointed when they discovered Santa was not there. That changes rather quickly.

Santa Claus Land opened August 3, 1946. This theme park includes a toy shop, a restaurant, children's-themed rides, and, of course, Santa Claus. Koch's son Bill soon became the head of Santa Claus Land. Over the decades, Santa Claus Land flourished. Children from across the country came to sit on the real Santa's knee and whisper their Christmas wishes all year around. As the park grew, the Koch family knew Christmas was not the only theming possibility for the park. In 1984, Santa Claus Land expanded to also include Halloween and Fourth of July sections, and the park's name was changed to Holiday World.

In 1993, Splashin' a great water park called Safari Water Park was added and is now over forty acres and features several water coasters and wave pools, a river, family raft rides, and water slides. The park, which was named the nation's number 1 water park by *USA Today*, also offers free sunscreen. In 1995 Holiday World expanded again. The Raven wooden roller coaster was created and has been voted one of the world's top wooden coasters almost each year since it first opened. The Legend wooden roller coaster, was added in 2000. In 2006 the park introduced a new holiday. The Thanksgiving section included a recording-breaking new wooden coaster, the Voyage, which helped catapult the park's seasonal attendance past the one-million mark for the first time. In 2013, *TIME* magazine named the Voyage one of the best wooden roller coaster in the nation, and since then, it has repeatedly been named one of the best around. Since then, another great ride (this one made of steel) was introduced in 2015, and this thrill ride is one of the best I have ever ridden. The park is one great place to take the family, and you will love the people you meet and the cleanliness you will find in this park. It is well worth the price of admission.

16. **Knott's Berry Farm,** in Buena Park, California, is a booming, 160-acre California theme park that started out as a small twenty-acre family berry farm but now boasts over 3.6 million visitors a year. Walter and Cornelia Knott bought Knott's Berry Farm during the Depression and began their business way back then. They sold berries, jams, and chicken dinners in order to make ends meet, and just eight decades later, Knott's Berry Farm is undisputed as one of the premiere amusement parks in the nation. With more than 150 attractions (including seven top coasters), restaurants, and shops scattered through six themed areas, Knott's Berry Farm is a destination park for just about everyone. Toddlers and elementary schoolers love the shows and rides in Camp Snoopy while older children and adults get a kick out of the thrill rides in Wild Water Wilderness and on the Boardwalk. Don't miss Old West Ghost Town, historically, the epicenter of the park itself. One of the best wooden coasters ever built, and one of the park's most popular attractions, resides at this location. Its name is Ghostrider. Ghostrider is an award-winning wooden roller coaster that opened in 1998 and truly needs to be ridden to be believed. Other great coasters include Xcelerator and the family coaster Jaguar. When the temperature climbs, cool off at one of the world's most high riding and steep rides in the world, Perilous Plunge. Now that is a serious water ride for the serious thrill seeker! It is the steepest flume ride every created.

One of the best times to visit this park is in October when Knott's Berry Farm transforms itself into Knott's Scary Farm, a fright fest that almost every other park has tried to copy. Get there and see the park. You will be glad you did! And if you tire of Knott's, just minutes away is another classic park. Most everyone knows it as Disneyland!

17. **Kings Dominion** located in Doswell, Virginia, is one of the best theme parks on the East Coast! You will find fourteen of the most hair-raising rides, the wettest water park, and stunning, innovative stage shows around. There are seven sections to this park, and it is safe to say that there is literally something here for just about everyone. If you are a roller coaster fanatic like I am, you can experience Intimidator 305, a three-hundred-foot mega marvel or visit the land of the Congo for Anaconda, Flight of Fear, Avalanche, and one of my favorites, Volcano. In the Grove section, get set for other top coasters such as Hypersonic XLC, the Rebel Yell, Hurler, and Shockwave. In the Old Virginia area of the park, you will find the wooden marvel Grizzly, and for kids, Nickelodeon Central, and Kidsville, site of the infamous Scooby Doo roller coaster. On International Street, you will be able to look over the park on a one-third scale, three hundred-foot model of the Eiffel Tower. And then there is the Water Works section of the park, nineteen acres of cool fun for the whole family, for those who just want to cool off and get away from it all.

Also at Kings Dominion's, there is the drop zone stunt tower. At 305 feet tall, it is one of the tallest drop rides in North America, promising daring riders a 270-foot descent at seventy-two miles per hour! This adrenaline-pumping adventure simulates the sensation of skydiving, offering to the public something new at this four-hundred-acre one-of-a-kind theme park. You will enjoy this park, but take your time. You will need a few days to complete your task. It is a pretty big one!

18. **Kings Island** near Cincinnati, Ohio, has a lot to offer its three million yearly visitors. There are great daily shows, and there is even an amazing miniature Eiffel Tower, which at three hundred feet, is a third the size of the original. Here, you can take a scenic elevator ride to the top of this tower for some awesome open views of the countryside. Overall, you will find more than eighty rides and attractions at Kings Island, with something for just every member of the family. You will also find a great whitewater ride in Whitewater Canyon, perfect for cooling off on those long hot days.

I think Kings Island, by far, excels in their roller coaster category. For the kids and family, there's a cool wood roller coaster called "The Racer" with twin--racing trains that run on the tracks side-by-side. You might remember this ride from an episode of the *Brady Bunch* where this coaster was headlined.

Moving up the scale, you have the Backlot Stunt Coaster and Flight of Fear. The Vortex is an intense metal coaster that features six inversions, one of which is a corkscrew. Let's not forget "the Bat," a classic ride for the masses. Now if you're looking for the bad boys at the park, look no further than Diamondback that twists and turns at eighty miles per hour around five thousand feet of track. Then there's "Banshee," one of the best thrill rides you will find at this locale.

Kings Island is also famous for its classic wooden coasters such as the "Beast," which truly lives up to its name. Although it is over twenty years old, it is still the longest wooden roller coaster in the country. It is a ride best enjoyed after dark and truly in a class by itself as it twists and turns through the woods with a spiral into a long tunnel that will leave you wanting for more. Although it is very safe, the aged-looking wood gives you the uneasy feeling that the whole structure could collapse underneath you at any moment. Something that adds to your enjoyment of the ride.

Kings Island also has a log flume ride, which is a relaxing, cooling way to ride through the treetops, ending with a splash that will feel great on a hot day! And if you like drop rides, then head to the Drop Tower and feel your heart drop when you plunge twenty-six stories from a height of 315 feet straight down at speeds that surpass sixty miles per hour. This is, at the time of this writing, the tallest gyro drop in the world! Let's not forget "Wind Seeker," standing at 300 feet, you can really experience the park swinging at over forty miles per hour. And if you can make it till closing time, you'll get to see a great fireworks display to boot. In addition to this, there is a huge water park that just in itself can be a day's worth of entertainment for the family. At Kings Island, as in other amusement parks, expect long lines at most e-ticket attractions and the usual fast-food places, but all in all, it is truly worth the trip.

19. **Knoebels** in Elysburg, Pennsylvania, made my top park list simply because it is an old-style park with many great rides and unique attractions that you just don't see any more. Comfortably nestled in the picturesque mountains of north-central Pennsylvania, Knoebels Amusement Park has been a popular family destination for more than three-quarters of a century. Officially, Knoebels opened in 1926 as Knoebels Amusement Resort. Today, Knoebels has over fifty rides and attractions, including two of the best wooden coasters you will find anywhere. First, there is the Phoenix, built in 1940 by PTC/Herb Schmeck and named Rocket when it resided at Playland Park in San Antonio, Texas. It became a classic in the park when it was relocated to its present site in 1985. All true roller coaster enthusiasts flock to this park in order to ride this wooden wonder.

You will find another woodie by the name of Twister here as well. The Twister is sure to give you an extreme ride with all the excitement you would expect from a world-class coaster. From over one hundred feet, you can experience some pretty good vertical drops, multiple twists, and hairpin turns throughout the ride. Both coasters are constantly on the top twenty-five lists around the country.

Then there is Whirlwind, a classic Arrow corkscrew coaster just right for those budding coaster aficionados, and finally, the "High Speed Thrill Coaster" built by the Overland Amusement Company of Saugus, Massachusetts. It first opened in 1955 and is believed to be the only operating "Overland coaster" left in the world.

If coasters aren't your thing, why not try the other rides and attractions you will find in this park. Like for example you can experience the Grand Carousel which was built in 1912. Its sixty-three horses were hand-carved by Master Carver George Carmel and used a Looff machine to spin the ride. Knoebels purchased the carousel in the first week of December 1941, and it is one of the few parks left that still actually offers a brass ring to reach for in order to get a free ride! In truth, the charm of this park really resides in the many old and classic rides that you just won't find elsewhere.

And you can't come to Knoebels without discovering one of the best dark rides in the nation. Their Haunted Mansion, which in many ways rivals Disney's Haunted Mansion, is a must see in this park. The Knoebels family marked the park's seventy-seventh anniversary season with the introduction of several new rides, but one that really stands out was the new Scenic Skyway, a triple-chair ski lift that takes guests on a fourteen-minute roundtrip 364 feet to the top of a mountain near the park's main entrance. It gives you truly one of the best views of the park you can get, and at times, it can get pretty steep. It is in fact one of the steepest (49.7 degrees) ski lift rides in the country. For those who don't like heights, this can be the scariest ride at the park. You can pay as you go here but pay-one-price plans are also available.

20. **Lake Compounce** in beautiful Bristol, Connecticut, can boast being the oldest operating amusement park in the United States. The park opened in October of 1846 and still offers the public a place to unwind and escape the realities of everyday life. Its picturesque lake still is home to many wild animals and birds of all kinds. And the sky ride, which takes you 750 feet up to the top of a nearby mountain range, offers an absolutely breathtaking view. In April 1996, the Kennywood Entertainment Company became the managing partner of Lake Compounce. Since then, this park has spent nearly fifty million dollars in new rides, attractions, and physical improvements added to the park. The park's transformation tastefully integrates its natural beauty and rich heritage with a blend of classic and contemporary rides, live shows, and unique attractions. As Lake Compounce, the nation's first amusement park still in operation continues into the new millennium, a balance between change and tradition continues to be important. From its vintage 1911 carousel, to one of the best wooden coasters ever created in Boulder Dash, you must make time for this park. The other coasters, Wildcat, Zoomerang and the kiddy coaster, are also well worth riding. The park's modern shows and attractions, plus a pleasure walk around the lake (that records life on the earth and how short a time period man has reigned supreme on this planet), are real eye-openers and very educational.

Also, on those really hot days, you can cool off on the Thunder Rapids raft ride. Or check out Splash Harbor, Connecticut's only water park! There you will find plenty of fun-filled water slides to get the whole family wet! The latest addition to the park is Mammoth Falls, a family raft ride that is sure to be wet and wild with a total drop of over fifty feet through a five-hundred-foot course.

21. **Luna Park** in Brooklyn New York. There's no shortage of excitement at Coney Island in the summertime. All of the rides and games at Luna park (as well as Deno's Wonderwheel Park and the Wonder wheel and some of the smaller parks here at Coney Island) will have you rushing this way and that way all day. It is truly a New York experience, and as a native New Yorker, it is one that I certainly can relate to. But you don't have to be a native New Yorker to enjoy these big parks? Will you find the most thrilling rides here? The answer to both questions is no. But what you will find is the atmosphere and old world charm of the place where the concept of modern-day amusement parks was created. This is the place where the very first modern-day coasters came into existence, the Switchback Railway, being the nation's first modern-day coaster. Also the infamous Tornado once stood here, and of course, this is still where the mother of all wooden coasters still resides.

Sure there are many new wooden coasters that can claim to be taller, faster, and longer, but nothing can take away the title of "most infamous coaster on the planet" held by the Coney Island Cyclone. Here you will still find the world-renowned and still operational coaster at Coney Island since its birth in 1927 and still packing a mighty punch for its size. After all, this is the coaster that noted aviator Charles Lindbergh once said was "scarier than flying." Another great (and new ride) for guests to experience is Thunderbolt, a steel roller coaster. This ride pays homage to the original wood roller coaster of the same name that was torn down in 1982.

At Coney Island, you can also visit the place where you get the original Nathan's hot dogs, the best hot dogs that you will ever taste. The building has been around longer than the Cyclone but still draws bigger lines than any other attraction in the area. Get a side of fries with the hot dog, and you will be in junk food heaven!

Also when you're talking Coney Island, you have to mention another park that defines the area. At Deno's Wonder Wheel Amusement Park, the Wonder Wheel is one of only two Ferris wheels in the world whose chairs slide back and forth. When you get to the top, the gondolas inch forward and slide across a path that will make you think you're going right off the edge. My pick for the best and scariest Ferris wheel in the world is this one. It also provides a great view of the beach.

At both parks, you pay as you go, and the price for the top rides is very affordable. There used to be a real problem with gangs and crime in the area. But since the new urban renewal program and the creation of a new minor league baseball team, it is a place I feel comfortable taking my family. That's right, between your park hopping, you will be able to watch a free ballgame from a minor league baseball team aptly named the "Brooklyn Cyclones."

Finally, if you are a beach lover, this is a place to go in the city where you can fly kites and run through the sand. You can find "polar bears" (the human kind), fishermen, sand sculptors, ice skaters, musclemen, sword swallowers, strollers, thrill seekers, old-timers, and sightseers of all sorts at the Brooklyn shore as well. You will even find the New York Aquarium not too far away. It is worth the day to visit the island—Coney Island that is!

22. **Michigan Adventure** may not be the biggest park around, but in my opinion, it has plenty to offer the entire family. Part of the Cedar Fair group (Cedar Point, Knott's Berry Farm, Worlds of Fun, Valleyfair, and Dorney Park), Michigan Adventure boasts over fifty rides and attractions and is a great place to have fun and get really wet. At the top of the ride list is Shivering Timbers, a world-class coaster with drops of 125, 105, and Ninety Five feet in its repertoire of thrill elements, truly one of the best wooden coasters ever put on this planet! If you are a wooden coaster fanatic, you have not ridden the best until you ride this one. Year after year, this coaster manages to be on everyone's top ten list.

Other good coasters to check out are Wolverine Wildcat, a Curtis and Summers design, and of course, the ACE family classic, Zach's Zoomer from Great Coasters International. Also at Michigan Adventure, you will find their newest thrill ride in Thunderhawk, as well as a colorful Mad Mouse and Big Dipper roller coaster that are perfect for the whole family. For the kids, Michigan Adventure recently added the Big Dipper, a family coaster from Chance rides that is a real hit with the little ones. And let's not forget Ripcord! For a few extra bucks, you can take a flight from the top of a 173-foot tower at speeds that can reach up to sixty-five miles per hour.

For water lovers, you have a choice of not one but three wave pools and a total of twenty-one water slides. If thrills and attractions aren't your thing, you will find a miniature golf course, lots of food stands, and many different gift shops all over the park to keep you busy. Okay, this one may not be the biggest or most exciting park around, but what puts this one on my list are the people and the overall atmosphere you get from visiting this park. The pace is a little slower here than in most places, but after a busy day in conferences, I surely enjoyed my visit. I am sure you will too.

23. **Morey's Piers** in Wildwood, New Jersey. Now here on the southern shores of New Jersey you will find the largest and most exciting set of amusement piers in the world! The beautiful beaches and Wildwood's famous boardwalk are the backdrop for three incredible fun-filled piers offering seven decent coasters, including wooden marvel Great White, the Great Nor'easter, and the Sea Serpent. You will also find family-style coasters there as well. When you add this to the beautiful beachfront water parks and family rides plus over two miles of boardwalk, you are truly in for a pleasant experience. Morey's Piers has been bringing thrills and laughter to families for over thirty years, and they seem to expand every year. In 1985, Raging Waters Water Park made its debut at the oceanfront end of Mariner's Landing, and following in the footsteps of its success, a second Raging Waters opened at Morey's Piers back in1988. This coincided with the purchase of a third pier, Fun Pier, which was renamed Wild Wheels, home to one of the largest Ferris wheels in the country.

Morey's Piers currently feature over 150 pay-as-you-go rides and attractions, hosting over three-and-a-half-million visitors per year. The staff, for the most part, are also very interesting characters too. Most are college students who come from around the world and work in the states during their summer breaks. The Piers do have a very odd rule of no hats or glasses on the majority of top thrill rides for safety purposes and even have horse-collar restraints on some of the small coasters, which I just can't understand, but overall, it is a pleasant park. For an added experience and nominal fee, you can also ride the *tramcar* up and down the two-mile boardwalk, enjoying one of the most long and pristine beaches on the East Coast. All in all, you will have a great time at Morey's Piers, but be warned that during the height of summer, this place gets really crowded! Over three million people from around the world visit this location yearly.

24. **Nickelodeon Universe (NU),** in Bloomington, Minnesota. This park was originally called Knott's Camp Snoopy, later known as the Park at the Mall of America (MOA) but whatever name it is, you're sure to be in for a thrill and a half. This seven-acre indoor amusement park is located in the center of the Mall of America (MOA in Bloomington, Minnesota. This location used to be the site of Memorial Field, home of the Minnesota Vikings and Minnesota Twins.

The park has over twenty-five rides and attractions, including five roller coasters. They are Avitar Airbender, Back at the Barnyard Hayride, the Pepsi Orange Streak, and SpongeBob SquarePants and Rock Bottom Plunge. There is also a Log Chute and Danny Phantom Ghost Zone. "Nickelodeon Universe." was announced on July 25, 2007. Construction began on August 27, 2007. Work was completed in sections so guests and about 80 percent of the park remained accessible while they were adding all those additions. Nickelodeon Universe was finally completed on March 15, 2008. Some of my favorites here include SpongeBob SquarePants Rock Bottom Plunge, a Gerstlauer Euro-Fighter-style coaster themed after the Nickelodeon show *SpongeBob SquarePants*, the Splat-O-Sphere, a tower drop-ride, and Avatar Airbender. The park is free to enter, but the rides require patrons to purchase tickets (points) depending upon which ride they would like to go on. Unlimited single rider wristbands or season passes are also available. NU is a great place to spend a few hours escaping one of the biggest malls in the country and having some fun with the kids while mommy is shopping.

25. **Quassy Amusement Park** in Middleberry, Connecticut. Quassy, which was once called Lake Quassapaug Amusement Park, was founded as an amusement park in 1908 and sits on the south shore of Lake Quassapaug in Middlebury, Connecticut. On twenty acres, it has two dozen rides, and while the park has mostly dry rides when I was there, it also has "Saturation Station," an interactive family water area that is connected to the park. Swimming in the lake is also something that one can do. Quassy offers many things including swimming, picnicking, a catering service, a huge family arcade, "Saturation Station," live entertainment, including comedians, magic shows, and of course, its twenty-two rides. Friday nights at Quassy have been called "quarter night," in which the park sells their hot dogs, soda, and cotton candy for just fifty cents.

26. **Santa Cruz Boardwalk**, in Santa Cruz, California. The Santa Cruz Beach Boardwalk is a beautiful oceanfront amusement park. Founded in 1907, it is California's oldest surviving amusement park and one of the few seaside parks remaining on the West Coast. The boardwalk portion of the park stretches along a wide and sometimes sandy beach that visitors can access easily from the park area. The eastern end of the boardwalk is dominated by the Giant Dipper roller coaster, one of the best-known wooden coasters in the world and one of the most visible landmarks in the Santa Cruz area. The Dipper and the Looff Carousel, which still contain its original 342-pipe organ built in 1894 and both are on the US National Register of Historic Places. They were–declared to be a National Historic Landmark. You will also find old-fashioned carnival games and snack booths throughout the twenty-four-acre park. Santa Cruz Beach Boardwalk has something that everyone can enjoy! The SCBB dates back to 1907 and is this state's oldest surviving amusement park. They have rides, arcades, and carnival games, as well as miniature golf, a pool hall and bar, shops, and a nice selection of foods to boot. In the summer months, they've have special discounts on weeknights and concerts take place here as well. In addition to the rides I mentioned, you will also find many other great rides at this park. A little trivia: This boardwalk was featured in numerous movies including *Lost Boys*, *Dirty Harry*, *Dangerous Minds*, *Sudden Impact*, *Lost Boys: The Thirst*, and *Harold and Maude*. The park is definitely worth the trip, especially along those long and winding roads you have to take in order to get there.

27. **SeaWorld** in Orlando, Florida may not have many roller coasters (four) or major flume rides, but to me, it stands out as one of the best parks around. The park attracts five million visitors a year, and even though I also like SeaWorld in San Diego and SeaWorld in San Antonio, the one in beautiful Orlando has risen above the rest with the invention of several rides, like Kraken and Manta. Kraken is a floorless coaster that will give you an experience like no other of its kind. Hanging from the top of the lift hill, you get a bird's eye view of the park, and what a view it is. You also have a great flying coaster in Manta and a cool family roller coaster called Shamu Express. However, if flume rides are your passion, get set for a Journey to Atlantis, which is the best of its kind in the nation. But these thrill rides are just part of this park's vast popularity. I know I like to talk about coasters, but this park doesn't need them to be successful. Like its counterpart at Busch Gardens in Tampa, it is very educational for the young and old alike. There are few places where you can pet "live" stingrays in a petting pool. You can also go to the Key West section of the park and touch a dolphin, or feed many different types of fish and mammals. And of course, there is the killer whale, Shamu, to

entertain the family! Whether you are six or sixty, you will leave the killer whale show greatly impressed with these wondrous and amazing whales. I know there has been bad press for this park in recent years, but I still think it is a great place to go and experience marine life at its best. Viewers get to see a fun and fanciful side to these massive and majestic creatures. Terrors of the Deep will give you a close look at the animals that horror films are made from. Among the sharks, barracudas, moray eels, and lionfish, there are many creepy creatures to thrill even the most steadfast visitors. The glass tunnel beneath the tank allows visitors to watch these creatures in their natural habitats.

Then there is the 3D Wild Arctic ride, and of course, the great SeaWorld tower where you get a 360-degree view of the entire park from over three hundred feet above the park. I have found the blue of the aquariums and the park lake to be breathtaking from these heights. I am pretty sure you will too. And new, as of 2003, is the waterfront at SeaWorld, a place where you can unwind and celebrate the sights, sounds (as well as food), and festivity of this vibrant city by the sea. Overall, there is so much to see and do at this park that it definitely makes my top list.

28. **Silverwood** in Athol, Idaho. This park is a fun one to go to. Located near the town of Coeur d'Alene and is less than fifty miles from Spokane, Washington. Original owner Gary Norton opened the park in June of 1988 and didn't have much to speak of back then. Originally having just a main street with shops, a few carnival rides, and an authentic steam train that traveled around the park, this park has gotten much bigger. As the years went by, Silverwood grew in size and popularity. In 2003, an adjacent water park "Boulder Beach" opened and is included with admission to Silverwood. In 2009 Silverwood began an annual Halloween event during the month of October called Scarywood. Garfield still is the official mascot of Silverwood Theme Park.

    Today Silverwood is the largest theme and water park in the American Northwest, with over two hundred acres and over sixty five rides, slides, shows, and attractions. With six roller coasters, including the wood roller coaster "Tremors" and a boomerang style ride called "Aftershock" the park has really become a destination location for many. In 2009, Silverwood opened Scarywood Haunted Nights, a nighttime fright fest filled with scare zones and mazes, and every year, thousands come out to see what scary attractions will be thought of next. It's a great park, and if you're in the area, a great place to escape your problems at least for a little while. Your kids will love it too.

29. **Six Flags America** in Largo, Maryland is a great park for those who like a little bit of everything. Located just fifteen minutes outside of Washington, D.C, Six Flags America started out primarily as a water park called Wild World in the seventies. The Adventure World name changed the park's focus away from water rides to a more traditional amusement park genre that is currently in operation. With the Six Flags changeover in 1999, it became the amusement park that we all see today, a modern-day, competitive amusement park chock-full of popular Six Flags Warner Brothers characters. Six Flags America features more than one hundred thrilling rides, shows, and attractions, headlined by eight fun and furious roller coasters! It is the home of the legendary coaster Superman—Ride of Steel, which, at two hundred feet tall, is one of the tallest and fastest hyper-coasters in the world. If you feel the need to fly like a bird, there is always Batwing, the incredible inverted coaster that literally has to be experienced to be believed.

Let's not forget the other great coasters this park has as well. They are the wooden coasters Roar and the Wild One, as well as great steel coasters like the Joker's Jinx and a great standup roller coaster called Apocalypse and Ragin' Cajun, a great family coaster. The park also features live Hollywood-style shows plus a huge water park called Paradise Island. (The "island" is filled with more than a million gallons of splashin' action.) Guests of all ages can enjoy the sensational rides, games, shows, and attractions, and recently, Six Flags America has cool new water ride like the Penguin's Blizzard River, the tallest spinning rapids ride (over sixty feet) in the world. This ride is the first to feature the popular Batman theme ride based on the legendary DC Comic book Super Hero series. You will find this to be a really enjoyable water park.

The other thing I really like about this park is the parking. There really isn't a bad parking spot in the complex. No need for trams or trains to move you to where the action is. All in all, it is a great place to spend the day.

30. **Six Flags Great Adventure** in Jackson, New Jersey, is one of the best parks in the nation and one of the most attended at 2.9 million visitors a year. Sure, I am a little prejudiced about it since I live just twenty minutes away from this park, but I say, "If you are going to have a park right in your backyard, there are only few others in the country that are better than this one." Originally built by Warner Leroy, the park received its trademark name of Great Adventure. In 1977 the park became part of the Six Flags chain, and today situated on 120 acres of land and boasting thirteen roller coasters, Six Flags Great Adventure is a destination park for just about everyone, especially if you are a roller coaster fanatic. If you truly want to be tested on your thrill factor, very few parks surpass the coasters (count um twelve) you will find here. First, there is the world's tallest roller coaster KingDa Ka, one of the best wooden roller coasters around El Toro, the floorless marvel Bizarro, the infamous Batman: The Ride, and of course, the huge 230-foot wonder Nitro. Also, if you want to witness the tallest drop ride there, you need to ride Zumanjaro: Drop of Doom. At 415 feet tall, it will surely knock your socks off. Boasting more rides and attractions than any other park in the country, Six Flags Great Adventure has recently added twenty-five new rides and attractions. One such ride is the flying coaster Superman: Ultimate Flight, a ride that allows you to fly like a bird underneath the tracks with nothing between you and the ground but a harness. Now that's sweet! You can also find the park's trademark two-hundred-foot parachute perch and a float down a pretty decent river rapids ride in Conga River Rapids. Plus if you like animals, right next door Safari Off Road Adventure which is now part of this park, making it the biggest amusement park in the world. "Safari Off Road Adventure" is a great way to experience the 350-acres of wildlife preserve that stretches over four miles and features over 1,200 animals. This is the place to go in the tristate area (New York/New Jersey/Pennsylvania) if you are truly looking for a great adventure on the East Cast.

31. **Six Flags Great Escape** is nestled in the foothills of the Adirondack Mountains and located in Lake George, New York. The Great Escape has gone under many different names since its inception in 1954, but I found this park to be one of the nicest places, especially if you want to get away from the city. Situated right next to Lake George, this park boasts the area's best thrill rides and roller coasters plus delicious food, games, and all the fun and excitement you can handle. There are seven roller coasters here, and if you like wooden coasters, one of the best can be found in this park. The Comet at Six Flags Great Escape Fun Park is, in a word, fantastic! A former nationally top-ranked wooden coaster, Comet continues to exhibit the attributes that made it so famous. Not too long ago, if you were looking for the best wooden

coaster in the country, you had to come here to find it.

Great Escape also boasts five other coasters you will surely enjoy. New is Canyon Blaster. Originally at Opryland USA in Nashville, Tennessee. Canyon Blaster in the Ghost Town section of the park is an outstanding family mine train ride, which dovetails nicely with the reputation of this family-style park. With two lift hills, a top speed of forty-five miles per hour, and a thrilling double helix, this ride is just great for the whole family. Canyon Blaster is just the latest in a string of improvements and innovative new rides that have been added at the Great Escape since Six Flags purchased the park in 1996.

Among the additions are four roller coasters—Frankie's Mine Train, Steamin' Demon, and the Alpine Bobsled (originally at Six Flags Great Adventure), and the Boomerang Coaster. Other additions to the park have been the Skycoaster, Lumberjack Splash Wave Pool at Splashwater Kingdom, Paul Bunyan's Bucket Brigade, and an Olympiad-style grand prix go-cart track. In addition to the many rides and attractions, when you add the beautiful lake, the majestic mountains, the nice people, and a great family atmosphere, you get the full picture of what this park has to offer. Add to these the great shows that this park puts together every year, and you will want to add this one to your list.

32. **Six Flags Magic Mountain** in Valencia, California, is another one of the e-ticket mega parks that is a must for all those who want to experience extreme rides. Just outside of Los Angeles, Magic Mountain is billed not just as a theme park, but also quite rightly as an "Xtreme park." It has nineteen roller coasters including Goliath, X2, Scream, to name a few. Since the park's inception in 1971, Six Flags Magic Mountain continues to deliver the next generation of thrill rides, and with the park now beats Cedar Point in total number of roller coasters offered to the public and, in fact, directly competes with Cedar Point as the top place to go to be thrilled. They also have classic rides like Déjà Vu, the tallest and fastest suspended, looping coaster in the world.

Also in the record books is another coaster worth mentioning: Superman: Escape from Krypton, the first ride to break the one-hundred-mile-per-hour speed barrier. You can also find Viper, the tallest looping roller coaster in the world at Magic Mountain as well. Colossus was, at one time, the tallest wooden coaster on the West Coast. For those who don't want to remain seated during a ride, the Riddler's Revenge is one of the tallest and fastest stand-up coaster on the planet. And of course, there is the steel legend, Revolution, the coaster that was the world's first 360-degree looping coaster and was highlighted in the blockbuster movie *Roller Coaster*. The park added Twisted Colossus, (the largest and most innovative} hybrid roller coaster in the park, replacing the original wood classic ride.

With all these coasters available, Magic Mountain also offers a fast-lane premium pass program. With this pass, you can ride the best attractions when you want and reduce your waiting time dramatically. Fast lane is a line management system that (for a fee) allows a limited number of guests the opportunity to all but eliminate the lines associated with Six Flags' most popular attractions. Like all Six Flags parks, its shows are also entertaining, the food is pretty good, and it has many rides for the kids and younger adults in the family.

33. **Six Flags New England,** located just over the Connecticut border in Agawam, Massachusetts, has changed its reputation quickly since Six Flags took over the reins in 1999. Keeping up the reputation of other Six Flags parks, the new management really cleaned up the place a lot. Rides were repainted over, litter seems to be less noticeable, and the park simply grew in name and stature. Changes also came from some new attractions.

One such attraction has made this truly a destination park. The coaster that was selected for this transformation was the third version of an already established legend, but this one literally broke the mold, offering more airtime, steep drops, and speed than the vast majority of roller coasters worldwide. I am talking about Superman—Ride of Steel, the ride which has literally put this park on the map. Since then, newer rides like Batman: The Dark Knight, Night Wing, and of course, Superman—Ride of Steel have continued to make this a destination park and one that the whole family will enjoy. There is also Gotham City Gauntlet and their new steel marvel, the Wicked Cyclone, to top off the eleven great coasters rides you will find in this park.

Like all Six Flags parks, this park offers the fast-lane service, which is very much like the Fastpass concept you find at all Disney parks. The fast lane allows you to get a ticket for one of the main attractions at Six Flags, so you don't have to wait in line. Like Disney's parks, you come back at a certain time and just get on the ride. Unfortunately, unlike Disney's, this privilege will cost you a little extra.

Overall, you will find more than 150 rides, shows, and attractions here, which make it the largest family theme park in New England. This sixty-five-acre theme park offers eight roller coasters and a two hundred-foot tower for you to be dropped down or shot up. It's your choice! Also you will find a nice water park, Island Kingdom, for kids as well as adults, with a nice wave pool to boot. It might not be the biggest park on my list, but overall, it truly offers a lot of excitement for the kid in all of you.

34. **Six Flags Over Texas** was the first park ever created for the Six Flags chain and is located in Arlington, Texas, a small city between Dallas and Fort Worth. From its humble beginnings, it has developed into one of the premier amusement parks in the country. It all started in 1961 when Texas oil baron Angus Wynne pioneered the regional theme park industry with the opening of Six Flags Over Texas. Wynne built a broad entertainment product close to where people lived, making it convenient and affordable. He got the idea to name his park from a little Texas history. It seems that six national flags have flown over Texas since the first European exploration of the region by Cortez, which took place in 1519. These countries consisted of Spain, France, Mexico, Texas as a lone republic, Texas within the confederacy, and Texas as a state in the United States. Thus the name of the park was created.

Six Flags Over Texas elevated the old amusement park concept to a true theme park experience with ingenious use of themed presentations, innovative rides, and action-packed shows geared to entertain the entire family. I found this park to be a real winner. You will find a slew of great roller coasters, themed rides, and special shows here, and it is well worth the admission price to get in. From the down-home country folk that man the rides, to the first-rate entertainment, it is top class. The best view of the park can be found on the Oil Derrick, a three hundred-foot observation platform. Today the park boasts twelve top coasters, including the 255-foot steel marvel Titan, the classic Shock Wave, Pandemonium, and of course, the notorious New Texas Giant. From this one park grew Six Flags incorporated, a company well known for the hottest coasters, thrill rides, and shows around the world. Six Flags Inc. is currently the world's largest regional theme park company, with a total of thirty-seven parks throughout the United States, Europe, and Latin America.

35. **Universal Studios** Florida (seven million in attendance) and California (six million in attendance) is all about Hollywood and the film industry with more big-ticket rides and more activities than Disney's Hollywood Studios but less moviemaking lore. Universal Studios Florida is larger than its counterpart in California (and does not have the second park Universal Studio's Island of Adventure) but both parks offer the visitor an inside look at how moviemaking is actually done. The park's key attractions are their thrill rides such as the following: The Revenge of the Mummy (which is my personal favorite), a roller coaster that hurdles you through darkness both backward and forward, Hollywood Rip Ride Rockit, a fantastic coaster that is one of the best I have ever ridden. Plus other attractions like the Men in Black, Alien Attack, The Simpsons Ride, Terminator 2 3-D (a 3-D movie with live action stunts), and also very popular is Transformers: The Ride-3D, Jimmy Neutron's Nicktoon Blast, based on the Nickelodeon cartoon, where you board a rocking and rolling spaceship and follow Jimmy into space and much more. There you will also meet a variety of Nickelodeon characters, including SpongeBob SquarePants. Capitalizing on the success of Shrek is Shrek 4-D, a 3-D movie that adds sensory touches to a continuation of the film as Lord Farquaad attempts to do away with the ogre, his bride, and donkey. Also, the classic rides are also there. Rides like Twister and Fear Factor Live are there as well. You can also find tamer attractions for small children as well. Like E.T which is a must-see experience event in the park. Indeed, there is a lot to do in this park and expect to be in the park several days to experience it all. If you like horror, you will love the Universal Horror Makeup Show. Try and seat yourself up front so that you really get a great view of all the makeup and blood making tricks used in movies scariest scenes. They call on volunteers to help them with this show. And it is one treat that kids all love. If you like magic and horror together, you will really love this show! There is also Beetlejuice's Graveyard Revue, and the Blues Brothers show at the park several times daily. One note to make regarding getting past those long lines at Universal Studios,, In Florida, if you are staying at any of the Universal Resorts, you can get in (most times) without even waiting just by showing your hotel key. At these hotels, you can most likely knock off Universal Studios in a day and a half and Islands of Adventure in about the same time period.

36. **Universal Studio's Islands of Adventure,** located in Orlando, Florida, is one of the newest parks (built in 1999) in the area and easily makes my list of top parks for several reasons. With over eight million visitors every year, it is simply a destination park to experience firsthand. First you will just love the Wizarding World of Harry Potter (and the Harry Potter and the Forbidden Journey 3D ride) as well as Diagon Alley. If you are a coaster fanatic, this park holds two of the sweetest coasters in the world, three if you count Dragon Challenge and the Harry Potter's twin-track experience. One of the best coasters around (and most surveys agree) is Islands of Adventure's the Incredible Hulk. And Islands of Adventure doesn't stop there. There is Flight of the Hippogriff for the kids and if you love water rides, you have a few options to choose from in this park. From Dudley Do- Right's Ripsaw Falls to the eighty five-foot drop at Jurassic Park's River Adventure, or Popeye and Bluto's Bilge-Rat Barges, it is a sure thing that you are going to get wet. For those who love heights and being shot up a 220-foot tower at speeds reaching forty-nine miles per hour, Doctor Doom's Fearfall is the ride for you. If 3-D is your thing, then you can experience the best simulated dark ride around, The Amazing Adventures of Spiderman's 3-D experience **that** will make you feel like you are right in the middle of the action. The kids will love "the Cat in the Hat" and "the High in the Sky

Seuss Trolley Train Ride" as well.

Overall you get many "Islands" to choose from here: Toon Lagoon, Marvel Super Hero Island, Jurassic Park, the Lost Continent, Wizarding Word of Harry Potter and Seuss Land for the kids. If you visit the park around Christmastime, do not miss the special Grinch show shown in three parts at Seuss Land. You will truly enjoy it. There is literally something for everyone in this park, and it is well worth the price of admission.

Like at Disney, you will find some of the best hotels right at the park. They are the Portofino Bay Hotel, the Hard Rock Café Hotel, and the last time I was there, the Royal Pacific Resort. Right next door you will surely have a blast at Islands of Adventure's sister park in Universal Studios, Florida. I like this park too! And if that isn't enough, and if rides, shows, and attractions don't really interest you, fear not, there is always "City Walk" for your shopping, dining, and live entertainment pleasure. They are so popular that both parks combined cater to over thirteen million people a year (five and a half for Islands of Adventure and seven plus million at Universal Studios Florida). These parks have it all, and I could literally write a book about all there is to do here. Oops, that was already done by someone else!

37. **Valleyfair** in Shakopee, Minnesota. Valleyfair was originally themed as a Coney Island-styled early twentieth century amusement park. I really do love this park and have talked about it on radio and television many times. This park is currently the largest amusement park in the Upper Midwest United States. It wasn't that way in 1976 when it first opened. That year it featured only twenty rides and attractions and is now a 125-acre park owned by Cedar Fair Entertainment Company, which features over seventy five attractions, forty eight of which are rides and that include eight roller coasters. Valleyfair also has a great water park called Soak City, which is included in the price of admission. It might interest you to know that Valley fair (as well as Cedar Point) were the two original parks under the Cedar Fair name and that name (Valley Fair) comes from this park. As I mentioned earlier, these coasters are fantastic and it is the home of one of the best around and one the tallest called Wild Thing (steel). There is a fantastic wood roller coaster called Renegade and an impulse coaster called "Steel Venom" (Steel) as well as many others. Here you will also find amazing entertainment in a ride called Dinosaurs Alive! There is also an all-new family area called, Route 76. Since we are in the northern part of the United States, Valleyfair's normal operation is from Memorial Day through Labor Day, but for all you Halloween maniacs, you don't want to miss "ValleySCARE" in October. This one is guaranteed to scare you silly. Overall this is a great park with such a friendly and accommodating staff. Your family will just love this park as much as I did.

38. **Walt Disney World** in Orlando, Florida, (with over fifty million visitors a year) is, in my mind, still one of top places to go when you want that "real family vacation." Does it have the most thrilling roller coasters around? Well, not really. Does it have the best live shows for adults? Possibly, but what it definitively does have can be described as pure magic to your senses! Talk all you want about other parks. You still have to give Disney World the highest marks for concept, theming, and overall presentation. As you all know, Disney World is comprised of many different parks. First there is the Magic Kingdom, home of Mickey and crew, with 1,001 things to do that will surely keep your four- to ten–year-old (as well as yourself) totally mesmerized. For the adults, you can't beat Splash Mountain or roller coaster favorites like Space Mountain and the Runaway Train. Children also have their own coaster in The Barnstormer and the new Seven Dwarfs Mine Train that will surely make everyone's day.

Other non-coaster top picks for me would include Mickey's PhilharMagic, It's a Small World, the Jungle Cruise, Pirates of the Caribbean, Peter Pan, and the new Under the Sea, Journey of The Little Mermaid.

Then there is Animal Kingdom, home of Disney's best roller coaster Expedition Everest, Kilimanjaro Safaris, Dinosaur, Kali River Rapids, It's Tough to Be a Bug, and Primeval Whirl, just to name a few. One of the best shows to experience here is the *Festival of the Lion King*, which is far better than your average show. Plus your kids will also love the hundreds of animals in the park. Animal Kingdom is very educational and an interesting departure from most other theme parks.

Another feature is Disney's Hollywood Studios, the home of the Tower of Terror, which, in my mind, is still one of the best drop rides around that you will find. For the roller coaster enthusiast, there is Rock n' Roller Coaster, a souped-up version of Space Mountain that really is well worth riding. Again, there are many rides, shows, and attractions that really make your trip including Star Tours, Toy Story Mania, Indiana Jones Stunt Spectacular, Light Motors, Action Extreme Stunt Show. For the kids, why not catch Muppet Vision 3D, Playhouse Disney, and the Voyage of the Little Mermaid. You will be glad you did.

Finally, there is EPCOT, which might be a little light on thrill rides, except for Test Track and Mission Space, but still an adventure for everyone who visits this park. I still love Soarin', the Living Seas with Nemo and Friends, Journey into Imagination (one of my all-time favorites). Also, while visiting the EPCOT's World Showcase around the lake, try seeing the Gran Fiesta Tour in Mexico. You might not know this, but at its inception, Epcot was labeled as the city of the future and Walt Disney's dream of what the modern world would look like in the new millennium. We now know that his vision in the seventies was not quite on track, but you will have a hard time hearing me complain about this masterpiece that he put together at this park. Nations literally come together in celebration of cultures and societies, all within walking distance from one another.

All in all, these four Disney parks are truly beautiful and absolutely amazing in their own unique ways with rides and attractions for just about everyone. They are set up for those of you who truly want to discover the child in yourself and to experience the sheer joy in your little ones' eyes. One thing for sure, make sure you get a park-hopper pass so you can go between parks and stay on Disney property if you can. Use the new fast pass system that you now connect to online and just have fun. The friendly staff and above-average service are also the best here. While you're there, you should also visit the Disney Springs area, the boardwalk, Typhoon Lagoon and Blizzard Beach water parks. Many books have been written about this magical theme park monopoly, as well they should. My review here is simply created to entice you to book a trip as soon as possible. You and your family will make long-lasting memories here that you will cherish for a lifetime.

39. **Worlds of Fun,** in Kansas City, Missouri. Worlds of Fun first opened on May 26, 1973, at a cost of (can you believe this) ten million dollars. It was situated near an industrial complex in the bluffs above the Missouri River. Mid-America Enterprises began construction on a new amusement park in 1969. The park was originally planned to complement a five-hundred-acre hotel and entertainment complex, but a lagging economy during the park's early years put this on hold for the time being.

The park opened in May of 1973 and currently has seven active roller coasters during this writing. Patriot is the newest ride (2006), a giant inverted coaster that flips guests four times at speeds of over sixty miles per hour. And then there's one of my favorites at this park called Mamba. This is a 205-foot-tall mega-coaster that takes the rider fly down a mile-long track at seventy miles per per hour. If you like wood roller coasters, there is the Prowler, a real beast of a terrain coaster and one of the best rides around. At the park for the kids you will find there is a petting zoo (as well as several other kiddy rides) at Planet Snoopy. At Worlds of Fun, you can also experience Dinosaurs Alive where visitors can step back in time to the beginning of the age of dinosaurs. In 1982, Oceans of Fun opened next door and has become one of the largest water parks in the world. If entertainment is what you're after, then you have come to the right place. Worlds of Fun has several great shows including the Great American Train Robbery, British Invasion Team Charlie Brown, and for the little ones, they can experience Sally's Sing a Long as well as meeting all the Peanuts characters at the park. Cedar Fair purchased this park in 1995, and it has increased in popularity ever since. It is a park you must not miss while in this city.

40. **Canada's Wonderland Park** in Toronto Canada is one of the best-attended seasonal theme parks in North America and, annually, almost four million visitors visit this Canadian roller coaster Mecca. This combination theme park and water park is located just minutes north of Toronto. At 330-acres, Canada's Wonderland is the one of the largest theme parks in Canada and offers more than to hundred attractions. This includes over sixty amusement rides around the park. Overall, Canada's Wonderland boasts fifty thrilling roller coasters and the largest selection of flat rides that you will find anywhere. It is here that you will find not one but two Mega-coasters including the 300-foot tall mega-coaster called Leviathan and the two-hundred foot tall Behemoth roller coaster at Canada's Wonderland. For the family, there is none better than the Backlot Stunt Coaster, and if you like swings, you have got to try Wind Seeker, a three-hundred foot swing that speeds its riders at forty five miles per hour at a fifty degree angle with nothing below them but air. The adjoining 20-acre Splash Works water park is also included with park admission and offers sixteen water slides, a lazy river, and the largest wave pool in Canada. Canada's Wonderland theme park is owned and operated by Cedar Fair Entertainment based in Sandusky, Ohio, and that was a great move in making this park one for the ages. The park opened in May 23, 1981, after several years of construction and has grown ever since. The park was eventually purchased by Viacom and rebranded as "Canada's Wonderland" In June 2006, Viacom sold the Paramount Parks chain to the Sandusky, Ohio- (Cedar Fair) based company called Cedar Fair, and a year later, the Paramount name was dropped, reverting back to its original name, Canada's Wonderland. If you are ever in the Toronto area, this amusement park is a classic and one that offers a little something for everyone. I absolutely love this park, and I am very sure that if you find yourself north of the border, you will too.

My Top Sixteen
European Amusement Parks
Across the Pond

In my first book, I talked about the best amusement parks in North America. Well, guess what? In this, I wanted to expand on that. There are many fantastic amusement parks across the pond in Europe, and I wanted to talk a little about them. In fact, there are so many great parks out there that I can only mention just a few of them in the book. To be truthful, I can only comment on those I've actually visited. Perhaps in my next book, I can expand on this list, but from what I have seen, these are my top pics for the area. Your favorites might be a little different and you can feel free to tell me about them.

1. **Alton Towers** in Alton, Staffordshire, United Kingdom. Yearly attendance is 2.75 million. This Disney-like park, which was built around a nineteenth-century listed gothic mansion also, has some pretty fantastic gardens. All in all, this unique park has eleven themed areas; an aquarium -Sharkbait Reef, featuring more than three hundred species of marine life. Thrill seekers will not be disappointed by the roller coasters they have here. Some of the best out there including Rita, Queen of Speed: Oblivion, the world's first vertical drop roller coaster, and of course, the one and the only… Nemesis, Europe's first inverted roller coaster. Overall this park has eight great coasters here including "Oblivion" and Thirteen. For the young tykes, children will enjoy Wobble World, an inflatable paradise, and also there's Squirrel Nutty, a ride where youngsters travel through the treetops in acorns. You will find rides and attractions that are great for the whole family. This also includes one of my favorites out there in the Charlie and the Chocolate Factory ride. This park is a one-of-a-kind treat and one you should not miss if you're in the UK.

2. **Blackpool Pleasure Beach,** in Blackpool, Lancashire, United Kingdom. This is indeed one of my favorite European parks that opens its gates to 1.8 million people yearly. Situated at the south end of Blackpool's promenade, the Pleasure Beach Resort is a place to enjoy the best thrill rides one can find in Europe. The resort was opened on the seafront back in 1896 (last century) with a mission to "make adults feel like children again." Well, that tradition continues even today. The park boasts more than 125 rides and attractions, including ten top-of-the-line roller coasters, including Europe's tallest roller coaster, "The Big One." Other great rides to try would be Infusion and two great wood coasters called Nickelodeon Streak and Grand National. They also have one of the oldest rides at the park built in 1923 called the Big Dipper. Also there, you will find an ice-skating arena and shows that even rival Broadway. There really is something here for all ages, and children can have their very own fun as well. It's a great park, the people are nice, and the park is very clean and easy to walk through. I have read that despite the millions of visitors every year, the size of this park means queuing is kept to a minimum. You will surely have a great time here, and if you can hook up with one of the local coaster clubs in the area and get some exclusive ride time on these monsters of the Midway, that would make your trip here perfect!

3. **Chessington World of Adventure and Zoo,** in Chessington, Surrey, United Kingdom. Total people that visited the park yearly is around 1.4 million. This theme park, which incorporates a zoo and sea life center, is separated into nine different themed areas with around thirty different rides to choose from including four roller coasters. Among the most popular and exciting rides here is one that is called "The Vampire." This is a suspended roller coaster that literally flies riders through the trees and throughout the park itself. Also in the park, you will find a great family roller coaster in Dragon's Fury. This one is a spinning marvel guaranteed to make some guests feel a little queasy. I love boat rides and Chessington has a good one as well. There are also a few hotels nearby especially one that I really like called the Holiday Inn Chessington. This is a safari-themed hotel and is located next to the park. Overall, it's a smaller park than most that you will find in the States but don't let that stop you from taking the trip. Here, it works well, and it is one that can be a lot of fun for the entire family.

4. **Disneyland Paris Cedex** in Marne-la-Valle, France. The park has about 10.5 million visitors a year. For those of you who know me, I love Disney, and this is one park that I think you will love as well. After the success of the Disneyland theme park in Anaheim, plans to build a European version actually started way back in 1975. Walt Disney had been gone almost a decade, but the plan was put together to put a new location somewhere in Europe. The Disney folks were looking at many different locations. Countries like Great Britain, Italy, Spain, and France were all considered possibilities. After a lot of thought on this, it was decided that the French location just outside of Paris would be the location of choice. All in all, I'd say it was a great decision. The park has over fifty attractions in five themed lands. The park is designed like a wheel with the hub on Central Plaza. The park itself is over 140 acres (has many of the classic rides you will find at other Disney parks) and is one of most successful parks that Walt Disney runs. The park contains all the lands that we know and love (Main Street, Fantasyland, etc), but in addition to this, you can now play with your favorite toys courtesy of some pretty familiar Pixar characters. Toy Story Playland is a pretty popular place to hang out and was the first complete land based on the Pixar smash-success trilogy. Here children can play with their heroes, and adults will be transported back to their own childhood memories as well with human-size green army men, a towering orange Hot Wheels race track, balsa wood airplanes, wooden railway track for benches, and much more. If you're in Paris, make sure to make this a stop on your "Must-Do" list.

5. **Drayton Manor Park** in Tamworth, Staffordshire, United Kingdom. 1.8 million visitors a year. Set among 280 acres of lakes and parkland, Drayton Manor features some of the biggest, wettest, and scariest rides you will ever encounter in Europe. Among them is one of my favorite. The ride is called Apocalypse, and it was the world's first stand-up tower drop, and that's one of the reasons I loved it. Among the five operational roller coasters, I also love Shockwave. This is Europe's first stand-up roller coaster, and standing at 120 feet tall, it does really pack a punch. The Buffalo Mountain Coaster is a great one for the family, and the tykes will love the Troublesome Trucks Runaway Coaster. As water rides go, Stormface is one of the best water rides in the country and one worth waiting for. Other family attractions include a 4D cinema that young children will enjoy and Thomas Land, a multimillion-pound attraction, which included a dozen rides and a spectacular indoor play area to boot. They also have a zoo, and the neat thing about Drayton Manor is the park's layout. You don't feel like you're walking miles to get to your favorite attractions. The United States might have hundreds of amusement parks, but I would put Drayton Manor (along with a few others in the UK) up there with the best we have here in the states.

6. **Europa-Park** in Rust, Baden-Wuerttemberg, Germany, has over 4.25 million people visiting their park on a yearly basis. Arguably this is Europe's biggest theme park and the second-most popular theme park behind Disneyland Paris. This park really does rock. It's located in a town called Rust, which is about Thirty-five-kilometers from Freiburg, Germany. The park has over fifty-eight different rides, including twelve roller coasters and four water rides for their guests. The oldest of them is a mine train called Alpen Express. One of their newest (and best) roller coasters is one called Blue Fire, and believe me, it's well worth the wait to ride this baby. You start this ride in the Energy Research complex before being launched about sixty miles per hour through various twists, loops, tunnels, and hills. Other rides to experience are the Wodan Timbur Coaster, a wood monster at 131 feet tall and built in 2012, and Silver Star, a steel marvel built by B&M that same year. The park is set up into twelve countries, each one with a different theme according to the European country that it represents. For example, all visitors in the German section of the park can see an original piece of the Berlin Wall, visit the Ancient German Fair, and many different types of German architecture. For children, Adventure Land and the many shows that take place at this park there are second to none. These productions range from traditional theatre, acrobatics, dance, and figure skating. Like most parks in Europe as well as here in the United States, the park was beautifully landscaped and pretty easy to navigate. Here you will find a very cool 4D cinema, a fully recreated Globe Theatre (based on one from William Shakespeare's day). The local culture and staff is extremely interesting, friendly, and helpful. Food prices inside the park are very reasonable too. It can accommodate up to fifty thousand guests per day, and many times it does just that. I'd definitely recommend staying in one of the park's hotels when you visit this amazing park.

7. **Efteling**. Located in Kaatsheuvel, Noord-Brabant, Netherlands. This park opens its doors to over four million guests yearly. This amazing park opened way back in 1952 and is actually one of the oldest running theme parks that you will find around the world. I think this is truly one of the most beautiful parks in the world, and when you add a great hotel on premises, you can't help but have a great time while there. The many other rides in this park are also pretty spectacular as well. There are elaborately themed buildings right down to ATMs find, one of which has been built into a giant treasure chest. Efteling is a fairy tale-style park that seems to come to life every night for its guests. You will find many family attractions in Efteling that everyone will love. Whatever their ages, there is always something for everyone! They even have an old steam train that rides you around the park and is very relaxing. There is a special carrousel, a railway for children, a 4-D movie theatre, boats, teacups, and so much more to see for the entire family. There is also the Fairy Tale Forest (or Sprookjesbos in Dutch) where well-known fairy tales are played out. Fairy tale figures like dwarfs, princesses, and dragons have been known to come out when you least expect it. In all, you will hear twenty-five different fairy tales stories that your family will love. The park contains some spectacular attractions including six wild roller coasters like the double-loop rollercoaster Python and the wood coaster Joris en de Draak. Three you will find the Haunted Castle, the Piranha river-raft ride, and about a half dozen additional rides and attractions (like the roller water coaster called the Flying Dutchman) too. They even have a pretty cool indoor roller coaster for the whole family that you just have to experience yourself. These attractions are great for the park in many ways and even rivals the best that Disney has to offer. Finally, you should know that this park is very big, so bring those walking shoes to be comfortable getting around the park.

8. **Flamingo Land,** in Malton, North Yorkshire, United Kingdom. On average, this park accommodates about two million people and is constantly ranked in the top ten in Europe. Like many amusement parks long before it ever became a modern-day amusement park, it started out as an old country club. Today with over 375 acres to walk around, Flamingo Land offers a theme park, zoo, holiday village, and a lot more. And yes, Flamingos were one of the first inhabitants at their zoo, hence the name Flamingo Land. Today, the zoo has more than one thousand animals, exotic birds, fish, and reptiles for you to enjoy. The theme park has over one hundred rides, ranging from crazy thrill rides for roller coaster aficionado to rides for the younger ones. That's right... Over one hundred rides and attractions can be found here and that includes nine great roller coasters. Among the best rides at this park you will find Hero, a great flying coaster; Zoom; Twistosaurus; and the Kumali, a suspended coaster that twists and loops over pretty long track. For kids, there is also the Go Gator coaster that they will just love. You will also experience a great water ride here called Splash Battle and Splish Splash. While in the park, families will get to experience some of the best shows around, and the food outlets are second to none.

9. **Gardaland**. Located in Castelnuovo del Garda, Veneto, Italy. **This** park boasts 2.8 million people visiting every year and thirty -plus rides and attractions for just about everyone in the family. Gardaland was founded back in 1975, and every year since then, this park has gotten bigger and bigger, adding new shows and attractions. Gardaland has worked hard to keep up with the competition (both in Europe and in the US) by improving attractions it offers and developing new theme zones. The park currently is home to seven roller coasters and over three dozen rides. When I was there, some of the best coasters to ride were Raptor, Blue Tornado, Magic Mountain, Sequoia Adventure, and Ortobruco Tour to name just a few. In 2011 Raptor was added to their list by the best Swiss manufacturer out there with the initials B&M. You might have heard of them? They also have three water rides at the park that takes up sixty-four acres and has a little something for everyone who visits. Even with all this to offer, perhaps one of the park's best features is the friendly and hospitable people you will interact with. Even if you don't speak the language, you will still feel at home.

10. **Heide Park** in Soltau, Niedersachsen, Germany. With an average of 1.4 million people attending this park, it is one of the most popular parks in Europe. Heide Park currently has about forty rides and many different attractions. It's not one of your biggest parks out there, but that's what I love about it. This is a great park to enjoy while on vacation because most of the rides here are geared to the family. They do, however, have fairly decent roller coasters as well, like Colossos, a wooden roller coaster, which until the opening of Balder in the Swedish amusement park Liseberg (that is also on my list), was the steepest wooden roller coaster in the world. Heide Park has now come full circle with the inclusion of a new launched roller coaster called "Desert Race." It was Germany's first launched roller coaster and accelerates from zero to sixty miles per hour in just two and a half seconds. Riders can experience as much as five positive gs during the trip. Overall the park has nine roller coasters and several water rides. Some other roller coasters to experience while here would be Krate, a B&M dive coaster; Flug der Damonen, a unique wing-style coaster and Limit a Vecoma SLC inverted ride. The shows there are pretty good too, and the people and staff are always so friendly. The park is very clean and pricing very competitive.

11. **Legoland Windsor** in Windsor, Berkshire, United Kingdom. Like the other parks here in the states, Legoland, is set in 150 acres of parkland and has more than fifty interactive rides, attractions, and live shows for the whole family. The one thing I love about Legoland is that

it's truly an amazing place to take your kids. Whether it's to take driving lessons and, in the end, get a special license or experience all the hundreds of things this place has to offer, it really is memorable for the entire family. For the older kids, there are several intermediate rides like the Dragon roller coaster and Vikings River Splash. The tykes can also ride its kid brother, the Dragon's Apprentice coaster. If I recall, Bob the Builder 4D movie is still there and a great place to hang with the kids. The newest addition to the park is called Kingdom of the Pharaohs and includes a new indoor ride as well. This attraction is a great place to get armed with laser guns and shoot your way through a labyrinth, battling skeletons, evil mummies, and dodging traps makes this a pretty exciting experience. Legoland may be the newest player in the theme park battle of the best, but they sure know how to keep the kids (and the adults) entertained. You will have a lot of fun and create new memories in this park. It may be over the pond, but the staff makes it feel just like home.

12. **Liseberg** in Gothenburg, Bohuslan, Sweden, is visited by almost three million people every year and is a great place to make memories. It's Scandinavia's biggest amusement park and offers many different attractions that everyone will enjoy. You will also find Sweden's top artists stopping by here often. Here, you will also find many fun games and plenty of flowers all around the park. Oh yea, at Liseberg, you can ride some pretty cool roller coasters too. Balder has been voted several times as the "world's best wooden roller coaster" and some say (including myself) that it really deserves this accolade. You can also ride their newest roller coaster called Helix, a LIM launch coaster (opened in 2014) that you will just love as well. Kanonen is also here, and this one will be fun for the entire family. It's safe to say, there's something for everyone here. Memorable attractions like, Uppswinget and SpinRock come to mind and a gentle children's carousel ride that give the little ones a thrill. If you prefer to take things a little easier, you can visit Evert Taube's World, take a walk in Liseberg Garden, or simply enjoy the dancing and music you will find here. In the park, there are games of fortune, plenty of shops, great food, and beautiful flowers all around this amazing park. And just like at Disney and Universal Studios, Christmas at Liseberg is truly one fantastic experience. The holiday celebration starts in mid-November, and it's a great time to visit this park. You can visit a traditional Christmas market, skate on the ice rink, or just enjoy the holiday atmosphere. You can also take home some unique Christmas gifts while there. So what are you waiting for? Come to Liseberg today!

13. **Parc Asterix** in Plailly, Picardie, France, sees over a million and a half visitors come through its gates yearly and truly is a destination park. It is especially known for its large variety of roller coasters (six in all) such as Tonnerre de Zeus, a wooden roller coaster; and Goudurix, an amazing steel multi-looping coaster built by Vekoma. This park also incorporates rides with great themes from historic Roman and Greek cultures. It is also home to the biggest wooden roller coaster in Europe! That roller coaster is called Zeus. This ride is over a hundred feet tall and propels riders down the steep track at seventy miles per hour. Another great ride here is their newest one called "Osiris," a five-element B&M inverted coaster that reminds me of the Batman series in the Sates. The park is large and has such a variety of attractions that everyone can enjoy. They also have great shows, and the food is absolutely fabulous. Park management was afraid that it wouldn't compete with the neighboring Disneyland Paris Resort that is close by, but it's safe to assume both parks have benefited in this situation. Parc Asterix is only open from April to October and has generally shorter opening hours than its Disney counterpart. This park doesn't really have the usual fast-food franchise giants and that makes this park unique. You will find only French food here, a change of pace that you'll just love. You also won't find all the craziness (as you will sometimes find here in the Sates) trying to get on a

ride. It's more civilized and informal here, so take your time and enjoy the view before you enjoy the ride. Parc Asterix is a fan favorite and one that you will not soon forget!

14. **Phantasialand** in Bruhl, Nordrhein Westfalen, Germany. This park is the host to two million visitors annually, which is more than the average amusement park in the United States. The park was opened in 1967 by Gottlieb Löffelhardt and Richard Schmidt. Although it started as a small family-oriented park, Phantasialand has done everything right and, over the years, has expanded with the addition of many cool rides. One of the best that I have ridden is a mine train called Colorado Adventure. Another favorite is Black Mamba and a cool elevator lift coaster by the name of Winjas. The park features the Seven Lands. Here you will find smaller versions of famous attractions like Brandenburg Gate. You will also find rides similar to what you will find at Disney World. like tea cups and bumper cars. There are a large variety of attractions at the Phantasialand theme park, and I'm sure there is one that will be your favorite. Laughter and excitement is universal, and even though you might not speak the language, you will bond with the other guests in this amazing park. I can promise you that.

15. **Thorpe Park** in Chertsey, Surrey, United Kingdom. Annually, this park is visited by over 1.85 million people. With more than thirty rides and attractions, this is a great park to just forget your troubles and enjoy yourself. Currently they have seven great roller coasters and one of my favorites is called "Saw-The Ride" the world's first horror movie-themed roller coaster on the planet. Adrenalin junkies will also enjoy Stealth, one of Europe's fastest coasters, which catapults down the track from zero to eighty miles per hour in under two seconds; Colossus, the world's first ten-looper, and my favorite, Nemesis Inferno -Their newest ride is also a good one as well. Built in 2012, Swarm, a B&M Wing Coaster has five nasty (and fun) inversions that you will just love. For those who really don't like thrill rides, you can also experience a 4D movie experience in the beach area, complete with sand and large pool. For the little ones, the Flying Fish can be logged into your book as one of their first thrill ride kiddy experiences. Thorpe Park was made for thrill ride junkies, so enjoy and try not to miss anything while there. Thorpe is a very special place, and you will have a great time. Try to get to the park early if you can because the lines get pretty long especially during midday.

16. **Tivoli Gardens** in Copenhagen, Denmark. Not many people know this, but the story of Tivoli Gardens dates back to 1843. Its founder, Georg Carstensen, grew up in a family that travelled a lot as his father was a diplomat. Georg Carstensen had seen many amusement parks around Europe and wanted to create one in Copenhagen. Tivoli sees more than 4.5 million annual visitors, and it is safe to say is one of the most popular seasonal theme parks in the world. It is without a doubt the most visited theme park in Scandinavia, and the second most visited in Europe, only behind (you guessed it) Disneyland Paris. The park is best known for its wooden roller coaster called Rutsjebanen (the Roller Coaster), which was built in 1914. It is one of the world's oldest wooden roller coasters still operating today. It's an old style ride, and like the Cyclone in Brooklyn, an operator controls the ride by braking down the hills so it won't gain too much speed. It is a classic roller coaster that is one of ACE's favorites. Their best steel ride called Daemonen (Demon) is also their newest. There is also Tivioli Hall, a classical concert hall, which features concerts often by big name talent like Elton John and Lady Gaga, which was built way back in 1956. There is also an open-air theatre called the Pantomime Theatre as well. The park is a great place for those who love thrill rides and enjoy the very best of family entertainment. I would recommend when you are in Denmark so stop by and say hello!

My Top (US) Amusement Parks to Visit During Christmastime

Amusement parks in the south have always been open for business during the holidays. However, not too long ago, amusement parks in the northern portion of the United States started to open for the holidays in order to extend their seasons. About 30 years ago it started out on a trial basis by a few theme parks, but before you knew it, there were dozens that became successful with adding Halloween events to their season. Later Christmas was added and even though it is bitterly cold in the Northeast states in late December, people kept coming to these parks, and they came in droves. These parks were not just about rides and holiday shows but serving kettle pop corn, hot chocolate, and even amazing light shows that rivaled what was already being presented down south. So my list includes these parks too. Some who have never experienced being in an amusement park in the dead of winter with temps that can reach ten degrees Fahrenheit may never understand why these parks are so popular, but believe me, they truly are. I have, and this is why they have been included here. Events do change from year to year but even with these changes these are my top pics for the Christmas Season.

1. **Disney World/Disneyland's Magic Kingdom Park and Hollywood Studios in** Orlando Florida and Anaheim California. When it comes to the holidays, and if you have kids (young or old), nothing beats "Mickey's Very Merry Christmas." There is no better place to celebrate the magic of the holiday season with your family than at Mickey's Very Merry Christmas Party. A special event held on select nights in November and December at the Magic Kingdom. For a separate admission fee, the Magic Kingdom Park also opens to ticketholders on select evenings. Featuring special Christmas themed parades, stage shows in front of the castle, and fireworks make this a great way to ring in the season. Snow falling on Main Street and complimentary hot chocolate and cookies add to the Disney magic. If you are in Orlando, Florida, you would never want to miss the tradition of the **Osborne Family Spectacle of Dancing Lights Show (which actually closes for good soon) at Disney's Hollywood Studios.** You will be glad that you didn't. Donated from a family in Arkansas, this light show features over four million lights. This synchronized light show is a definite must see. Disney even has "glow with the show" merchandise available for purchase that synch with the holiday festivities. For more info, you can visit their website at http://disneyworld.disney.go.com/.

2. **Silver Dollar City** in Branson Missouri. An Old Time Christmas. The event runs from November 3 to late December weather permitting and many of the park's rides are open for the event. They are truly one of the best around when it comes to getting you and your family in the holiday mood. Silver Dollar City features four million lights and also a Christmas on Main Street tree-lighting presentation. You also have the Gifts of Christmas Holiday Lights parade and some of the best shows and musical performances you will ever see. They even do a great presentation of *"A Christmas Carol"* for all to experience. Santa also holds court in Kringle's Krossing. In addition to this, there are special holiday treats that include hot wassail and ginger cookies. You got to check out the Mother Goose Guild and the Nativity Pageant as well. Silver Dollar City is a park (especially during the holidays) that you will not soon forget. If you get the chance to visit during the holidays, you should. You can visit their website at

silverdollercity.com

3. **Universal Studio's Islands of Adventure** in Orlando, Florida. What can I say? It's not Christmas until you visit here! First, you have the Macy's Holiday Parade to start things off. The Grinch makes personal appearances throughout the day, and you will love the show in Dr. Seuss land. There is a live retelling of the Dr. Seuss's *Holiday Classic*, and many times during the day these characters really come to life right before your eyes. After, you can meet the Grinch and his dog, Max, and get a photo up with this pair if you like. You can also ride "Cat in the Hat" while you're there, and you will truly have a great experience in this park especially during the holidays. This is one place where there is something for everyone and since we're in Florida and the weather is always perfect and all rides stay open during this holiday celebration. You can visit their website at universalorlando.com/Theme-Parks/Islands-of-Adventure.aspx.

4. **Hershey Park** Christmas Candy lane and Hershey Sweet Lights in nearby Hershey, Pennsylvania is open from November 18 to December 31, and it is open most days. Yes, it gets a little cold here during the winter, but the park does open many rides (weather permitting) and presents great shows to get you in the Christmas spirit. When visiting, it's not hard to tell that you are literally in the sweetest place in the world all year around. During your trip, you even get to see Santa's real reindeer, and I'm telling you, your kids will just love it. In the past, one of my favorite shows included the musical, *"A Rockin' Music Box Christmas."* Hershey also offers a drive-through holiday light display up the hill that is second to none starting on November 16. It's called Hershey Sweet Lights, and it is two miles of trails (in the car, of course) with over one-million lights on more than five hundred animated displays along the way. Hershey also offers hotel packages (for the hotel and the lodge) and other holiday promotions as well that you can take advantage of. You can visit their website at Hershey Park.com.

5. **Dollywood.** For many years, it has been called the "Smoky Mountain Christmas Festival and is located at Pigeon Forge (near Knoxville). It is open from Early November to December 30th and is a great time to be in this park. Not all but many of Dollywood's fantastic rides will be operating during the holiday festival. When it comes to attractions creating the holiday mood is very important. With 3.5 million twinkling lights all around and synchronized to holiday tunes, this is a great place to celebrate with your family. The staff is also very nice, and you know you are with great folks when you come visit here. The park also features "Twas the Night Before Christmas" and several other new productions that are sure to put a big smile on your face. There's also the Polar Express 4-D Experience, a ride/film based on the popular Christmas film that the whole family will just love. Also at Santa's Workshop, children will be able to make their own holiday craft projects. There is nothing like being in Pigeon Forge, especially during Christmastime. It is really safe to say that you and your family will surely love your visit. You can visit their website at Dollywood.com.

6. **Busch Gardens Williamsburg** in Virginia. During the holidays, Busch Gardens transform its European hamlets, including Ireland and England, into Christmas Town Williamsburg, an Old World Christmas village that you will just love! There's Retro lane, an old-school Christmas light display, and when I last visited, they have had great shows like *"Miracles," "Gloria!," "Deck the Halls," "O Tannenbaum,"* and *"A Sesame Street Christmas."* Many of their rides and attractions are also open on selected days and weather permitting. As with most parks this time of year, there's delicious holiday-themed food and dining, and of course, you can meet the

man in the big red suit as well. The fun starts From Thanksgiving until Christmas Eve. You can visit their website at http://seaworldparks.com/en/buschgardens-williamsburg.

7. **Busch Gardens Williamsburg** in Tampa. If you like Christmas in Virginia, you will love the goings on that you will find here in Florida. You and the family will have a lot of fun as "Christmas Town" transforms this amazing park in a holiday wonderland. You have some great shows, live entertainment (like *"Elmo's Christmas Wish"* and the ice skating extravaganza *"Angels of Peace"),* a million plus brilliant lights, and visits from Santa for the kids. The local train becomes Christmas Town Express and when you visit, you will find real snow in the park and snow sledding opportunities as well. The sights, smells, and sounds of the holidays are all here plus thousands of different animals to get you in the mood. Christmas Town runs from November 27th through December 31st and is a great place to take the family.

8. **Holiday lights** at Lake Compounce in Bristol, Connecticut. This park is one of the oldest in America and, in my mind, a great place to go during the holidays. Holiday Lights usually starts every year on Fridays, Saturdays, and Sundays from November 30 through December 22. This includes a North Pole railway train ride, cookie decorating for the kids, storytelling for everyone, carolers that will make you feel quite festive, and a selection of kiddie and family rides, if the weather permits. Santa has also been invited, and there are millions of festive lights of too! This park is one of the best in the nation, and you won't find a better way to celebrate the holidays than at this park. You can visit their website at Lakecompounce.com.

9. **Dutch Wonderland.** Everyone knows about the holiday celebration at Hershey Park, but not too far away in Lancaster County, you will find Dutch Winter Wonderland. Dutch Wonderland in beautiful Pennsylvania might be small, but it's a great place to take the family this holiday season. Again this year, the Princess of Dutch Wonderland will be offering some Christmas stories that the family will love. Rides will also be open for everyone, but know that it will be cold, so dress accordingly. Santa will be on hand to see who's been naughty or nice. And the Dutch Winter Wonderland Royal Light Show will again feature colorful lights synchronized to holiday music and fun for everyone. The action starts in mid-November and runs through December 30th. You can visit their website at Dutchwonderland.com

10. **Holiday Lights** at Kennywood in West Mifflin, Pennsylvania (just outside of Pittsburgh), is open for holiday celebration starting on the weekends from November 23 to December 30. Kennywood might be new to the game, but take my word for it, they do a great job in setting the holiday mood. There is something about being here in the north during the holidays that is just amazing. The people are so nice here and with carolers caroling, twinkling lights twinkling, and the rides in operation, you are sure to have a great day in this park. Every year, Kennywood presents Holiday Lights, and it's a fantastic addition to all the fun stuff they offer to their guests. Santa is going to be there with kettle corn on hand as well as hot chocolate to keep everyone warm while visiting. The holiday shows are great, the staff festive, and the fun index is listed as high for everyone who stops by. You can visit their website at Kennywood.com

11. **Six Flags Over Texas's Holiday in the Park** in Arlington, Texas (near Dallas) is truly a cool place to be. This holiday tradition was started back in 1985 and as of 2015 is still going as strong as ever. I love this park during the year, but it really is a special place to be during the holidays. It is truly one of the most popular seasonal events you will find in this park, and I was lucky enough to experience the magic firsthand over the years. Everything you need for

you and your family to get into the holiday spirit can be found right here at Six Flags Over Texas and during "Holiday in the Park." From more than a million twinkling lights, holiday shows, toasty campfires, delicious hot cocoa, and roller coasters to the nearly sixty-foot Holiday Tree of Trees, Santa Land, to having the kids see Santa Claus it's a destination location for the whole family. They even have a snow hill that you can sled down! Special moments and thrills await you at North Texas's largest holiday festival running until December 20th. You can also visit their website at sixflags.com/overtexas/index.aspx.

12. **SeaWorld San Antonio Theme Park** in San Antonio, Texas and Orlando, Florida. Sea World's San Antonio's Christmas Celebration select dates, are from November 17 to December 31. There you see many holiday attractions like Shamu Claus, as well as Santa Claus who will be on hand to greet guests. Special shows will include *"Clyde & Seamore's Countdown to Christmas,"* featuring the park's sea lions, as well as *"A Sesame Street Christmas."* Candy Cane Forest will be decked out with over one-hundred thousand lights. In Florida, you will find many of the same holiday shows, and there is also the Polar Express experience, and the Sea of Trees, which is a synchronized light show set to holiday music. Shamu's *Christmas Miracles is a* great holiday themed production as well. You and the kids will just love it! You can visit their website at seaworldparks.com.

13. **Legoland** in Lakeland, Florida. Now this is one surefire place to take the kids during the best time of the year. You will find a cool thirty-foot Lego Christmas tree on site and, of course, appearances from Santa Claus all day. You will find many specialized events at the park with nightly fireworks over Lake Eloise. There is a Lego Santa scavenger hunt in Miniland USA. The Christmas Bricktacular and Kids' New Years Eve event is held on weekends in December starting on December 26th and running until New Years Eve. Legoland is all about kids and this a great place to take them during the holidays. You can visit their website at Legoland.com

14. **Sesame Place.** A Very Furry Christmas in Langhorne (near Philadelphia) is open from November 17 to December 31. The park is just outside of Philadelphia and easily accessible from major highways. Not only do they have a great little Halloween event, but their Christmas shows are some of the best around especially for the little ones. The event includes a parade, shows such as *"Elmo's Christmas Wish,"* loads of decorated trees, and some of the park's rides (if the weather cooperates) stay open for everyone. This is not a big park, but one of my favorites, and the kids just love it. You can visit their website at http://www.sesameplace.com/sesame2/.

The Best Amusement Parks to Hit for Halloween

By the light of day, America's biggest amusement parks entertain families in friendly, wholesome ways. But be warned that at night, in October, it is a very, very different experience. Amusement parks spend millions of dollars to make sure their guests are scared out of their wits and everyone has a great time. Whether it's spooky haunted houses, scary pathways, crazy ghoul shows, or riding thrill rides "in the dark."Here are just a few of the best parks that celebrate this holiday. Events do change from year to year but even with these changes these are my top pics for the Halloween Season. Enjoy!

1. **Fright Fest (Six Flags).** Fright Fest is not just a name, but a business for Six Flags Entertainment Corporation. One of the best parks to deliver the scares can be found in New Jersey at Six Flags Great Adventure. This Fright Fest features thrills and chills. If you arrive before dark, enjoy some rides and not—so-scary shows. As night falls, be sure to make your way over to the Awakening, a show that marks the transformation of the park as the nighttime creatures "awaken". Terror trails and attractions change from year to year. Some of my favorites have included Shipwreck Cove - where zombies have come ashore; Wasteland, a mutant-filled forest; Voodoo Island, a perennial favorite,; the Manor, home to (where my daughter performed); and Insanity. The shows are amazing here, and on top of that, you will also enjoy and experience the biggest thrill rides at the park. Ya can't beat it. The park runs on select nights through October 28. I do love (and hate) to watch Circus of Thrills. You got to see it to believe what you are seeing here.

2. **Halloween Horror Nights (Universal Studio's).** Universal Studios knows movie magic, and they ain't too bad at scaring people as well. Universal Studios Orlando's Halloween Horror Nights is a true thrill seeker's dream. The fun of these live shows is amazing. The scary street encounters and haunted houses themed around AMC's hit horror show *"The Walking Dead"* are fun to watch. Alice Cooper's nightmares and the popular video game Silent Hill can also be quite intense. Word of warning: this is not a place for young tikes or those who are squeamish. Held on most nights throughout October, this hard-ticket event is now in its twenty-second year.

3. **Halloween Haunt (Knott's berry Farm).** Knott's Berry Farm in Buena Park, California, has been known as the place to be for the Halloween season for almost four decades. This is the park that most everyone tries to emulate. Sure there are zombies, clowns, witches, and monsters, but there are a few things you won't find anywhere else. An attraction based on the cult film *Evil Dead* sends guests into a cabin in the woods where they discover the "Book of the Dead" and attempt an escape with a truly twisted take on the Pinocchio tale. In this, the marionette seeks human flesh to cover its wooden skeleton. Let's hope it's not yours.

4. **Phantom Fright Nights (Kennywood).** One of the nicest parks I have visited is also one that doesn't do a bad job for Halloween as well. Crazy ghouls, goblins, and witches roam the pathways at this fabulous park in West Mifflin, Pennsylvania. When darkness overtakes this Pittsburgh suburb, the Raging Rapids area becomes Voodoo Bayou, the Dancing Waters transforms into a creepy cemetery, and one of the best dark ride attractions around becomes the Haunted Ark. You can visit Kennywood and this amazing park every Friday and Saturday night through October 27.

5. **Halloween Haunt (Kings Island).** Now one of the best places you can find yourself in is the city of Cincinnati in a park affectionately called Kings Island. When I say that they pull out all the stops here, I really mean it. Most parks will train their actors to do a great job, but here, you have a cast of murderous characters that are second to none. There is nothing like riding the Beast on a fright night or being chased around by the most realistic chainsaws you will see at an amusement park. During the day, the park is great for the family and teens, but at night, watch out! A blood-spattered meat cutter haunts the Slaughter House, while the twisted Madame Fatale has been released after a decade of incarceration to curate a museum of oddities and wax. These are just a few of the many attractions and shows you will find at this park. Halloween Haunt takes place on Friday and Saturday nights through October 27.

6. **Hallo Weekends (Cedar Point).** Cedar Point (Sandusky, Ohio) is known as the Roller Coaster Mecca for the thrill ride community, but they are also known for throwing some pretty cool (and scary) Halloween events. From some very realistic wax figures, creepy clowns, numerous mazes, and their first-class shows, you are sure in for a real treat. One of several amazing thrills you will find throughout this theme park. While there, you can walk the dark corridors or stumble through an eerie cornfield populated with denizens waiting to pounce. HalloWeekends runs Friday, Saturday, and Sunday nights through October 28, and it's a great place for you to bring in this special holiday!

7. **Mickey's Not-So-Scary Halloween Party (Disney).** At most Halloween special events, you will find attractions that were created for those who want to be scared out of their wits. Not here. Walt Disney World's version of the nighttime Halloween transformation is a mild, kid-friendly affair where families dress up in costumes and trick or treat at selected locations around the Magic Kingdom. The main event here is, of course, a parade, and this one is called the Boo-to-You parade. Of course there will also be Disney characters in costume and a special fireworks display called HalloWishes. Like their Christmas event, this one is going to be very crowded. However, with the entire park being open and Disney magic in the air, it is still well worth it.

8. **Hershey Park in the Dark (Hershey Park).** Okay, we all know Hershey Park is the sweetest place on the planet. It also has some of the best rides and attraction that you will ever find. So how do they stack up when it comes to Halloween events? I'd say quite well. There is always so much to do here, and if you have children twelve or under, they can gather sweets at Hershey's Chocolate World (which is right next door to the park) and continue into the Treatville area. Yes, it gets a little cold in the hills of Pennsylvania, but you will still find fifty rides and almost a dozen roller coasters that will be open during this event, which runs until just before Halloween. At night, creatures of the night let visitors get up close and personal with them, and while with them, you can play with the snakes, turtles, alligators, and, yes, even spiders...

9. **The Count's Halloween Spooktacular (Sesame Place).** Just a stone throw away from Philadelphia, Pennsylvania, you will find a great place to take the kids for Halloween. You will not find any spooky characters, no scary music, no strobe-lit haunted houses, or eerie cornfields to try and run through. No clowns for those who are afraid of them, and of course, no one to chase your kids around with chainsaws. What you will find here are smiles on the faces of your little ones as they celebrate this holiday in a different way. You can enjoy walking with the kids through mazes, seeing several kid-friendly shows, and experiencing a

character hayride that your family will just love. There's is also Ernie's Rubber Duckie Costume Party, which is a hit at this park as well. It's a fun place for the kids, and the park is open on weekends until October 28th.

The Top Ten Water Parks Around the Nation

In addition to Amusement parks, thrill rides, and roller coasters, I also would like to mention that our nation has some of the best water parks around. Many are attached with established amusement parks, which, in the end, actually saves them and you. It's smart because for years now, I have been telling people to stay out of the amusement parks during the heat of the day. Midday is a great time to hit the pool or a water park and even better if that park is owned by that same amusement park. For a few bucks more, you can actually buy a season pass ticket that includes the rides, shows, attraction, and a water park to boot. What better way to cool off during the day than to take advantage of this? Also, these days you will find thrill rides at these water parks that will rival just about every ride you will find at your local amusement park. So I say if you can try out a water park on your next vacation, why not incorporate both amusement and water parks together? Here are my favorites in North America.

1. **Schlitterbahn Water Park** in New Braunfel, Texas, and several other locations). In my mind, one of the world's biggest secrets has got to be Schlitterbahn Water Park with several locations that includes the New Braunfel location and another just north of Galveston, Texas. What can you say about a park that seems to have every water attraction that you can think of? I mean, they have everything! Not surprisingly, Schlitterbaum has paved the way to creating the best water rides around. In fact, it was Schlitterbahn that opened the first ever uphill water ride back in 1994. It was called Dragon Blaster. Since then, they have led the way and, over the years, added several other uphill water rides like the Master Blaster and the Family Blaster. The Master Blaster, in particular, has often been voted as the best water ride in the US by many different publications. Open from mid-May through mid-September, this park has over sixty-five acres of crazy entertainment including seventeen water rides and over three miles of tubing. If you like uphill water coasters, Schlitterbahn has three of them. A fantastic soothing lazy river and a kids' section of the park that is second to none. In the kids section of these parks, you will find most of them padded and not just kid friendly, but it's also adult friendly as well. Still most of the great rides and activities there are designed for children and those who are young at heart. The younger kids will love areas such as Sliden Polywog, Kinderhaven, and "Squirt 'n' Slidein" just to name a few. The parking is (and always has been) free. Like most water parks, lifejackets are provided and are not optional on many of their high intensity rides. There are plenty of lounge chairs (thank the Lord!) that come with open umbrellas (very important item to have in Texas) for when you need a break and for those who prefer to watch. And like most first-rate water parks, it is well worth it to get a cabana for a few dollars more. The food is also quite good, and if you get there early enough, you might just be able to experience the entire park during your stay. If you love water rides, good food, and getting wet, then this destination park located in Texas should be on your list of things to do on vacation.

2. **Typhoon Lagoon (Disney)** - in Orlando, Florida. Well, it is safe to say that no one does it like Disney and that can also be said for their water parks as well. This fabulous park features incredible theming and great rides like Crush 'n' Gusher, Gang Plank Falls, and so many other rides to choose from. It's almost sixty acres of pure fun, all wrapped up with Disney magic. Disney's Typhoon Lagoon features attractions for the entire family—including thrill rides, chill rides, family-style raft rides, areas for little ones, and plenty of tropical lounging for us grownups. This water park opened on June 1, 1989, and still has the world's largest outdoor wave pool around. The theme of the park is the "Disney Legend" where a typhoon (called by

the name of Hurricane in the west) wreaked havoc on what can be described as a tropical paradise. Anyone who has ever experienced a typhoon or hurricane (I was hit by Sandy a few years ago and once was enough) knows what a storm like that can do. At the time of this writing, the centerpiece of the park is "Miss Tilly," a shrimp boat impaled upon a mountain named "Mount Mayday" and is clearly visible from just about anywhere in the park. Mount Mayday erupts from a fifty-foot geyser of water each and every half hour and truly is fun to watch. The park's mascot is "Lagoona Gator", who is related to Blizzard Beach's mascot, Ice Gator. At Typhoon Lagoon, you can also swim with the sharks at "Shark Reef.' There you can enjoy the underwater world and see some incredible saltwater sea life up close. If you want and if you're courageous enough, you can have the opportunity to actually swim with leopard and bonnethead sharks, stingrays, and schools of colorful tropical fish in their home environment. If you ever wanted to know what it's really like to be an extra in *"Finding Nemo"*, you have come to the right spot. The reef itself surrounds an overturned sunken tanker. Less adventurous guests, or anyone who just wants to get a spectacular view of the sharks without actually getting wet, can enter the tanker and view the undersea creatures through little portholes. Everything you will need to go into the Shark Reef tank like masks, snorkels, and lifejackets are provided to all guests and are free. As you may have guessed, children under age ten must be accompanied by an adult. Typhoon Lagoon is by far the most visited water park in the world with over two million guests visiting the park yearly. It's truly a fun place to be with family and friends.

3. **Dollywood's Splash Country,** in Pigeon Forge, Tennessee. If you like down home and country water fun (and who doesn't), then you have to head east from Nashville and head to Splash Country. Opened in May 2001 in a little town called Pigeon Forge, Tennessee, Dolly's Splash Country was a welcome addition to Dollywood Company's theme parks. They also held a special contest to come up with the best original name, and I am told there were over sixteen thousand entries to the contest. The winner was a gentleman by the name of John Torres, and no, I'm not sure if he met Dolly after that. The park was built around the natural and very beautiful terrain that holds the twenty-five acres of mountain area that just happens to be right next to (you guessed it) Dollywood theme park. The park was a twenty-million-dollar investment by the Dollywood Company and is amazing! In this water park, you will find twenty-three of the most creative water (and thrill) rides around. Experience white water rafting at its finest on Big Bear Plunge, and the corkscrew tunnels of Mountain Scream are just amazing. There is also the Cascades, a lagoon-style pool that has more than twenty-five different and exciting elements that kids can explore. It also features a giant rock grotto (sorry, Ariel) with a centerpiece of cascading waterfall with an active geyser that shoots water twenty feet into the air. They even have two interactive children's playground areas. They also have the Lazy River and Little Creek falls where you will surely find many family fun activities that can be experienced by the entire family. Unlike other water parks and due to its location, Dollywood Splash County also has *many* shaded areas for you to escape the heat. For those who love to shop and eat, Splash Country has many fine restaurants and concession stands with a variety of choices. You can shop until the park closes to get those souvenirs that will make your trip even more memorable, The Park opens in late May and runs all the way to around mid-September. If you really want to experience great water rides and Southern hospitality at its best, look no further than Dollywood's Splash Country.

4. **Raging Waters** in San Jose, California. Raging Waters is actually three water parks, and they are located in Sacramento, San Dimas, and San Jose, California. Together they are without a doubt the largest water park system in the state of California. The three parks are owned by Palace Entertainment and each contains very different attractions. Because of their location in Northern California, they are generally closed during the winter months. Of all three, the San Jose location's twenty plus acres make it Northern California's largest water park and offers millions of gallons of family fun and attractions, including one of the newest rides called Dragon's Den. Raging Waters features thrilling high-speed slides and family attractions like a fantastic 350,000-gallon Wave Pool and the "Pirate's Cove"-an interactive themed water fort. This particular location has a nice feel to it, and I can truthfully say that the food, the people, and the California culture make this one of my favorite water parks across the country. Raging Waters is located on the grounds of beautiful Lake Cunningham Regional Park in San Jose and is just a stone's throw away from major highways in the area. Raging Waters (as a whole or separately) is always ranked high in many surveys and always shows up in the Travel Channel's top ten list of best water parks nationwide. I know I talk about RW almost every time the media brings up water parks.

5. **Six Flags Hurricane Harbor** in Jackson, New Jersey. Six Flags Great Adventure is already home of the largest amusement park and a fantastic safari park to boot and they have now added one of the best and most exciting water parks called Hurricane Harbor. Hurricane Harbor is a forty-five-acre water park with over twenty-five major water rides and attractions set in a tropically themed island hideaway. A 42,000-square-foot wave pool (it's a lot of fun too) that contains almost a million gallons of water and runs three to five foot waves every fifteen minutes. Being within an hour's drive to the Atlantic Ocean, it is in fact the closest thing to being at the shore. Adventure River Tube Ride is a 2,150-foot-long one with waterfalls and rapids going every which way but loose .The dual Family Raft Rides are rafts that hold up to six people adventuring down a winding path, which I would compare to a level 3 white water rafting experience (I like that word!). Speed slides are three body slides that flip you over at around forty miles per hour through dark tunnels and at forty-degree angles. There are many more fabulous attractions to mention, but I could spend all day to do that. For the younger ones, they have an interactive family water lagoon with over seventy water activities including climbing nets, water blasters, and tipping buckets, which soak you every five to ten minutes if you let it. Numerous food courts, shops, changing areas, restrooms, and showers are located throughout the park. Hurricane Harbor has a separate entrance, parking area, and admission fees from their amusement park, and combination passes are available. Again, coming here is a great way to escape the heat during midday before heading back to the adjacent park.

6. **Noah's Ark** in Wisconsin Dells, Wisconsin. This one just happens to be America's largest water park. Residing on over seventy acres in the heart of Wisconsin Dells, Noah's Ark truly has everything you could ever want or imagine from a water park. With a total of forty-one (count um, forty-one) waterslides, two huge wave pools, two fantastic lazy rivers, great children's water play areas, Paradise Lagoon activity pool, two group amusement rides, three arcades, and an eighteen-hole mini golf course, you won't ever be bored while you are at this park. One of America's largest and longest water coasters resides here as well. Black Anaconda is in the park, and if you really like water rides with a kick, you will just love this one. Recently they also added a new ride called "Time Warp", which is the world's largest family bowl ride ever created! I can't think of a better place for the kids to have fun with so many areas devoted to just younger children. Whether it is Tadpole Bay Kiddy Play Zone, the

"Endless River" Kiddie Area, or the Big Kahuna Kiddie Area, there are countless slides, fountains, swings, and water to keep everyone pretty busy. Also where else than at Noah's Ark can you also find a 4D drive-in theatre. Pretty cool stuff. You will also find plenty of places to go shopping and many first-rate restaurants with gourmet desserts and much more. The cast of the Middle is ever present here in the Midwest, and the people are all just so friendly! Noah's Ark is continually evolving, offering the most variety of water rides anywhere in the nation, and they are usually open from Labor Day until Memorial Day. If you tried the rest, you should visit one of the best and that would be Noah's Ark located in Wisconsin Dells, Wisconsin. It's a destination park and one that will provide you with many long-term family memories.

7. **Water Country USA,** in Williamsburg, Virginia. They might not be the biggest water park around, but I can tell you honestly, they truly have some of the best water rides around. Billed as the mid-Atlantic's largest water park in that they recently added a new epic drop slide called Vanish Point. The seventy-five-foot drop is extremely exciting, and it now joins the forty-plus acres of pools, children's play areas, lazy rivers, and water rides that make up Water Country USA. The park also includes "Rock 'n' Roll Island," featuring two football fields (over six hundred feet) of body slides, a seven-hundred -foot lazy river, and a 9,000-square-foot pool all set to a 1950s and a 60s surf theme so you are guaranteed to have fun. For the guests, you will also find over 1,500 free lounge chairs, which is something where most parks fall short. You can also rent sixteen exclusive private cabanas. The park is owned by SeaWorld Parks and Entertainment, a division of the Blackstone Group and is just a few miles away from Busch Gardens Williamsburg where most of the parks patrons go after they visit this magnificent water park. Multipark passes are available, and a parking pass at Water Country USA is valid for same-day entry to Busch Gardens Williamsburg. The food is great, and at their shops, you can get just about everything you will need for an enjoyable day at the park. Water Country USA is open from mid-May until the first week of September, and if you love both amusement parks and water parks, this is a destination area for you to visit.

8. **Morey's Pier Raging Waters** in Wildwood, New Jersey. This water park might not make the top ten list for many people, but it sure does make it on mine. For me, it isn't really the summer without visiting Morey's Pier Raging Waters. It is actually two water parks adjacent to Morey's Pier Amusement Park on the Wildwoods Pier. Originally opened in 1985, the parks have over ten million gallons of water combined with over fifty slides, tube rides, and attractions. Just a couple of hundred feet away, you will also find the Atlantic Ocean as a nice backdrop to your Morey's Pier Adventure. For the younger set, Morey's offers two water areas: Hydroworks, -an interactive water play area and Shipwreck Shoals, a 5,000 square-foot pirate adventure featuring water-shooting cannons and waterslides. If you start to get waterlogged, you can take a break and play a round of miniature golf at their award winning eighteen-hole adventure golf course complete with waterfalls, hand-carved rockwork, and scenic landscaping. When the hunger sets in, they have beach grills, which will prepare a variety of foods, and have poolside waitress service. The parks features numerous gift shops, lifeguards, lockers, showers, and changing facilities. Information for Morey's Amusement Park can be found at Amusement Parks in New Jersey.com Once on the boardwalk, you can take the tramcar up and down the two-and–a-half-mile boardwalk to get the most of your Raging Waters' experience.

9. **Water World** in Denver, Colorado. Water World in Denver Colorado is still one of America's largest family water parks, and guess what? It's located just fifteen minutes north of downtown Denver. When you get there, look for this beautiful park that can be found on sixty-four beautifully landscaped acres of fun. It's America's second largest water park behind Noah's Ark Water Park in Wisconsin Dells, Wisconsin. Water World has been open for almost thirty years, and it features the biggest variety of attractions (over forty) in America from Wally World for the tots to Voyage to the Center of the Earth for the entire family, Water World can boast having more family tube rides than any other water park around. Thrill rides of every shape and size are in abundance as well. The park has several unique water attractions with one of the most notable called "Screamin Mimi." A ride where guests take board-type vehicles down a roller coaster-like track, reaching speeds of thirty miles per hour before landing in a pool and bouncing across the water. Another ride is called the "Space Bowl," and this one sends riders down a slide, and it opens into a circular bowl, which drops out into a pool of water. The park is clean, and there are many picnic areas around for the family to choose from. Something that is usually hard to come by is shade at water parks, but I am happy to report this one has many shaded areas, covered pavilions along with grass areas to just stretch out. The park has not one but two wave pools, and they both are very crowded much of the time. The park first opened in 1979 and is open from Memorial Day through Labor Day.

10. **White Water** in Atlanta, Georgia. Six Flags White Water is a seventy-acre water park located northwest of Atlanta, Georgia. First opened in 1984 as White Water Atlanta, the park became part of the Six Flags family of parks in 1999. Today, it is part of Six Flags Over Georgia, and the two parks usually cross promote together. This is a great idea and one that most parks do in order to get more guests to their parks. Like an amusement park, Six Flags White Water is made up of five different sections, each with a number of different attractions. The thing I like about White Water is that this park is always clean and the staff is always there to give you a great experience. The staff is trained well and incidents at the park are very few and far between. Atlanta is also a beautiful city, and there is just so much to do in the area. This is why I say this is a destination water park that you should definitely put on your bucket list.

Non Roller Coaster Adventures Worth Mentioning

There are many great roller coasters out there, but I thought I would add another section here. What about those thrill rides (that we all go on) that are not classified as roller coasters but are just downright thrilling? Those rides may not have rails to ride on, but they will still thrill us and scare us all at the same time. There are many out there, and we all have our favorites. Rides like Tower of Terror and the new Zumanjao: Drop of Doom come to mind for me, but I'm sure you all can mention a few that are not on this list. These are simply the ones that made my short list. You would literally need to write another book to name them all. In this chapter you will find just a few worth mentioning, especially if you haven't already experienced them. These thrill rides are listed in no particular order.

1. **Extreme Supernova** at Six Flags Magic Mountain. It's not a roller coaster, but you'll have fun seated with fifteen other bold riders and are loaded into the giant pendulum-shaped structure. Suspended from the axis above, you'll face outward as the floor literally drops right below you. You'll first complete several back and forth swings, high and low, elevating you to what seems like (but not quite) a near-vertical back and forth sway for what seems like an eternity. The thrill ride plays on your mind as well while you watch others as it sways right over your head. This ride will spin you almost upside down in countless gut-wrenching inverted spins that are sure to make you sit up and take notice. The Extreme Supernova offers fantastic inverted views of the park and Splashwater Kingdom as well. But you better look quick because as you hang up in the air and twist, the view changes quite rapidly... You'll love it!

2. **Zumanjaro: Drop of Doom** at Six Flags Great Adventure is a ride hard to describe. Sure it's a drop tower, taller than any before, but it is indeed in my mind so much more. First of all, your eight-person gondola will take off up the 415-foot structure in approximately thirty seconds. Now that's pretty fast! This is a good thing because if you had longer to think about this, I'm sure many wouldn't do it. You'll pause for a moment at the top and get the most outrageous view of the park and safari. If you're lucky, you may get to see the Kingda Ka train as it heads up the side of the tower and above you. But don't take your eyes off this ride, because at the moment you least expect it, it happens, or doesn't, because as your heart races, you seem to still continue to wait for the bottom to drop out. After what seems like forever and it feels like it does, the plummet occurs and it is fast! Reaching speeds of over ninety miles per hour. Everything soon becomes a blur as gravity pulls your gondola downwards, reaching ground level again in less than ten seconds. Almost before you have a chance to scream. The lines are long, but I assure you it's well worth it. What a drop!

3. **Insanity the Ride (Stratosphere Tower)** in Las Vegas, Nevada. It might not be a roller coaster, but it is a ride that you surely will not quickly forget. I know I won't. Let me say that this ride is not recommended for weak hearted individuals, and if you hate heights, better not try this one. Insanity the Ride is a truly mind-blowing experience! Picture this massive arm extending out sixty-four feet over the edge of the Stratosphere Tower. (This just happens to be the tallest building in Vegas.) At a height of over nine hundred feet, this Vegas ride will spin you and several other passengers right over the edge with nothing below you at high speed with 3 g's pushed into your face. You'll be propelled up to a top angle of seventy degrees and then you look straight down when the seat changes direction. When you do that and if you are brave enough to keep your eyes open, you'll be looking at nothing but open air and a

breathtaking view of historic downtown Las Vegas. Experience Insanity at night, and you would have gone pretty far to overcome your wildest fear. Something you will never forget and one that will make that Vegas trip one to remember.

4. **Test Track (Disney EPCOT)** in Orlando, Florida. When at Disney World, one of the best attractions you simply *must do* (Stacey Aswad would agree) is Test Track. The ride is a simulated trek through the rigorous testing procedures that General Motors uses to evaluate their new concept cars. The ride builds up from simple high-speed skid breaking tests to a high-speed drive around the exterior of the enormous attraction. Because of some incidents, the ride closed for refurbishment in the spring of 2012 and reopened in December that same year. Test Track officially opened on March 17, 1999, after many, and I mean many, technical delays. It was over a year from its planned opening when this ride became fully operational. The ride had replaced the aging World of Motion and still uses part of the same building. The ride illustrates what goes into assessing an automobile's ground performance in very adverse conditions. The highlight of the attraction was (and still is) the speed trial on a track around the exterior of the building while achieving top speeds of over sixty-five miles per hour. This would make Test Track one of the fastest rides you will find at Walt Disney World. After the ride, guests can see how their car did overall, and there is also a great place to buy souvenirs in the shop after your ride experience. One should know that the line for this attraction gets pretty long, so it would be advisable to Fast Pass this one when planning your thrill ride experience.

5. **Harry Potter and the Forbidden Journey** at Universal Studios in Orlando, Florida. For those of you who loved the *Harry Potter* movies, you will truly love this 3D attraction. Harry Potter and the Forbidden Journey is a dark ride located in The Wizarding World of Harry Potter themed areas of Islands of Adventure and at Universal Studios Japan in Osaka, Japan. You know you're in for a treat when you enter through the towering castle gates and make your way down the familiar passageways and corridors of (you guessed it) Hogwarts School of Witchcraft and Wizardry. It's like you have been transported into the movie, and before the ride ends, you'll visit iconic locations such as Dumbledore's office, the Defense Against the Dark Arts classroom, the Gryffindor common room, and much more. Then look out! At this point you'll be ready to soar above the castle grounds as you join Harry and his friends on an unforgettably thrill ride experience! This amazing attraction (like everything Universal does these days) uses groundbreaking, state-of-the-art technology to create a one-of-a-kind ride experience and one you and the family will never forget. I highly recommend it, and if you are staying at one of the many Universal Studios hotels, lines will be a bad memory from the past.

6. **Big Shot, (Stratosphere Tower)** in Las Vegas, Nevada. Now if you really want to do something very different, then this ride is right up your alley. Sure there are many towers around, but I can assure you, they are nothing like this one. Built in 1996, Big Shot is the world's highest amusement/thrill ride. Even though the tower may only be 160 feet tall (small in size next to the newest ones out there), this particular tower is actually built at the top deck of the Stratosphere Hotel. This makes it a 1,000-foot-tall marvel. Big Shot is a pneumatically powered tower ride, created by S and S Worldwide that features a rapid ascent from an elevation of 921-foot mark to 1,081feet. The ride accelerates to forty five miles per hour (seventy-two kilometers per hour). The ride generates 4gs during the rapid ascent and is pretty short at about a half a minute, but it is well worth it. I recommend riding this puppy at night. If you're afraid of heights, this one is not for you. You will be able to really get a bird's eye view of the Las Vegas Strip and one you will not soon forget.

7. **Mission Space (Disney Epcot)** in Orlando, Florida. This ride opened in August of 2003 and is still one of the best five=and-a half minute rides you will find at Disney World. Mission Space is a centrifugal motion simulator thrill ride, and I am told by my astronaut friends that it accurately simulates what an astronaut might experience aboard a spacecraft on a mission to Mars. From the high g-force of liftoff to the hypersleep one might experience, this ride is actually very intense (it's actually set up like an eggbeater with pods) and, in the past, has actually caused injury, so you might want to also take this into account when riding it. You also have the option to just experience the visual aspect of this ride if you choose. If you choose the intense version, here are a few tips you might need to get through this ride and have a positive experience. First, always, and I mean always, keep your head back and your eyes focused on the video screen in front of you. You will be subjected to extreme g forces, and if you turn your head away from the screen or close your eyes, you might also become a little disoriented and develop motion sickness. As I mentioned earlier, this ride also offers a less intense 'experience, and this means choosing the ride that bypasses the centrifuge (spinning action) of Mission: Space. Just let a cast member know which version you prefer, and you'll be directed to the appropriate queue line. I love this ride and even the real Astronauts who were invited to test it before it opened did as well. This is another ride at Epcot that you will need to Fast Pass if you plan on seeing most of the park that day.

8. **Revenge of the Mummy (Universal Studios)** in Orlando, Florida (and elsewhere). If you truly like dark rides, then you will love this one. Based on the movie *the Mummy*, this is not just a simulation ride, but it is also a full-fledged roller coaster as well. The original Revenge of the Mummy opened on May 21, 2004, in Florida. Revenge of the Mummy roller coaster uses three linear Induction motors launches, to propel riders from a complete standstill to speeds reaching. Forty Five miles per hour. The Queue line and preshow is a nice start to this attraction. Guests enter the complex by entering the massive Museum of Antiquities facade, browsing through the film setup of a fictional sequel entitled "Revenge of the Mummy." You will find that the film's props, molds, and concept drawings are on display inside. The inside queue morphs into a 1940s archaeological dig inside an Egyptian tomb, where guests climb to the second floor to board plain but interesting mine cars utilizing individual lap bars for their safety. After that, the ride begins. Overall, the track is 2,200 foot long and is intense even though it has no inversions. There are some pretty high banked turns and at one point, a fifty-degree angle of descent is experienced. There is a track like a roller coaster and I will tell you, it does move rather quickly down the track. When you add the incredible special effects, the ride becomes unbelievable. You will find several versions of this ride, including Universal Studios Hollywood, and Universal Studios Singapore, but my favorite will always be the original at Universal Studios, in Orlando, Florida. This attraction is a high-speed thrill ride and can be pretty disorientating for some, so keep those eyes open at all times. For your money, this is one ride you can't pass up.

9. **Soarin' at Walt Disney World.** Soarin' is located both in Disneyland and at my favorite spot, the Land Pavilion at Epcot. It is a pretty realistic motion-base simulator attraction that combines both physical motion, in-theater effects and an amazing IMAX film backdrop to recreate the feeling of flight. As a pilot, I can tell you they come pretty close to the real thing. The attraction sends riders through in an amazing flyover above such iconic structures like the Golden Gate Bridge and beautiful California for a bird's-eye view of the rich landscape and topography this state provides. "Soarin Over California" was so popular in that state it was only a matter of time that Disney World would also have this attraction as well.

No one does it like Disney, and this ride successfully combines cinematic artistry and winning state-of-the-art motion base technology. When you enter, you are placed in a ride that literally lifts you forty feet inside a giant projection screen dome and completely surrounds you with amazing images of the state of California, and except for a few quick scenes where the picture gets a little blurry (and some pretty noticeable scene changes), you get to see much of California from the air. It's a scenic tour over the Golden Gate Bridge, the Redwood forests, Napa Valley, Yosemite and other iconic places in the Golden State and ends with a night shot of Sleeping Beauty's Castle. The flight experience also feels so real due to the simulation of sweeping winds and smells of the orange blossoms and pine trees that you really feel like you're actually there. It's a ride that is fun for the entire family and one that, no matter how many times you ride it, never loses its wonder and excitement.

10. **Tower of Terror,** at Disney's Hollywood Studios in Orlando, Florida, and Anaheim, California. What can one say about the Tower of Terror? We have all been on drop towers, and they are indeed a lot of fun, but what if you take that simple idea and expanded upon it? What if you put an entire story together (in this case, the popular television series *The Twilight Zone*) and created an attraction like no other? Bingo! The original version of the attraction opened at Disney's Hollywood Studios in July 1994 and was the basis of the 1997 made-for-television movie *Tower of Terror* starring Steve Guttenberg. Since then, this attraction has been placed in several other locations including Disney California Adventure, Tokyo Disney Sea, and Walt Disney Studios Park in Paris. The ride takes guests in the old dilapidated "Hollywood Hotel" and presents riders with a cool (but fictional) back story in which people mysteriously have disappeared from a hotel elevator under the influence of some kind of supernatural element. This occurs in the late 1930's, but the ghosts of this place are still very alive and well. The tower itself is over two hundred feet tall, making it one of the tallest attractions you will find in any of these parks. After an amazing queue and preshow (I don't want to ruin it for you), guests enter the hotel and are told their room isn't quite ready for them. Eventually they are led to the elevators. Everything in this hotel has apparently been preserved ever since it closed on that fateful night all those years ago. Before the drop, you will head to certain floors with the one and only Rod Serling (host of the TV series *Twilight Zone*) appearing to guests. You won't find just those on these new drop rides, and that's a good thing. Top speed of the drops is just over thirty miles per hour, but it seems you are falling a lot faster. However, if you don't like that negative g feeling, this might not be the best ride for you, but it is indeed one that I truly enjoy. When you add the imagination and illusion that this ride provides for their guests, it's truly a fan favorite for most!

11. **Texas SkyScreamer,** at Six Flags Over Texas. We all know that there are many swing rides out there, but this one takes the cake. At four-hundred feet in height, this unique ride opened on May 25, 2013. SkyScreamer was designed by Funtime, a very popular ride manufacturer, and since 2011, Six Flags has installed SkyScreamers in eight of their parks with this one in Texas being one of the tallest thus far. Riders are carried aloft in two-person swing-like chairs attached to a rotating gondola mounted on a central tower. When the gondola reaches the top of the tower, riders are swung in a wide circle at speeds of about forty miles per hour. The views you get at these dizzying heights are amazing, but if you don't like heights, it might not be the best ride to experience for you. The ride is both a thrill ride but, at the same time, not that intense, so it is a great ride for the entire family. The ride can be run forward as well as backward, although at this location, it only moves in a forward direction. It may not be a roller coaster, but this type of ride does attract a great following. Unfortunately with only thirty two seats available during each ride, the lines can get quite long, waiting to get a spot at the top.

12. **Supreme Scream**, at Knott's Berry Farm, in California is a vertical ascending and descending amusement thrill ride, and it is a doozy. Designed and manufactured by the experts in this area, S&S Worldwide, it opened to the general public on July of 1998 and, at 312 feet high, was the tallest turbo drop-type amusement ride in the world. The ride actually has three individual towers arranged with what can be described as a triangular footprint. The actual drop is 252 feet and drops its passengers at a top speed of fifty-five miles per hour, exposing riders to over four positive gs of force and a few negative g's to boot. Supreme Scream carries twelve riders per tower in octagonal carriages upward, pausing for what seems like forever before it drops you rather quickly and without warning. You actually fall faster than a freefall due to the fact that this pneumatic system accelerates a passenger faster than gravity. It's a great ride and one you should try out when visiting this park.

13. **The Amazing Adventures of Spider-Man,** at Islands of Adventure, in Orlando, Florida, and Universal Studios Japan. Now if you are looking for the best dark ride on the planet, the one that pretty much set the standard for all dark rides would be Spiderman. The Amazing Adventures of Spider-Man can also be found at Universal Studios Japan theme park. The ride first opened in1999, and this attraction combines special motion half-enclosed vehicles, state-of the art 3D projection, elaborate physical sets, and imagination that literally has run wild. The ride takes park guests, who are invited to be last-minute-reporters (for the *Daily Bugle*), into the crazy and exciting world of Marvel Comics and the one we all call Spider-Man. Guests board a ride vehicle called the Scoop for the *Daily Bugle*. The news reporters are told that the Sinister Syndicate has actually captured the Statue of Liberty and he has something called an antigravity gun. This evil group consists of some of Spider-Man's biggest enemies like Doctor Octopus, Electro, Scream, Hydroman, and Hobgoblin, and when they all get together, that's when the fun on this ride really begins.

The attraction took about three years to produce with many new technologies and techniques that were never used before. The Amazing Adventures of Spider-Man has been well received, winning several awards, and it looks like they are continuing to win the converted Golden Ticket Award for the Best Dark Ride. This ride, my friends, is the one that started the new generation of dark rides and one that you and the entire family will absolutely love. If you go on one attraction when you are in the parks that have this ride, one is all you will ever need.

14. **High Roller** is a 550-foot-tall, 520-foot–diameter "Giant" Ferris wheel located on the Las Vegas Strip in Paradise, Nevada. The wheel, which began construction in 2011, was created by Arup Engineering for Caesars Entertainment at a cost of over $550 million. It officially opened to customers in March 2014 and is now the world's tallest observation wheel. High Roller features twenty-eight spherical passenger cabins, which can carry up to forty passengers each, and is illuminated with dynamic multicolored LED light system that can be seen for many miles. High Roller is three yards or 9 feet taller than the 541-foot Singapore Flyer, making it the world's tallest observation wheel ever built (others include The Star of Nanchang at 535 feet, the London Eye, at 443 feet and rounding out the top five is the Orlando Eye at over 400 feet in height). It might interest you to know that High Roller was the name of a former roller coaster atop the Stratosphere Las Vegas tower. A ride that many truly loved. Following this tradition, this amazing wheel was built to achieve new heights, and it has succeeded famously toward that end. One revolution on this gigantic wheel takes about thirty minutes, so you might want to have the kids (and the adults) hit the restrooms before climbing aboard.

Tips for Families
When Traveling on Vacation

During my interviews on both television and radio, I am always asked questions on traveling and preparing for upcoming family vacations. The hosts usually ask me if there are any tips I can give one to make this experience as hassle free as possible. The answer is most definitely yes! When enjoying that trip to Disney World, Universal Studios, SeaWorld, Cedar Point, Busch Gardens, or any of the hundreds of amusement parks out there, I have talked about some things you will need to know. These tips are good for you and for the whole family and don't just apply to amusement park visitation. They apply to anyone who wants to travel and is looking to minimize the headaches that are associated with putting together memorable experiences. Hope you enjoy them.

Always book your trips well in advance.

Whether it is just taking a long trip by car or flying, it is imperative to always try and book your vacation well in advance of your travel date. I frequently travel on business (as well as pleasure) and one of the first things I do is make sure I know where I am going, and where I can find the best deals possible. It is true that in business situations you can't always do this, but when it comes to family vacations, it is absolutely a must! For a typical family vacation, I can't emphasize to you that it is best to book your trip at least eight to ten months in advance, especially if you are going to your favorite thrill ride destinations in-season. If it is off season, three to four months would be more of the norm. If you attempt to book your vacation in less time, the odds are quite good that your vacation will not be nearly as much fun as it should be. It will also be very time consuming for you and your family as well. Remember you are not just going on vacation, you are also making memories, and trust me, it all starts at the planning and booking stages. If you really want to get that hotel room, best flight, Disney character breakfast or dinner, you simply have to book early. Don't leave anything to chance. I have seen cases (in particular, Disney character breakfast or special theatre shows) where you absolutely must call at least a year in advance or more to get that perfect table. If you want to book a last-minute trip, you may be successful, but unfortunately, the odds are against you, and you are more likely to get a secondhand vacation as an end result. The last thing one wants to hear after a vacation are phrases like "next time" or "it would have been nice" thrown into the conversation. This is not how you want to remember your two weeks on vacation. Booking early saves headaches!

Do I use a travel agent or book direct?

Another question to ask yourself is when do i book this trip? Do I use a travel agent, go online, use a travel search engine, or call the airlines and hotels directly? It's a good question, and the answer quite frankly depends on a few factors. Like what are you planning on doing and how long in advance are you booking this dream vacation. It doesn't have to be just visiting an amusement or water park. If you are planning a cruise, I would definitely use a travel agent, especially if you are planning a trip that lasts longer than ten days. The reason for this is simple. These agents go on vacation tours themselves and experience firsthand what these packages have to offer. They know where the vacation pitfalls are or where the hidden away values can be found, so why not utilize their expertise when it comes to booking your vacation. Unfortunately, not everyone has the time or can afford to do this. For those that do not want to, the best way to plan a trip for these individuals is by using a travel search engine like Orbitz, Expedia, or Priceline.com. These online travel services can find you that affordable flight, hotel, and car much "faster" than any other options you might encounter. Most importantly by using them, they will also save you a lot of money. The last option is, of course, booking your trip yourself. Personally, I am not a big fan of doing this, but some people have gotten this down to a science. Take for example my wife. She can get a fantastic flight deal, hotel, car, and also book dinner shows and any other events that you can think of quicker than most travel search engines. One can find that there are always bargains that can be found online and at the last minute if you have the where-with-all, the time, and the patience that it takes to find these specials. One last thing to consider when you are booking your vacation is to make sure that you and your family are all on the same page. I have personally seen family vacations go down the tube very quickly because everyone had their own vision of what they were planning on doing during their trip. In the end, most vacations end up having people settle for something less than what they were expecting. This is why it is imperative for you to sit down with your family "first" and ask them what they really want to do. Don't assume that it is the same as what you and your travel agent had already planned out. Case in point. Let's say you like amusement parks. "Not a far stretch since this is the subject of my book" but your wife likes the beach and your kids love fishing. The goal in any memorable vacation is to find a place that will be able to cater to everyone. In the above example, certain places that come to mind would be the Jersey Shore's "Morey's Pier" and Cedar Point in Sandusky, Ohio. At both of these locations, you would not only find an amazing amusement park, but a fantastic beach and an ample amount of chances to fish as well.

Do I fly or drive?

This is a question that many people continue to argue about even to this day. There are some people who simply love to get in their car and drive and drive and drive some more. It might be a quick trip somewhere or a trek across the country. It doesn't matter to them, and they will always choose to drive themselves then have to deal with the airlines, bus depots, or crowed railways. Others (like myself) simply hate to drive long distances and that's my choice. If you have a job that demands you to drive from point A to point B, this is understandable. But when planning a vacation, I tend to use the five-hour rule. If your drive takes longer than five hours, I say fly! Sure it is great to get in your car and see the countryside and share with your family the different flavors and local culture that each city and town brings. But remember, some of your family members do not travel well, especially if they are just toddlers. Video games and DVD movies will only get you so far down the road. Not to mention the constant bathroom breaks along the way. Your family may not share your love of the open road, so keep that in mind when planning that special trip.

What to pack?

One of the most important "costly" and "cost efficient factors" you need to consider is how much should you bring with you (and for the family) when you take this trip. My standing answer to this is to always pack as lightly as possible. There are many that love to pack everything including the "kitchen sink", but in today's economy and with airlines charging for all checked baggage, it is no longer the smart way to go. A family of four can expect to pay a minimum of $250 just for one checked bag each. In most cases, that would be like paying for an additional passenger on your trip. My advice is to pack light and leave heavy. It would be advisable to try to tow as much carry-on luggage as possible. Fifteen shirts for a six to seven-day trip with pants and underwear included will take up a lot of room. Don't do that! When you times that by two, three, or four other individuals going on the trip, it does get quite costly. Let's not forget you are on vacation and, if you are like most of us, will be buying clothes and souvenirs during your trip anyway. Make sure to put these shirts (clothing) into rotation and wear them while you are on holiday. Also that coat that you would normally pack in your bag, why not wear it when you pass through the jet way, and if you have a garment bag on you, why not wrap it around your briefcase or pocketbook so you can make that two-items-per-person airline limit. Only surrender that additional piece of luggage if asked to. You can also save space by packing as little toiletries as possible. Let's not forget you are going to hotels that have complementary toiletry items, so why carry your own? It's these little things that will take all that space, and by removing them from your luggage will save you from having a costly and expensive headache.

Getting through security (remember, you're vacation starts here).

In my mind, any vacation starts as soon as you hit that airport, train station, or bus terminal. Sometimes it's hard to remember, but when flying, know that the TSA is actually on the same side as you are. Most of us remember that tragic day in September 2001 and because of this, the TSA's primary concern is for the safety of all passengers that fly and that means you and your family. They have a tough job to do, and by doing their jobs correctly, it can sometimes be a hassle for you and your family. Fortunately, there are several ways you can get around this. One of the first things that need to be done is to prepare your family to be mentally ready to go through that checkpoint. This specifically means don't wait until the last minute to get ready for your inspection. Make sure your jackets/sweaters and any metal items are off and put on the track. This means belts, rings, watches, cell phones, and of course, coins. There is nothing more embarrassing than to have people behind you throwing you the evil eye while they and the friendly people of the TSA wait. Before you reach the final turn, make sure your shoes, belt, and personal items, as well as your computer and electronic items have already been removed. Make sure that you talk with your children (especially if they are very young) and let them be aware of the process. If by chance they are picked to be searched, tell them to not be afraid of this. Tell them it's just a game that adults sometimes play. Chances are pretty good that one of your group may be singled out. In most cases, it's just the luck of the draw and sometimes you're it. If you have a baby in a stroller, make sure to remove everything from it. If you have a toddler, the order of operation I would recommend is to have a family member go first and wait on the other side while you follow. For infants, the procedure is similar except that you will be able to walk through with the baby. The one thing to always remember is that you are on vacation... *Period.* Don't sweat the small stuff and don't let long lines and crying babies ruin your trip!

Most importantly, don't allow any incidents during your travel to spoil the whole trip. I have experienced this firsthand myself, and if you allow bad incidents to fester while at the airport, train terminal, or bus depot, it will stay in your mind and will become a lasting memory of that trip. A trip you will not soon forget.

Overcoming jetlag—an important factor.

Nothing can ruin a business trip or a vacation faster than what is commonly referred to as jet lag. This occurs when you are traveling between several different time zones and will cause your body to be a bit confused. Usually, two or more zones will just about do it. It's called jet lag, and it is the end result of using a method of transportation that gets to your destination quickly. When flying, proper sleep and lighting conditions are important to alleviating these negative effects. Today newer aircraft (like the 787 Dreamliner) have sophisticated light systems to help alleviate jet lag in its passengers. So what tips can you do yourself to avoid this condition?

Well, for one thing, sleep is the best remedy. It's best to try and put yourself and your family in the time zone of your destination. For example, if flying east, passengers should advance their sleep schedule (move bedtime earlier) to reflect the time change. Going westbound, one should do the exact opposite and delay your bedtime to later on in the flight. Also try to get on this new sleep schedule several days before you fly so that it is not a complete shock to your system. This is true, especially on the first day of arrival.

In order to try and sleep better, your seat can be most important. The more legroom you have, the better. Now with a family, first class is most likely out of the question, but the airlines do have aisles that are wider than others in coach. Look for them and book those seats on your flight. As for me, I always prefer the window seat because you can at least put a pillow by the window, for extra padding. Not to mention you won't be the person who disturbs everyone when you do need to get up to use the restroom. You should also be aware that the back of the plane (like on a roller coaster) is rougher than the front, so keep that in mind when flying yourself and especially your family over two or more timelines.

So on westbound flights, try and stay up, and when flying two times zones eastbound, you will need to sleep early. You need to turn off all computers, cell phones, and movies. The blue spectrum light they emit is very activating and can delay the sleep process. On the other hand, if you are trying to delay sleep, turn them all on and keep your mind as occupied as possible.

It has been said that having a cocktail to help you fall asleep really does work. I say the opposite is actually true. It's all about dehydration, and when flying in an aircraft at thirty thousand feet, this is what happens to you. Alcohol has a tendency to dehydrate you and will lead to a fragmented sleep, which will leave you feeling groggy upon waking. Also stay away from caffeinated products as well like coffee for obvious reasons. Drink water instead, but not too much, or you will be heading to the restroom more often than you had planned.

For longer flights (seven hours or more), you might want to also take a sleeping pill if you really need it. I don't usually do this and, with a family in tow, would is not recommended, but in extreme cases, the right sleep cycle is the key to overcoming jet lag, and the lack of it will ruin your trip (as well as your children's) faster than anything else. If you decide to take a sleeping pill, make sure you get clearance from your doctor, and if traveling with a spouse, or significant other, make sure they are aware of your intentions.

It also gets pretty loud in these cabins, so to get the right amount of sleep, you might need noise canceling headphones. If you don't have those, you might want to invest in simple earplugs before your flight. It can get pretty uncomfortably loud in an aircraft hurtling through space at five-hundred miles per hour, so it's a good idea to have these available for your kids as well, especially for those long duration flights.

Finally, one of the biggest mistakes people will make when traveling westbound and over two time zones is to try and make a day of it immediately after landing. Not a good idea. Chances are, you will need a little time for your body to adjust to your new environment. Take at least a half a day to do that. Relax, nap, or just take it easy for a bit. Your vacation will still be there when you've rested and relaxed a bit. Jet lag can be beaten, but you need to be smart about its lasting effects on family vacation planning.

Amusement Park Safety- Have fun but be Safe

In most cases, a little knowledge can actually prevent many injuries sustained on vacation, especially at a theme park. When you're on vacation, the excitement and fun of doing something different can lead to some slight errors in judgment and common sense. Here are my top ten tips to help you and your family stay safe on your next vacation to Walt Disney World, Disneyland, Universal Studios, SeaWorld, Busch Gardens, Six Flags, Cedar Fair, or any other park you wish to visit. These tips are not just for theme parks, but for anytime you leave the comfortable confines of your home dwelling.

1. First off, stay hydrated, cool, and watch out for that nasty sun.

One of the biggest problems one will find when visiting an amusement park occurs when you are in the sun for a sustained amount of time. I've seen more visitors suffer from sunburn, rashes, heat exhaustion, and heatstroke than all other injuries combined. Not to mention the long-term effects of too much sun without the right precautions. This is serious business, and you need to know all the harmful effects of being in the sun too long without proper hydration.

Drinking to stay hydrated is so very important but don't drink too fast. Water on those long hot days is, in fact, your best friend and will help prevent heat stroke while in the park. Many think that drinking water quickly might seem like a good idea, but it is the worst thing one can do. Some of the best athletes out there during their training will usually hydrate three or four times a day. They also make it a habit not **to** gulp water down in one sitting. You need to replenish yourself frequently on a hot dry park in order to make up for the energy and sweat you lose. This is true, especially during the popular summer months when visiting the Sun Belt of Florida, Texas, Arizona, and Southern California.

So what should you drink? There are a lot of drinks out there, but in my mind, water's your best choice for hydration. Drinks with sugar additives don't really do the trick for me and alcohol dehydrates, leaving you more susceptible to risk of heat exhaustion and sunstroke than anything else.

Most importantly, always, and I mean always, put on waterproof sunscreen before and even at the park. This goes for anytime you are outside. Some of these amusement parks (like Cedar Point in Ohio) have beaches, and the same is said when in between rides and when relaxing by the lake. The sun itself can be your worst enemy, and I always apply sunscreen (thirty SPF or higher) whenever I am outside. It's always safer to do this than suffer the consequences later, especially when one is on vacation. Also, personally, I always try and wear a hat and sunglasses when I am at these parks for added protection against the scorching sun. You should always wear comfortable shoes and clean, dry socks as well. The heat reflecting off the asphalt pavement has also been known to give you a nasty rash, so be aware of that. If you plan on wearing sandals or no socks, you should remember that the average amusement park guest will walk almost eight miles during the course of the day, and a good pair of shoes will help your feet survive the experience.

2. Stay aware of your surroundings. When you add crowds, rides, and people together, accidents do occur.

Never forget, there are literally thousands of people in these parks and sometimes very limited space to sometimes walk. Simple collisions are pretty common at these parks and are a major source of many theme park injuries. Be aware of where you are, and who is around you while walking around. Looking up and away from your path is not a good idea in a crowd. Sure, it is normal to want to look around and take in the mega-coasters, shows, games, and attractions but don't get too carried away. By not paying attention, you run the risk of stumbling into someone else, or worse, tripping over a child in a stroller. I have seen this happen, and it's not pretty. Also if you're the one pushing the stroller, always be courteous when you walk. Many people forget to add the extra four to five feet in front of them and sometimes ram (unintentionally) the front of the stroller (and the baby) into unsuspecting people walking ahead. It's pretty simple in practice. Always watch where you are walking so that you don't crash into legs and feet. Also if you are a frequent visitor to these amazing theme parks, you've probably heard park employees telling people not to run, especially when the park just opened. Best advice one can give. I always tell people, don't worry, the ride will be there, so just walk to it. It's really not worth it to take out several people trying to be the first on line. Finally, please don't stop suddenly while walking. In crowds, this could end up being a minor catastrophe. Always look around and scope the area and the best bet is just to move to the side, and find a bench so that you can pull your map out and get the lay of the land.

3. Stay away from where you don't belong.

Never, and I mean never, enter a restricted area in a theme park unless you have approval to do so. Restrictions are there for a reason and most times are put up for your own safety. I have seen many injuries, park ejections, and in some cases, emergency room visits because someone was curious about what was on the other side of that manmade barrier. Don't climb or hop fences or walk through employee-only gates. If you lose something like your keys while on a ride (or it falls in a restricted area), ask a park employee for help. They will be glad to recover that item for you.

4. Know your limitations both physically and emotionally.

It is a very good idea to read the ride restrictions *before* you get in line for a ride you have never ridden before. If you are pregnant, have pain or injuries in your back or neck, or have a heart condition, you should not take a chance and go on high-intensity thrill rides without a doctor's approval. If pregnant, you can do serious harm to your baby, and if you have a physical condition, there can be some serious consequences (and even death) if you continue down that road. Always check with your doctor before doing these things. It's better to play it safe on a family or kiddy coaster than in the hospital ER on your vacation. Also, be aware that some of the newer thrill rides also have height and sometimes seatbelt restrictions as well. If you are shorter than five feet, or taller than six feet, you'll also encounter rides where you will either not be permitted or simply won't be comfortable. Many rides in addition to having a safety harness also have a seatbelt that is attached to the rider. They only go so far, and if you can't get that seatbelt on, be aware you will not be allowed to ride. I actually had to move my wallet and take a deep breath to ride Millennium Force one time, and it's pretty embarrassing when this happens. Some parks make special seats available on select rides for larger visitors. Just ask if you think this may apply to you. If you have high blood pressure, or think you might, it's probably best to skip the big roller coasters and simulator rides until you get the ok from your doctor.

One important note: Most parks issue special guidebooks for persons with disabilities. This will also include the restrictions on rides not suited for small kids or larger riders. You can always stop by the park's guest relations office if you have any questions or unsure if a ride is appropriate for you or your special guest.

5. Know your health condition before taking that risk.

One of the very first thing you need to do before attempting any ride is know your health condition before you ride and anything. If you haven't had a check-up within the past year it's best to do so just in case. Too many negative incidents can occur in theme parks are the result of undiagnosed medical conditions so know before you go.

6. Follow the safety rules

Accidents happen when you don't obey all the rules. The ride might look safe enough to try and bend the rules but too many times this has ended in disaster, a hidden drop or turn, a sudden stop, which is unexpected can lead to danger if you're not prepared for it. Never think that you know more about a ride than the park employees do. If they tell you not to ride, then don't. Please don't try to get out of ride until it completely or try and make your kids appear taller than they actually are. Height and safety restrictions are there for a reason, and the end result of not heading these warnings can be catastrophic.

You might also be advised that jumping the line is an easy way to get thrown out of the park. It's simply not worth paying the high price of admission, just to get thrown out of the park. If you see line-jumping, don't make a big scene. Just report it to the nearest employee at the ride or, if possible, a security officer. Remember, you are on vacation and the family is with you.

7. Stay in your seat to stay safe.

One of the most dangerous things you can do is try and fix it so you can get out of your harness (and seat) while the ride is in motion. Also, your hands and feet should always remain in the car at all times. If you happen to be riding a "floorless" roller coaster, relax your legs and let them dangle underneath you. Don't kick them out to the side or towards the front as this can lead to a loss or limb or life. If you are on a ride with a lap bar, seat belt or safety harness, make sure that it is in place, snug, and locked. If the ride starts to move and your restraint is not in place, immediately yell (loudly) for help. We have seen too many incidents occur where a fatality occurred because this was not done. Also, always be aware of your children's surroundings and make sure they stay safe as well. Sometimes, vehicles stop short of the unload platform to wait for groups up ahead to exit so stay seated until told otherwise.

8. Ride the ride and don't let it ride you.

Some rides, especially roller coasters and simulator rides, can whip your head around, leaving you at risk for headaches as well as more serious head injuries. On those types of rides, sit in the middle of the chair and don't slouch or lean to one side. Relax, but do not go limp. You want to keep your balance in the seat as much as possible. When the seat pitches you to the left, relax your torso and bend to the right to keep your head upright and centered and vice versa. Think of riding a horse, or surfing. You want to ride the seat—not have it throw you all around.

Also keep your eyes open so you won't suffer vertigo and don't forget to scream. Doing this keeps the blood in the upper torso and is a great way to avoid browing out (and getting tunnel vision) or blacking out altogether.

Note" If you are prone to headaches, have any neck or back problems, or have been diagnosed with aneurysm, do not get on any roller coaster or simulator ride until you have been cleared to do so.

9. Please… Help your kids!

We sometimes go back to our childhood when we visit these amusement parks, but remember, you're still the parent. If you are responsible for children that are with you, take a moment to explain the ride to them, and tell them how they should behave. They are depending upon you to keep them safe, so set a good example for them by following the rules yourself. If you follow the rules, they will too. Always tell them to stay seated. Like I said earlier, have them hold the grab bar and not to stick their knees and feet outside the ride vehicle. Make them look to you for the okay to get on or off a ride too.

One thing I always stress is never try and put a crying child on a ride. If your child starts to cry, let others pass you in line. Ride only when he or she is ready to do so. If this doesn't happen, just exit the queue and find something better to do. Finally, remember that young kids can't keep an adult's pace in a theme park. Let them take plenty of breaks and have them take as much time as they need. The result of not doing this is often a tired, cranky and unhappy child. Even if your child handles being tired well, remember that their bodies experience a loss of balance and coordination and they are more prone to getting injured. Consider a mid-day break, perhaps a swim back at the hotel, to avoid mid-day heat and crowds.

10. Alert staff about problems.

If you see something wrong—a broken restraint, a person jumping the line, a backpack that has been left unattended or anything else that could jeopardize the safety of a park guest—alert a park employee immediately. They are there to help keep you safe. In the end, safety for you and your family is the most important thing that matters. If you follow the above suggestions, you will surely go a long way towards achieving that goal.

The Future of Coasters

The Sky is Still Literally the Limit!

Well, as you can see, the future of roller coasters looks very promising. Was it just thirty years ago when we were building roller coasters less than 150 feet tall? Now when you look at the best coasters in our nation and in the world, we are talking 450-to 500-feet in height. Even our drop towers and swing rides are achieving these heights and it looks like the sky is literally the limit. I believe the best is still yet to come. In the coming years, I am very confident that the next scream machine will be even taller, faster, and more exhilarating than what we could ever imagine. Coasters like *X2(the first of many new concepts)* show us that we can change the angle and perspective of the ride at every second. Flying coasters (like Superman the *Ultimate Flight*) do indeed give a new perspective of what a coaster should look and feel like, and today's drop, launch and my favorite floorless coasters give the feel that we are sitting in our most comfortable easy chair while experiencing all the fun that comes with a thrill ride. .

Also, with today's hydraulic launch coasters, we can now experience a zero to 150 mph cannon launch much like a fighter pilot would experience being shot straight up to dizzying heights in just seconds! The true test of how fast and high we go will not rest in the limits of our imagination, but in how much stress and strain the human body can actually endure. When does a ride go over the boundaries of excitement and fun into an area where the rider has a clear potential of getting permanently hurt physically from the attraction? That will be the key question in the minds of those who manufacturers who continue to build these mega marvels into our future. Simulation rides that are roller coasters (like the *Revenge of the Mummy*) are popping up and new and innovative thrill rides are becoming standard at amusement parks worldwide.

It looks like the bar is getting higher and higher every year and it's indeed a very exciting time to be a Thrill Ride Maniac. With the addition of *Polarcoaster* rides like Skyscraper set to hit the Orlando Skyline (at over 550 feet tall) in 2017, who knows where that bar will go next? One thing is for sure. I will still be looking forward to the next ride, the next rush, and the next gigantic roller coaster attraction to hit the market. I hope I will be able to ride that newest attraction with all of you right next to me.

Roller Coaster and Dark Ride Clubs

Now that you are ready to ride the rails and experience all there is to do, you might want to share these experiences with like minded people. Clubs are a great way to meet people who have the same interest in roller coasters and thrill rides as you do. The excitement of being with a group of people on the best rides around can be a definite plus and many of these clubs receive discounts from the parks and are able to get special (and exclusive rides) on many different attractions. Trips are also set up by these groups allowing family and friends to vacation together at less cost. I belong to a few of these clubs myself and they are well worth investigating. Here are just a few of them.

1. **American Coaster Enthusiasts (ACE).** ACE is the largest roller coaster club in the world. It was founded as a not-for-profit, all volunteer that promotes better knowledge and appreciation as well as a mission to conserve classic wooden roller coasters. They also have a thing or two to say about steel contemporary coasters too. Since 1978, ACE has grown to over 7,000 members representing 49 states and over 12 countries. A good group of people here and in addition to a national event called CoasterCon. They also sponsor several local events every year as well. You can get more information about ACE at Aceonline.org.

2. **CoasterBuzz Club.** It's a club that is a good fit for roller coaster enthusiasts just about everywhere. Its mission is to bring roller coaster enthusiasts (and their families) together to enjoy the best thrill rides around. If you go to the CoasterBuzz website, you will find many different events to choose from and there is a little something for just about everyone in the family to enjoy. These include a myriad of roller coaster events at many amusement parks around the country. For more info, go to http://coasterbuzz.com/Content/Club.

3. **Coaster Zombies.** I am told the name comes from the way we feel after a long road trip riding the best roller coasters around the nation. It seems a member once proclaimed "I feel like a Coaster Zombie," and the name just stuck. Today the Zombies are several hundred strong and come from all over North America. Their events are comprised of many park visits and an annual road trip every year. It all builds to their biggest event that usually takes at Six Flags America in Largo, Maryland. Visit Coasterzombies.com.

4. **Club TPR.** Theme park reviews is an official club for enthusiasts of theme parks, roller coasters, and fun rides across America. They are growing every day and their website is very professionally done. Visit Clubtpr.com.

5. **Darkride and Funhouse Enthusiasts (DAFE).** If you like dark rides, this is a club that you really need to get involved in. Not as large as other clubs, these individuals really know where the best of the best dark rides reside, and they can plan trips for those interested. It's a great opportunity to visit one every year with a chance meet many people who love dark rides too. Annual membership includes the quarterly newsletter, *Barrel O' Fun.* Visit Dafe.org.

6. **European Coaster Club (ECC).** When you join the European Coaster Club, you become part of a group that consists of several thousand members from all over the world. Sure they plan trips in Europe, but that's not all. Every year's special events are set up for its members to cross the pond and head to the United States as well. I have met many of these individuals, and they are a lot of fun to be with. All of whom share your enjoyment of roller coasters and thrill rides no matter where in the world they might be. There is nothing like visiting another country and talking the universal language of thrill rides and roller coasters with a stranger who just might end up being a future friend. They also have a great newsletter called *First Drop,* and the stories you will find in this publication cover not only what's happening locally but what's going on across the world as well. You can visit their website at Ceoasterclub.org.

7. **Florida Coaster Club.** One of my favorite clubs that you will find out there. The members in this group are the best, and their mission statement really says it all. "To bring together people who share the love and thrill of riding roller coasters." They travel near and far in the quest of that ultimate coaster ride. They are in search of "the endless summer of roller coasters" and being located in the Sunshine State, there are many different rides around the country or even locally in Florida for you to choose from. And the good news is that you don't have to live in Florida to be a member. This is one club that I highly recommend joining. For more info, go to Floridacoasterclub.com.

8. **Great Ohio Coaster Club (GOCC).** We all know that Ohio has some of the best amusement parks and thrill rides in the nation. The GOCC is a roller coaster enthusiast social organization dedicated to the enjoyment of the ultimate scream machines that one can find out there. They talk about "and ride" the best roller coaster, thrill rides, and amusement parks that you can find out there. Though many of its members are from Ohio, potential members are invited from all over the world. Visit Greatohiocc.org.

9. **Mid-Atlantic Coaster Club or MACC** is a roller coaster club based out of northern Virginia. Its events cover many different parks throughout the year, and I believe this is truly a fun group to hang out with. Two examples of some of their event are "Screamfest" and "Summer Send Off." Like many other coaster clubs, members get lots of Exclusive Ride Time. This means that members get to ride their favorite roller coasters over and over again usually before or after that particular park is closed. Also MACC has sponsored picnics at predetermined amusement parks and during these events it is safe to say you will make many new friends with similar interests. Visit http//www.coasterdan.com/macc/

10. **Southern California Coaster Club.** The Southern California Coaster Club is a coaster club based in California and primarily focuses on the Southern California parks including Six Flags Magic Mountain, Knott's Berry Farm, Disneyland, and Sea World. The people here are very nice, and it is safe to say you will make a lot of friends here. Again when you join this group, Exclusive Ride Time is benefit that you have to experience firsthand. http://www.westcoaster.net/sccc/

11. **The Coaster Crew** is a growing roller coaster club with just over one thousand members across the United States and Canada. Like other roller coaster clubs, they offer special events at many amusement parks, and its members are given exclusive ride time as well. Members also get special discounts on tickets, Fast Passes, and several special events that take place during the year. I like them a lot. Visit http://coastercrew.net/

12. **Western New York Coaster Club.** This group is a specialized regional coaster club promoting preservation, knowledge, and enjoyment of all roller coasters. The club hosts an annual convention on Memorial Day Weekend and membership dues include ten issues of the *Gravity Gazette* newsletter. Like all other clubs out there, you have many choices, but what I like about this group is that being smaller in size, every member has a say in what events the group will do and finding a coaster buddy for life is a definite possibility. You can visit Wnycc.org for more information.

Listing of North American Amusement Parks

United States:

Alabama

Alabama Adventure (Visionland) - Bessemer, Alabama
Southern Adventures - Huntsville, Alabama
Waterville USA - Gulf Shores, Alabama

Arizona

Castles N' Corners - Phoenix, Arizona
Enchanted Island - Phoenix, Arizona
Funtasticks Family Fun Park - Tucson, Arizona

Arkansas

Magic Springs and Crystal Falls - Hot Springs, Arkansas

California

Adventure City - Stanton, California
Belmont Park - San Diego, California
Blackbeard's Family Fun Center - Fresno, California
California's Great America - Santa Clara, California
Disney's California Adventure - Anaheim, California
Disneyland - Anaheim, California
Gilroy Gardens Family Theme Park - Gilroy, California
Knott's Berry Farm - Buena Park, California
Legoland - Carlsbad, California
Nut Tree Family Park - Vacaville, California
Pacific Park - Santa Monica, California
Pixieland Park - Concord, California
Raging Waters - San Jose, California
Rotary Playland - Fresno, California
Santa Cruz Beach and Boardwalk - Santa Cruz, California
Scandia Amusement Parks – Ontario, California
Sea World San Diego -San Diego, California
Six Flags Discovery Kingdom - Vallejo, California
Six Flags Magic Mountain - Valencia, California
Universal Studios Hollywood - Universal City, California

Colorado

Elitch Gardens - Denver, Colorado
Lakeside Amusement Park - Denver, Colorado
Santa's Workshop - North Pole, Colorado

Connecticut

Lake Compounce - Bristol, Connecticut
Quassy Amusement Park - Middlebury, Connecticut

Delaware

Funland, Rehoboth, Delaware

Florida

Adventure Landing - Jacksonville Beach, Florida
Busch Gardens Africa -Tampa, Florida
Celebration Station - Clearwater, Florida
Disney's Animal Kingdom - Lake Buena Vista, Florida
Disney's Hollywood Studio's - Lake Buena Vista, Florida
Disney's Magic Kingdom -Lake Buena Vista, Florida
EPCOT - Lake Buena Vista, Florida
Fun Spot America – Kissimmee and Orlando, Florida
King Richards's Family Fun Center- Naples, Florida
Legoland - Lakeland, Florida
Old Town - Kissimmee, Florida
SeaWorld Orlando - Orlando, Florida
Universal Studios Florida - Orlando, Florida
Universal's Islands of Adventure - Orlando, Florida
Wet and Wild Orlando - Orlando, Florida

Georgia

Lake Winnipesaukee - Rossville, Georgia
Six Flags Over Georgia - Austell, Georgia
Wild Adventures - Valdosta, Georgia

Idaho

Silverwood Theme Park - Athol, Idaho

Illinois

Haunted Trails - Burbank, Illinois
Kiddieland - Melrose Park, Illinois
Safari Land - Villa Park, Illinois
Six Flags Great America - Gurnee, Illinois

Indiana

Fun Spot - Angola, Indiana
Holiday World and Splashin Safari - Santa Claus, Indiana
Indiana Beach - Monticello, Indiana

Iowa

Adventureland - Altoona, Iowa
Arnold's Park - Arnolds Park, Iowa

Kentucky

Beech Bend Park - Bowling Green, Kentucky
Six Flags Kentucky Kingdom - Louisville, Kentucky

Louisiana

Carousel Gardens - New Orleans, Louisiana
Celebration Station - Baton Rouge, Louisiana
Dixie Landing - Baton Rouge, Louisiana

Maine

Funtown Splashtown - Saco, Maine
Palace Playland - Old Orchard Beach, Maine

Maryland

Adventure Park - New Market, Maryland
Baja Amusements - West Ocean City, Maryland
Jolly Roger Amusement Park - Ocean City, Maryland
Jolly Roger at the Pier - Ocean City, Maryland
Six Flags America - Upper Marlboro, Maryland
Trimper's Rides - Ocean City, Maryland

Massachusetts

Six Flags New England - Agawam, Massachusetts

Michigan

Jeepers Great Lakes Crossing - Auburn Hills, Michigan
Jeepers Northland Mall - Southfield, Michigan
Michigan Adventure - Muskegon, Michigan

Minnesota

Como Town - St. Paul, Minnesota
Nickelodeon Universe - Bloomington, Minnesota
Paul Bunyan Land - Brainerd, Minnesota
Valleyfair - Shakopee, Minnesota

Missouri

Big Shot Amusement Park - Linn Creek, Missouri
Miner Mike's Adventure Town - Osage Beach, Missouri
Ocean's of Fun - Kansas City, Missouri
Route 66 Carousel Park - Joplin, Missouri
Silver Dollar City - Branson, Missouri
Six Flags St. Louis - Eureka, Missouri
Worlds of Fun - Kansas City, Missouri

Nebraska

Fun-Plex - Omaha, Nebraska
Scateland - Omaha, Nebraska

Nevada

Adventure Dome - Las Vegas, Nevada
Buffalo Bill's Hotel and Casino - Jean, Nevada
Las Vegas Mini Gran Prix - Las Vegas, Nevada
NASCAR café - Las Vegas, Nevada
New York, New York Hotel and Casino - Las Vegas, Nevada
Playland Park - Reno, Nevada
Stratosphere Tower and Casino - Las Vegas, Nevada
Wild Island Family Adventure Park - Sparks, Nevada

New Hampshire

Canobie Lake - Salem, New Hampshire
Fun World - Nashua, New Hampshire
Santa's Village - Jefferson, New Hampshire
Story Land - Glen, New Hampshire

New Jersey

Blackbeard's Cave - Bayville, New Jersey
Bowcraft Amusement Park - Scotch Plains, New Jersey
Casino Pier - Seaside Heights, New Jersey
Clementon Park and Splash World - Clementon, New Jersey
Fantasy Island - Beach Haven, New Jersey
Funtown Pier - (being rebuilt) Seaside Park, New Jersey
Gillian's Wonderland Pier - Ocean City, New Jersey

A Personal Guide to the Best Thrill Rides and Amusement/Water Parks

I-Play America - Freehold, New Jersey
Jenkinson's Boardwalk - Point Pleasant Beach, New Jersey
Keansburg Amusement Park - Keansburg, New Jersey
Land of Make Believe - Hope, New Jersey
Morey's Pier's - Wildwood, New Jersey
Playland's Castaway Cove - Ocean City, New Jersey
Six Flags Great Adventure - Jackson, New Jersey
Steel Pier - Atlantic City, New Jersey
Storybook Land - Egg Harbor Township, New Jersey

New Mexico

Cliff's Amusement Park - Albuquerque, New Mexico
IT'Z - Albuquerque, New Mexico
Western Playland - Sunland Park, New Mexico

New York

Adventureland - Farmingdale, New York
Adventurers Family Entertainment Center, Brooklyn
Boomers - Medford, New York
Coney Island Boardwalk - Brooklyn, New York
Coney Island Bowery - Brooklyn, New York
Darien Lake - Darien Center, New York
Deno's Wonder Wheel Park - Brooklyn, New York
Great Escape and Splashwater Kingdom - Lake George, New York
Great Escape & Splashwater Kingdom, Lake George
Hoffman's Playland, Latham
Hoffman's Playland - Latham, New York no website to confirm
Kids N' Action - Brooklyn, New York
Luna Park – Brooklyn, New York City
Krazy City - West Nyack, New York no website to confirm
Magic Forest - Lake George, New York
Martin's Fantasy Island - Grand Island, New York
Midway Park - Bemus Point, New York no website to confirm
Playland Park - Rye, New York
Seabreeze Amusement Park - Rochester, New York
Sports Plus - Lake Grove, New York
Sylvan Beach Amusement Park - Sylvan Beach, New York
Victorian Gardens, New York City

North Carolina

Carowinds - Charlotte, North Carolina
Cherokee Fun Park - Cherokee, North Carolina
Ghost Town in the Sky - Maggie Valley, North Carolina
Santa's Land - Cherokee, North Carolina

Ohio

Castaway Bay - Sandusky, Ohio
Cedar Point - Sandusky, Ohio
Coney Island - Cincinnati, Ohio
Geauga Lake and Whitewater Kingdom - Aurora, Ohio
Kings Island - Mason, Ohio
Memphis Kiddy Park - Brooklyn, Ohio
Putt 'N Pond Speed Park - Fostoria, Ohio
Stricker's Grove - Ross, Ohio
Tuscora Park - New Philadelphia, Ohio

Oklahoma

Bartleville Kiddie Park - Bartlesville, Oklahoma
Celebration Station - Tulsa, Oklahoma
Frontier City - Oklahoma City, Oklahoma

Oregon

Enchanted Forrest - Turner, Oregon
Oaks Park - Portland, Oregon
Thrill-Ville USA - Turner, Oregon

Pennsylvania

Bushkill Park - Easton, Pennsylvania
DelGrosso's Amusement Park - Tipton, Pennsylvania
Dorney Park - Allentown, Pennsylvania
Dutch Wonderland - Lancaster, Pennsylvania
Hershey Park - Hershey, Pennsylvania
Idlewild and Soak Zone - Ligonier, Pennsylvania
Kennywood - West Mifflin, Pennsylvania
Knoebels Amusement Park - Elysburg, Pennsylvania
Lakemont Park - Altoona, Pennsylvania
Sesame Place - Langhorne, Pennsylvania
Waldemeer Park - Erie, Pennsylvania

South Carolina

Family Kingdom Amusement Park - Myrtle Beach, South Carolina
Hard Rock Park - Myrtle Beach, South Carolina

Tennessee

Dollywood - Pigeon Forge, Tennessee
NASCAR Speed Park Sevierville, Tennessee
Sir Goony's Family Fun Center Chattanooga, Tennessee

Texas

Joyland Amusement Park - Lubbock, Texas
Kemah Boardwalk Amusements - Kemah, Texas
Kiddie Park - San Antonio, Texas
Oasis Lanes - El Paso, Texas
Schlitterbahn - New Braunfels, Texas
Sea World San Antonio - San Antonio, Texas
Six Flags Fiesta Texas - San Antonio, Texas
Six Flags Over Texas - Arlington, Texas
Wonderland Park - Amarillo, Texas
Zuma Fun Center - Houston, Texas

Utah

Lagoon - Farmington, Utah

Virginia

Busch Gardens – Europe - Williamsburg, Virginia
Kings Dominion - Doswell, Virginia
Motor World Virginia Beach - Virginia Beach, Virginia

Washington

Puyallup Fair - Puyallup, Washington
Remlinger Farms - Carnation, Washington
Riverfront Park - Spokane, Washington
Wild Waves and Enchanted Village - Federal Way, Washington

West Virginia

Camden Park - Huntington, West Virginia

Wisconsin

Bay Beach - Green Bay, Wisconsin
Little A-Merrick –A - Marshall, Wisconsin
Noah's Ark - Wisconsin Dells, Wisconsin
Riverview Park and Waterworks - Wisconsin Dells, Wisconsin
Timber Falls Adventure Golf - Wisconsin Dells, Wisconsin

Canada

Atlantic Playland - Lower Fackville, Nova Scotia, Canada
Au Pays Des Marveilles - Sainte-Adèle, Québec, Canada
Burlington Amusement Park - Burlington, Prince Edward Island, Canada
Caloway Park, Calgary, Alberta, Canada
Canada's Wonderland - Maple, Ontario, Canada
Centreville Amusement Park - Toronto, Ontario, Canada
Chippewa Park - Thunder Bay, Ontario, Canada
Crystal Palace - Dieppe, New Brunswick, Canada
Galaxyland - Edmonton, Alberta, Canada
Kingston Family Fun World - Kingston, Ontario, Canada
La Ronde - Montréal, Québec, Canada
Marineland - Niagara Falls, Ontario, Canada
Park Safari – Hemmingford, Quebec, Canada
Playland - Vancouver, British Columbia, Canada
Sandspit - Hunter River, Prince Edward Island, Canada
Santa's Village - Bracebridge, Ontario, Canada
Upper Clements Park - Annapolis Royal, Nova Scotia, Canada

Roller Coaster Terminology

A

acceleration - Describes when the coaster's cars or trains are gaining speed. The term is most commonly used to describe how fast a train reaches a specific speed particularly on a launch coaster.

airtime - Term used to describe the feeling created by negative-g forces. Airtime is the sensation of floating while riding a roller coaster when your body is forced up from the seat creating air between the seat and your bottom. Airtime or negative-g forces are most commonly experienced on a drop or at the crest of a hill.

anti-rollback device - A ratcheting device used on a lift hill or section of a roller coaster that prevents the cars or trains from rolling backward. That familiar clicking sound you hear on the track on the lift hill up the coaster is this device in action.

ascend - To rise up a hill, tower, or any incline in the course of a ride.

B

backward riding - This term refers to riding a roller coaster while seated facing in the opposite direction you are traveling. Amusement parks will on occasion run a roller coaster backward by placing the train backward on the track so the rear car goes down the hill first. On shuttle coasters (Vekoma is a good example) riders will travel backward and forward since the roller coaster track does not form a complete circuit.

banked turn - Describes a section of track that is banked (laterally angled) while turning. Designers bank the turns on roller coasters to reduce the lateral G forces inside the train.

Barrel Roll - An inversion term that basically is a corkscrew maneuver on a roller coaster. See corkscrew.

bench seats - A flat-seat designed with no divider between the riders. Bench seats were common on older wooden coasters and mine train coasters. A bench seat allows riders to slide across the seat. Today, most coasters are designed for more safety and security and have seat dividers or bucket seats to meet modern safety specifications.

boomerang - A type of inversion with two half loops connected to each other. Boomerang is also the term used by Vekoma to describe one of their shuttle coaster models. A similar maneuver would also be called a cobra roll.

brake run - A section of track usually before the loading station where brakes are installed to bring the incoming trains to a complete stop. Brake runs may also be installed midway through the course to slow a car down and decrease replacement of the wheels for that train.

brakes - basically used to slow or stop the train on a roller coaster. Brakes are placed on the brake run, but may also be located along the course the train travels to slow the train down if necessary or stop it. Brakes can be physical in nature or can use magnetic forces to stop or slow down a train.

C

camel back - A series of hills on a steel or wooden roller coaster where each preceding one is slightly smaller than the proceeding one. Camel backs produce negative gs or "air time."

car - A car is a part of the overall coaster train. A car consists of one or more rows where riders are seated in individual or bench seats. A coaster train should consist of two or more cars linked together to form the train.

catapult launch - The coaster train is launched to give it power instead of using a lift hill and gravity. The catapult system connects with the train and accelerates the train using a flywheel or weight drop. More recently, compressed-air (thrust air), linear synchronous motors (LSM's) and linear induction motors (LIM's) are being used as well to launch a train.

chain lift - The chain lift is one of the fundamental elements of most roller coasters. The chain lift pulls the car or train to the top of a hill and then releases the train to coast down a hill where gravity takes effect and the train accelerates down the course. On some coasters more than one lift hill may be used.

circuit - Used to describe a complete roller coaster track from start to finish.

cobra roll - A term describing a signature element on some roller coasters designed by Bolliger and Mabillard. The cobra roll is a double inversion similar to a boomerang element. Riders enter the element and are sent upside down twice and leaving going in the opposite direction they were as they entered.

corkscrew - A corkscrew is a twisting inversion designed like a corkscrew. Arrow Dynamics designed the world's first corkscrew inversion. Barrel roll is the term used by Bolliger and Mabillard to describe their corkscrew inversion.

D

diving loop - A term used to describe an inversion similar to an acrobatic stunt plan maneuver. This inversion involves half a vertical loop and a twisting curve leading either in or out of the inversion. On the B&M inverted coasters, this inversion is also referred to as an Immelman.

dive coaster - (previously known as Diving Machine). This is a steel roller coaster manufactured by Bolliger and Mabillard. On this ride you experience a moment of freefalling. The drops are usually 90-degrees. Unlike other roller coasters where the lift hill takes the train directly to the first drop, a Dive Coaster stays at the top. It is followed by a holding brake which stops the train (from 5 to 10 seconds) just as it enters the vertical drop. The train will then be released into the drop. Development of the Dive Coaster began in the mid 1990's, and it is safe to say has been very successful since their inception.

double dip - A hill that has been divided into two separate drops by a flattening out of the drop midway down the hill. The Jack Rabbit at Kennywood is one of the most famous coasters that utilize this maneuver and still running today.

double loop - A term used to describe an element of two vertical loops together or may be used to describe a roller coaster with two vertical inversions, and no other inversions.

double out and back - A term used to describe the layout on a roller coaster where the track heads away and returns to the station twice. See related terms: out and back, triple out and back.

dual track - The term used to describe a roller coaster with two different tracks or circuits. A dual track coaster shares the station and may share some parts of the structure including the lift hill.

dueling coaster - A dual track roller coaster that is designed to produce the effect of near, head-on collisions through the circuit. Dueling Dragons at Universals Studio's Islands of Adventure is a classic example of this type of coaster.

E

enclosed - A roller coaster where the entire track is housed inside a building or some sort of structure. Theme parks generally build coasters inside a structure so they may theme the ride with lighting, sound, or other special effects.

F

figure eight layout - A roller coaster track layout that resembles the number eight from above.

First Drop-The first major drop on a roller coaster and generally the first drop following the lift hill.

fixed lapbar - A restraint on a coaster train that a rider sits under that locks in a designated position and does not adjust. Because of an increase in safety awareness fixed lab bar (for each individual) restraints are replacing full train restraints.

flat spin - A term used by coaster designers to describe their banked, high-speed helix turns.

flat turn - A turn where the track remains flat and gives the sensation that the train my tip due to the lateral forces. Most turns on a coaster are banked, but in some cases, a flat turn may be used to increase the thrills. *The Cyclone* in Coney Island, New York is a good example of utilizing these flat turns.

G

g-force - The Amount of gravitation force that is put on the body. For example, two g's would equal twice the force of gravity on your body. If you weight two hundred pounds in a two g maneuver, you will be carrying four hundred pounds on your body at this time.

giga-coaster - A marketing term used by Cedar Point and manufacturer Intamin to describe a roller coaster that stands more than three hundred feet tall. Millennium Force a 310-feet high.

H

heartline - A term used to describe an inversion where the center of gravity is designed around the rider's heart line.

helix - A turn on a roller coaster course that forms a radius of more than 360-degrees.

hyper-coaster - A term used to describe a steel roller coaster designed for speed and airtime. Hyper-coasters have large drops for speed, have no inversions and have plenty of camelbacks, bunny hops, or speed bumps for airtime.

I

immelman - A term used to describe their diving loop on inverted roller coasters. This element was named for an airplane maneuver invented by a German pilot in World War II.

indoor roller coaster - An indoor roller coaster operates inside a building, such as an indoor amusement park, mall, or other venue. They can also be dark rides such as *Space Mountain* located at both Disney Land and Disney World parks.

inversion - A term used to describe any portion of a roller coaster track that turns the riders upside down.

inverted roller coaster - A roller coaster with trains suspended beneath the track above.

J

junior coaster - A term also used to describe a kiddie-coaster or a simple roller coaster designed especially for children and frightened parents.

L

lapbar - A type of restraint that secures the rider by placing a bar across the passengers lap. A lapbar restraint can be designed to secure an individual rider or multiple riders.

lifthill - The section of the coaster that contains some device or mechanism that pulls or pushes the roller coaster train up a hill. The majority of lifthills use a chain connected to a motor that pulls the train to the top. Some roller coasters contain multiple lifthills and the lifthill may be midcourse or at the end of the circuit.

linear induction motor (LIM) - A magnetic motor commonly used to launch a roller coaster train along or up a section of steel track. LSM or Linear Synchronous Motors are the same idea, but the technology used to propel the train is different.

looping corkscrew or loop screw - A type of roller coaster that features a vertical loop and a corkscrew.

loading platform - The part of the station where the riders board the roller coaster train.

M

manual brake - A hand operated brake requiring a human to operate that slows or stops a roller coaster train. Many classic wooden roller coasters have manual brake systems, but in recent years, they're becoming rare as parks replace the manual brakes with computerized brake systems. The Cyclone in Coney Island, New York still operates this way.

mine train - A genre of early steel roller coasters with a layout that features fast, quick turns, drops, and helix turns. Most are themed after a runaway mine train. One of the first of these appeared at Six Flags Over Texas in Arlington, Texas.

N

negative Gs - Negative gs generate airtime or the sensation of floating while on a roller coaster. Negative Gs are usually found on a roller coaster at the top of a hill when the rider's body is accelerated upwards. These types of g-forces are more uncomfortable to riders than positive g-forces that press you into your seat.

O

out and back - A term used to describe a type of layout on a roller coaster. An out and back roller coaster layout is where the train leaves the station and heads out to a point where there is a turnaround to send the train back to the station. Sometimes variations can be found like an L-layout out and back where the turnaround is not the only curve in the roller coaster. Some out and back coasters like Shivering Timbers at Michigan's Adventure will have a helix at the end of the layout but still maintain a correct out and back layout.

over-the-shoulder restraint (OTSR) - A device that goes over the riders shoulders to restrain and protect them while riding a roller coaster. Another name for these types of restraints are commonly called horse collars.

P

partially enclosed - A roller coaster where only a portion of the track is within an enclosed structure or building.

pay-one-price - Amusement Park admission structure where you pay-one-price for all rides, shows, and attractions and is often called a POP ticket. The other option if available is to pay-as-you-go, in which case you would use tickets for the rides, attractions, and shows. Disney Theme Parks are examples of POP admission parks, and Knoebels Amusement Park is an example of a park that has POP as an option on selected days, but always offers the option to pay-as-you-go.

positive Gs - Gravitational forces that pull you downward that are often found in inversions, highly banked, high speed turns and at the bottom of hills. Positive G-forces are when the gravitational force exceeds one g, giving you the sensation of feeling heavier than you actually are.

R

racer - A dual track roller coaster designed where the trains leave the station at the same moment and race each other through the circuit. Most racing coasters like Colossus at Six Flags Magic Mountain feature parallel tracks. Other coasters like Rolling Thunder at Six Flags Great Adventure or Lightning Racer at Hershey Park race, but each track is entirely different.

restraint - Some sort of device to prevent the rider from leaving the roller coaster train while it's in motion. The fundamental idea of the restraint is to protect the rider and keep them in the proper riding position throughout the duration of the ride. Commonly found restraints include lap bars, over-the-shoulder restraints, and seat belts.

running rails - A term used to describe the track or rails the train or car on a roller coaster rides on.

S

seats - The location where the rider sits in the car or train while riding the roller coaster.

seatbelt - A rather simple device used to help restrain and protect the rider. On some roller coasters like the Matterhorn at Disneyland this is the only restraint device, but on many other coasters seat belts are being used in addition to another restraint like a lap bar.

shoulder harness - A device used to secure a rider's shoulders by placing a bar over the shoulder area, but unlike an over-the-shoulder restraint it does not go down over the chest, stomach, and cross the riders lap. Also see Over-The-Shoulder Restraint.

shuttle - A term used to describe a roller coaster track that does not form a complete circuit. Instead the train or car is required to traverse the track in one direction and then reverse directions and return by repeating the course over again going in the opposite direction. The Boomerang at Morey's Pier in Wildwood, New Jersey is a good example of a shuttle coaster.

side friction - A roller coaster designed with guide rails above and on the outside of the track or running rails. The guide rails keep the train or car on the track without the use of guide wheels or upstops. Leap the Dips (the oldest operational coaster in the world) at Lakemont Park is an example of a side friction roller coaster.

single loop - A roller coaster layout that only contains one, vertical loop. California Screaming at Disneyland's California Adventure in Anaheim, California, is the best example of this type of ride.

speed bump - A small hill placed in a location where it will be taken at a high speed and will produce negative g-forces or airtime lifting the riders out of their seats.

spinning wild mouse - A Wild Mouse coaster designed with cars that spin during the entire course or parts of the roller coaster. The spinning is not controlled by mechanics, but instead by gravity, weight distribution, and other forces caused by the ride.

stand-up roller coaster - A roller coaster design that permits the riders to stand during the entire ride instead of being seated. This is not a ride for someone with bad knees!

station - The station is a building or structure that houses the loading and unloading platforms for a roller coaster. The station may also contain the ride's control panel, maintenance shed and a train storage area or transfer track.

steel roller coaster - A roller coaster built with steel rails as opposed to an all wood construction.

suspended - A roller coaster designed where the trains ride below the track rather than on top of the track. The Arrow Suspended like Big Bad Wolf at Busch Gardens Williamsburg have special trains that are designed to swing freely from side to side.

suspended looping coaster (SLC) - A term used by Vekoma to describe its inverted roller coaster design.

T

terrain roller coaster - A term used to describe a roller coaster layout that makes use of the terrain and natural surroundings. The coaster track is generally kept low to the ground and the surrounding terrain generally adds to the ride experience. A good example of this is Boulder Dash at Lake Compounce in Bristol, Connecticut.

theme park - A term used to describe an amusement park that is designed to carry a theme in one or more areas of the park. The theme may carry over to the rides and attractions in that area as well. Examples of theme parks include Holiday World, Islands of Adventure, Disneyland, Magic Kingdom, and Knott's Berry Farm.

traditional amusement park - A term used to describe an amusement park that continues to operate in a manner similar to the way parks operated in the early 1900's. Examples include Kennywood, Knoebels Amusement Resort, Lake Compounce, and Playland Park in Rye, New York.

train - A group of one or more cars linked together to form a roller coaster train.

turnaround - A term that describes a turn on a roller coaster that sends the train back going in the opposite direction it came from. Turnarounds are common on roller coasters with an out and back layout.

twister - Describes a roller coaster layout that features many turns, crossovers, and track that runs in many directions. A twister is a roller coaster layout that is unpredictable. Examples include Roar at Six Flags Marine World, Cyclone at Luna Park, and the Wildcat at Hershey Park.

two lift hills - A roller coaster that includes two lift hills.

U

unloading platform - The part of the station where the passengers unload from the train or car. On many roller coasters the loading and unloading platform is the same thing.

upstops - A part of a train that is generally a flat piece of steel with a nylon or rubber surface that is attached to the train and placed underneath the track or to keep the train from flying off. If the upstop comes in contact with the track due to the train rising from negative g-forces it will slide along the track and prevent the train from rising any further.

V

vertical loop - A term used to describe an inversion that is a 360-degree loop placed in a vertical position where riders are sent upside down once.

W

weight drop launch - Found on some versions of the Schwarzkopf shuttle loop roller coasters. The weight drop launch uses a large weight attached by steel cables to pulleys that when released pulls the train from the station, accelerating it to its top speed.

wheels - Describes the part of the roller coaster car or train that rolls on the rails or track. Wheels are typically steel with a nylon or rubber coating on the outside to reduce the noise steel to steel contact would make and the heat generated by friction. There are three types of wheels on a roller coaster. Also see Guide Wheel, Road Wheel, and Upstop Wheel.

wild Mouse - A term that describes a type of roller coaster with sharp turns that are not banked and quick steep drops. Wild Mouse coasters typically run with two or four passenger individual cars as opposed to trains.

wing Coaster - This is a steel roller coaster that is manufactured by B&M where the riders sit on either side of the actual track. There is nothing below the rider. Development of this type of coaster began in 2007 and the following year the first of these type of roller coasters was released. It was called the Raptor. Right now, there are about a dozen of these rides operating worldwide.

wooden structure - Describes the support structure of a roller coaster that is made out of wood.

wooden roller coaster - A roller coaster that uses layers of laminated wood with a flat steel rail attached to the top and inside as the track.

About the Author

Pete Trabucco

Pete has been an avid pilot and roller coaster enthusiast for the past 15 years. He has traveled all over the country and has ridden over a thousand roller coasters in this time period. Pete is a nationally known travel and vacation expert. He has appeared on over 1500 radio and television shows (in every major market) in the United States and Canada. This includes multiple appearances on the Fox News Channel, MSNBC, CNBC, and CNN. Bloomberg Television, Fox Business and the CW network and the Travel Channel to name just a few. For many years Pete was a weekly guest on the weekly morning magazine program "Daybreak USA" which aired daily on the USA Radio syndicated network. Talking what else??? Travel! He has worked as an executive in sales for several Fortune 500 companies including Staples Inc. and BP Corporation.

Pete has also been involved with the American Heart Association serving as Director of Regional Sales and Training for AHA in the state of New Jersey. His responsibilities at AHA included helping this organization by successfully lobbying for several health bills at the statehouse including the Automated External Defibrillation or PAD (Public Access Defibrillation) bill. This legislation would eventually become the model that would be utilized by all fifty states and was signed into law on the federal level in 1999. AED's are now the "Standard of Care" worldwide.

A graduate of Kean University, Pete worked several years as The New Jersey State Assembly Chief of Staff in the nineteenth and thirty-fourth New Jersey legislative districts. He has been a major in the US Air Force Auxiliary New Jersey Wing Civil Air Patrol (CAP) program based out of McGuire Air Force Base in Wrightstown, New Jersey. He has been involved with this organization since 1987 and has held the position of *Central Jersey Squadron Commander* for the New Jersey Wing. Pete received his pilot's certification in 1991 and has been twice been awarded the Air Force Chief of Staff award at the Pentagon for his work with this organization. Pete has devoted many long hours in his spare time teaching others "search and rescue" and most recently "homeland defense" preparation tactics for this wing.

Finally, Pete has written and has published dozens of national articles in the fields of aviation, healthcare and politics. He has interviewed several Space Shuttle crews over the years and has strapped in with one of these crews (STS 132 Atlantis) in NASA's full motion flight simulator. He is constantly asked to speak at conferences and seminars on many topics. Pete is married and has a daughter named Jennifer.

Starry Night Publishing

Everyone has a story...

Don't spend your life trying to get published! Don't tolerate rejection! Don't do all the work and allow the publishing companies reap the rewards!

Millions of independent authors like you, are making money, publishing their stories now. Our technological know-how will take the headaches out of getting published. Let "Starry Night Publishing.Com" take care of the hard parts, so you can focus on writing. You simply send us your Word Document and we do the rest. It really is that simple!

The big companies want to publish only "celebrity authors," not the average book-writer. It's almost impossible for first-time authors to get published today. This has led many authors to go the self-publishing route. Until recently, this was considered "vanity-publishing." You spent large sums of your money, to get twenty copies of your book, to give to relatives at Christmas, just so you could see your name on the cover. Now, however, the self-publishing industry allows authors to get published in a timely fashion, retain the rights to your work, keeping up to ninety-percent of your royalties, instead of the traditional five-percent.

We've opened up the gates, allowing you inside the world of publishing. While others charge you as much as fifteen-thousand dollars for a publishing package, we charge less than five-hundred dollars to cover copyright, ISBN, and distribution costs. Do you really want to spend all your time formatting, converting, designing a cover, and then promoting your book, because no one else will?

Our editors are professionals, able to create a top-notch book that you will be proud of. Becoming a published author is supposed to be fun, not a hassle.

At Starry Night Publishing, you submit your work, we create a professional-looking cover, a table of contents, compile your text and images into the appropriate format, convert your files for eReaders, take care of copyright information, assign an ISBN, allow you to keep one-hundred-percent of your rights, distribute your story worldwide on Amazon, Barnes & Noble and many other retailers, and write you a check for your royalties. There are no other hidden fees involved! You don't pay extra for a cover, or to keep your book in print. We promise! Everything is included! You even get a free copy of your book and unlimited half-price copies.

In four short years, we've published more than fifteen-hundred books, compared to the major publishing houses which only add an average of six new titles per year. We will publish your fiction, or non-fiction books about anything, and look forward to reading your stories and sharing them with the world.

We sincerely hope that you will join the growing Starry Night Publishing family, become a published author and gain the world-wide exposure that you deserve. You deserve to succeed. Success comes to those who make opportunities happen, not those who wait for opportunities to happen. You just have to try. Thanks for joining us on our journey.

www.starrynightpublishing.com

www.facebook.com/starrynightpublishing/

CPSIA information can be obtained at www.ICGtesting.com
Printed in the USA
LVIW01n1446110417
530415LV00011B/148